Selected Essays

The Romantic Survival. A Study in Poetic Evolution
The Characters of Love
Tolstoy and the Novel
Pushkin. A Comparative Commentary
The Uses of Division. Unity and Disharmony in Literature
An Essay on Hardy
Shakespeare and Tragedy

Selected Essays

JOHN BAYLEY

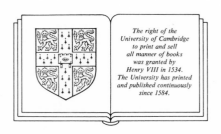

The right of the University of Cambridge to print and sell all manner of books was granted by Henry VIII in 1534. The University has printed and published continuously since 1584.

CAMBRIDGE UNIVERSITY PRESS

Cambridge
London   New York   New Rochelle
Melbourne   Sydney

Published by the Press Syndicate of the University of Cambridge
The Pitt Building, Trumpington Street, Cambridge CB2 1RP
32 East 57th Street, New York, NY 10022, USA
296 Beaconsfield Parade, Middle Park, Melbourne 3206, Australia

First published 1984

Printed in Great Britain at
the University Press, Cambridge

Library of Congress catalogue card number: 83–15222

British Library cataloguing in publication data

Bayley, John
Selected essays.
1. Literature, Modern
I. Title
800   PN 710

ISBN 0 521 25828 6 hard covers
ISBN 0 521 27845 7 paperback

Contents

Acknowledgements

These essays originally appeared, in whole or in part, in the following periodicals: *The Times Literary Supplement, The London Review of Books, The New York Review of Books, The Listener, The Guardian* and the *New Statesman.* The essay on Pushkin has not previously been published.

Songs of a furtive self: Whitman

The English writer Edward Carpenter, who inspired both E. M. Forster and D. H. Lawrence in his time, had a number of conversations with the aging Walt Whitman, and was startled to hear him remark of himself, in the third person: 'There is something in his nature *furtive*, like an old hen.' It is a most endearing remark, and shows the kind of lordly shrewdness and self-awareness that must be in the bedrock of Whitman's genius. Carpenter, and many of his disciples, had more than a bit of the old hen in them too, but one cannot imagine them coming out with it like that. Their image of social and sexual emancipation, on behalf of which they fought a courageous but necessarily devious campaign, did not include that particular sort of avian behaviour pattern; but Whitman, who in the preface to *Leaves of Grass* inserted what Ivan Marki in *The Trial of the Poet* well calls 'a veritable ornithological litany'–

The wild pigeon and highhold and orchard-oriole and coot and surf-duck and redshouldered hawk and fish-hawk and white-ibis and indian-hen and cat-owl and waterpheasant etc., etc.,

–found room for a hen in it, and would no doubt have celebrated hen-like behaviour in his barbaric yawp, as he celebrated most other kinds.

None the less, furtiveness is a vital ingredient in the extraordinarily rich and autonomous world of Whitman's poetic language, all the more so because – as Marki implies in the course of his analysis – it mostly masquerades as an extreme and challenging openness. The 'curious triplicate process' of *Song of Myself* may in some ways remind us of Henry James's dream of pursuit by a shapeless terror in a nightmare in the Galerie des Glaces at Versailles, and how he nerved himself at length to round on it and chase it all the way back down the hall. It is of significance that James understood Whitman, accepted and admired him to the point of hardly troubling to comment, or to isolate him safely on the pedestal contemporaries had hastened to provide. He knew what it was all about; and it would not be fanciful to see an alembicated cousin to Whitman's in the style James evolved, a medium as equal to startlement as it was at home in depths of equivocation, adapted to agility as to repose – just as an old hen is in fact.

'The expression of the American poet is to be transcendent and new. It is to be indirect and not direct or descriptive or epic.' Whitman's words in the preface are certainly true although, as Marki implies, the indirectness has often been overlooked, even by such sympathetic and perceptive scholars as Allen, Rubin and Catel. The fact is that Whitman was not really doing anything American at all in *Song of Myself*, whatever the appearances; he was creating a new language and style for self-expression – the physical sense of self – as Keats had done thirty years or so before. Keats's sensuality of language can often be slightly shamefaced, but it is not furtive: furtiveness implies a carefully worked out undercover programme, such as the genius of Whitman could organize.

The effects of Keats's language, though, are remarkably similar to Whitman's – 'The Eve of St Agnes' and *Sleep and Poetry* are in terms of their verbal world the nearest kind of poetry to *Song of Myself*. Even Keats's neologisms have an exact parallel in Whitman's exuberances and demotic oddities. Marki observes disapprovingly:

Whitman's silly habit of flaunting the five or six [foreign] words that he knew has been, from the first, a matter of so much gratuitous mirth on the part of his readers and therefore has become so tediously familiar that beyond a short note of 'acknowledgment' it can be safely ignored.

This is surely on a par with the critics who wince at Keats's verbal ardours and gentilities; Whitman's gallicisms are an essential part of his style, its total and original 'campness', and like Keats's intuitions in language of the nature and feel of the body, Whitman's sense of it seems also to need that posture of touching and unwitting absurdity and vulnerability which belongs to human nakedness. This his fervency of language, like Keats's provides.

> The young men float on their backs, their white bellies bulge
>   to the sun, they do not ask who seizes fast to them,
> They do not know who puffs and declines with pendant and
>   bending arch,
> They do not think whom they souse with spray.

Like Keats's Whitman's language has what might be termed erectile tendencies ('Those movements, those improvements of our bodies', as Byron blandly remarks) and its exuberance and oddities seem wholly natural for this reason. There is nothing pretentious or metaphysical about the neologisms of either poet; they seem to expand into a world not of ingenuity but of vivid physical simplicity, a verbal equivalent of what Whitman calls 'the curious sympathy one feels when feeling with the hand the naked meat of the body', and its 'thin red jellies'.

Discovering the body in poetry was not quite the same thing as discovering America. More fortunate than Keats in this as in other ways, Whitman did not feel that he had to pass himself for the higher life in order to discover America. Furtiveness came naturally to him, but it had the simple health of inner shamelessness: he was not in thrall to romantic ideas of the European tradition, the spirit and its lofty destiny, as Keats was. The age and the expectations that ordained for Keats the romantic hero's role, in opposition to his own poetic genius, left Whitman wholly free to loaf about on fish-shaped Paumanok, clam-digging and declaiming Shakespeare to the waves.

The impressive thing about his poetic self, and the language in it, is the freedom it achieves – from the self as an abstract identity – by remaining as it were bewitched by the body. In what James called 'the spacious vacancy' of America, the way to be alive was to touch oneself, a strangely original activity for the poetic. And it is no sense narcissism. Berryman, who achieves in *Dream Songs* something of the marvellous insouciance of Whitman's style, is none the less a self watching itself pen in hand in the rocking chair, and making poetry out of finding this 'I' to be a case. The new American *sum* soon became as absorbed with itself as the European *cogito*. Hemingway addressing himself as 'you', drinking the whisky, putting the bait on the hook, feeling good, is a kind of ghastly parody of Whitman, even down to the use of foreign words – before the hero of *A Farewell to Arms* is blown up by a shell, and finds himself leaving his body, he has just been consuming a mass of cold 'pasta asciutta' with some Italian privates: mere macaroni would not have been worthy of his style of self-intentness.

Tocqueville observed that Americans do not converse but address, and that they will instinctively address a single interlocutor as 'Gentlemen'. Whitman virtually addresses his body as 'Gentlemen' in *Song of Myself*, and the effect is seraphically funny. It is the nuances of this process in which Professor Marki is interested, and he has many admirable and penetrating things to say. He uses a more or less formalistic technique to analyse the under-cover workings by which Whitman arranges either to address us, or to be overheard addressing himself; and this can lead to whole paragraphs in which we seem to be nowhere near the poetry at all. But, most endearingly, the critic has caught from his great original some of the inability to be afflated and rhapsodic for long, so that he drops down again into a simple exclamation of pleasure or the expression of a personal preference.

In *Walt Whitman Reconsidered* Richard Chase analysed some time ago what he called 'the paradox of identity' in the poet, and traced the 'comic drama of the self', unfolding in the great poem through the self's 'escaping a series of identities which threaten to destroy its lively and various spontaneity'. 'A comic drama' might not appear to consort with 'I lean and loafe at my ease . . . observing a spear of summer grass', but it is just Whitman's trick (again one might think of Keats and 'I stood tip-toe upon a little hill . . .') to present physical indolence and self-absorption in terms of a dynamic process of courting and evading the kinds of experience and identity which consciousness plays with and is threatened by the consciousness that

> Looks down, is erect, bends an arm on an impalpable certain rest,
> Looks with its sidecurved head curious what will come next.

Marki handsomely acknowledges Chase's book, as also E. H. Miller's *Walt Whitman's Poetry: A Psychological Journey*; but he has his own individual method of feeling the way into the world of the poetry and exploring the nature of its originality. He lays particular stress on the preface to *Leaves of Grass*, which in its way demoralizes the reader by its very lack of commitment and clarity, preparing him for the real clarity and unexpectedness of the poem. I think Marki is too ingenious when he claims that 'the sketchy, improvisational quality of each single image or phrase is the most convincing proof of the validity of the total effort', which is as much as to say that *because* the preface is so muddled and evasive it is doing its work properly and saying what it has to say; but this is undoubtedly a notion along the right lines, for like some preliminary recitative of poor quality, the nullity of the preface ('America does not repel the past' – what *does* it do then?) makes the sudden bursting forth of the aria all the more impressive. Even the 'nationalistic turgidity', as Marki calls it, is not very positive, giving as it does muffled hints of the poem's joyful peculiarity – the rivers and 'beautiful masculine Hudson' being there to 'embouchure where they spend themselves', and also to 'embouchure' into America's bard.

The permament scaffolding of Freudian interpretation has always been wasted on Whitman as his more enlightened critics have realized – 'Did you fear some scrofula out of the unflagging pregnancy?' the poet enquires – and the same is probably true of other theories and interpretations of the self, Hegelian or otherwise. Lawrence, who much admired Whitman but could not resist trying to cut him down to size, as he did with all manifestos but his own, replied to his expansive query, 'What is impossible or baseless or vague? . . . all things enter with electric swiftness softly and duly without confusion or jostling or jam' with 'if that is so, one must be a pipe open at both ends, so everything runs through'. This metaphor of aliment and excretion – 'a pipe open at both ends' – 'is indeed perfect for Whitman, and higher praise than Lawrence presumably realized. It expresses the physical relief and freshness ('The bowels sweet and clean') he gets into poetry, and suggests, too, the lapses into vacancy when we are not concentrating on it. It leaves little or no mark on the memory or mental consciousness, and is then renewed when we go back to it again and plunge in.

Hence he is a poet of release rather than accretion – we do not add to our knowledge of him and our participation in him, as time goes on, in the way that we do with every other great poet. The slate is wiped clean each time: coming back to him we immerse ourselves afresh. Hence, it must be admitted, the comparative pointlessness of academic criticism, even though the stylistic analyses of Professor Marki and his predecessors do give us a clearer view of Whitman, as 'the equable man' in his poetry, than do the more straightforward earlier debates about his attitudes and message. In fact probably the best as well as the briefest thing about him is Louis Simpson's poem, 'Walt Whitman at Bear Mountain', with its epigraph from Ortega y Gasset, 'life which does not give the preference to any other life . . . which therefore prefers its own existence'. In this admirable poem Simpson speaks of 'the realtors, pickpockets, salesmen and actors performing official scenarios' who turned a deaf ear to him, having 'contracted American dreams'. But:

> the housewife who knows she's dumb,
> And the earth, are relieved.
> All that grave weight of America
> Cancelled!

Naturally enough the grave weight of Soviet Russia does not see it like this. Whitman must there be seen to be (and he is immensely popular) an American poet in the sense in which a Soviet poet is a

Soviet poet. Maurice Mendelson is an experienced and erudite scholar, in the admirable tradition of Russian critical scholarship on poetry which has produced so many good Pushkinists, but given the Soviet line on Whitman he has no chance to say anything of interest, although the biographical side of his book, *Life and Work of Walt Whitman*, is well done. The 'puzzles' of Whitman, however, are of a different kind to those which receive the attention of Professor Marki. Leslie Fiedler is indignantly castigated for his view of Whitman the impostor, and the correct dialectic is set forth:

> Was Walt Whitman a skilful demagogue playing at democracy, or a poet whose world view was that of the democratic masses . . . was the poet bound hand and foot by bourgeois individualism, or did his strength lie in an emotional and intellectual leaning towards collectivism?

Gorki saw Whitman as 'Calling on man to merge with mankind', and Commissar Lunacharsky 'shrewdly remarked' that the 'real foundation of his poetry was not individualism but just the opposite'. This is all perfectly rational in terms of Newspeak, but one suspects that the Soviet masses in fact simply read their Whitman with the same kind of relief that the rest of us do.

On the Civil War and slavery Mendelson's attitudes have a better cause, for Whitman was more deeply involved in the war between the states than any other great poet has been in a national or civil war, not even excluding poets who have fought in one. The Soviet imagination has always been caught by the Civil War – on the side of the North of course: a recent Soviet novel by Alexander Borshchag-ovsky tells the true story of a Tsarist officer, Turchin, who emigrated to America and became a colonel in the Illinois regiment. Soviet society would feel much more at home with Whitman's letters from the military dressing station where he worked, and the articles he wrote about it, than with his poetry, and indeed these are deeply moving in what they express about the war and Whitman's feelings about it, feelings common to all good men. There is of course not a whisper in Mendelson's book about Whitman as homosexual, 'Extoller of armies and those that sleep in each others' arms' – only a commendation in the preface for Emory Holloway's book *Free and Lonesome Heart*, which condemns speculation about his 'alleged homosexuality'. Specific queries here are certainly beside the point, but it is surely impossible not to feel that the war for Whitman was a profoundly, indeed sublimely homosexual experience, of which his great work among the wounded was very much a part, and to which the most moving poems in *Drum-Taps* – 'The Wound Dresser' or 'As Toilsome I wander'd Virginia's Woods' – bear witness in a manner as uncompromising as it is dignified.

State of the nation: American poetry

One feels inclined to say: life is bad enough but not quite so bad as it becomes in certain kinds of modern American poetry. Where now is the poetry of feigning, of splendid inventions and devices, the poetry that not so long ago could turn 'five dead wet nuns', as a reviewer recently remarked, into a sisterly apotheosis? –

> sealed in wild waters,
> To bathe in his fall-gold mercies, to breathe in his all-fire glances.

The art of inventing in poetry, which is what Shakespeare meant by 'feigning', was designed – whether consciously or not – to solace the reader with imagined and pretended beauty, to tell him what Keats fervently if embarrassedly called 'the most heart-easing things'. The poetry of invention is always a solace. And maybe it is harder to escape from than the poetry of impoverishment is aware, the poetry that only wants to offer something bleak, meagre and true, what Helen Vendler, in her book on modern American poets *Part of Nature, Part of Us*, calls 'an interior state clarified in language'. The consciousness of Elisabeth Bishop, or Louise Gluck, would have rendered those nuns as just very wet, very dead: but out of the accuracy with which they registered the wetness and deadness the inevitable solace that right language brings would none the less have come.

It remains true, however, that, some kinds of poetry cheer us up more than others; there remains a distinction between the comfort that the 'cool web' of language realized as poetry brings, and the sort of world to which it is directing our attention. This distinction may not exist for structuralists, but it does for the ordinary reader. Life, in modern American poetry, does seem a gloomy affair, and gloomy because almost wholly interiorized, the soul hung up in chains of nerves and arteries and veins. 'Day by Day' (as Lowell called his last collection) the remorseless and obsessive concentration of words on experience goes on; the exactness of the labour, like an automatic manufacturing process monitored by micro-chips, becomes its own point and justification. Berryman is the same. Their manic misery is life-enhancing, of course, in its own obsessed way – 'awful but cheerful' as Elisabeth Bishop calls the domestic scene – and creates something that never existed before, but it is also claustrophobic. Its air of reality appals us even while, as reality, it cannot wholly convince.

The paradox there, perhaps, is that consciousness is not best represented in poetry by the techniques that suggest they are representing it most closely. Our persisting illusion is of literature coming always closer to life, coinciding with the feel, tempo, continuity of it. The poet also needs this sense of just about to break through, the right words producing the exact sense of being, as it is. He needs it, and his reader responds to it, however illusory it may be. It is significant that structuralism can be seen, in this context, as an attempt – in protest against this aspect of modernism – to lay once and for all the ghost of 'life' in literature, and as something which literature strives to come close to. The structuralist shows that all that is in question is a verbal code, relating to other verbal codes; but the poet, and his reader, know that looking in the heart and writing is a way of getting close to life. And in each generation, and to its readers, this closeness will seem to have come about as far as it can come. Take Frank O'Hara's poem about a gay-bar scene, 'At the Old Place':

> Joe is restless and so am I, so restless.
> Button's buddy lips frame "LGTTHOP?"
> Across the bar. 'Yes' I cry, for dancing's
> my soul delight. (Feet! Feet!) 'Come on'!
>
> Through the streets we skip like swallows.
> Howard malingers. (Come on, Howard.) Ashes
> malingers. (Come on, J. A.) Dick malingers.
> (Come on, Dick.) Alvin darts ahead. (Wait up,
> Alvin.) Jack, Earl and Someone don't come.
>
> Down the dark stairs drifts the steaming cha-
> cha- cha-. Through the urine and smoke we charge
> to the floor. Wrapped in Ashes' arms I glide.
>
> (It's heaven!) . . .

This expresses, and most happily, animation and enjoyment – as Lovelace's poem 'Gratiana Dancing' does – but it also assumes it *is* that animation, an echo of it in words. It is very characteristic of modern American poetry that the more it enacts living the more conscious it is of what this might mean as a theory of poetry. O'Hara is very clear about what he is doing.

> I don't think my experiences are clarified or made beautiful for myself or anyone else; they are just there in whatever form I can find them . . . It may be that poetry makes life's nebulous events tangible to me and restores their detail.

O'Hara also remarks, rather surprisingly, that it's depressing 'when you feel you relate more importantly to poetry than to life'. Honest remark, which Yeats himself would hardly have dared to make, at least in that form, and which goes oddly with the business of putting the gay-bar life so imitatively into words. Like Lowell and Berryman, O'Hara is well aware that his apparent obsession with the momentary and actual in living is really an obsession with the techniques and machinery of poetry.

It is the same with ideology. You dispense with it entirely and find you still have it on your hands, so you give it a name – 'Personism'.

> It was founded by me after lunch with LeRoi Jones, a day in which I was in love with someone (not Roi by the way, a blond). I went back to work and wrote a poem for this person. While I was writing it I was realising that if I wanted to I could telephone instead of writing the poem, and so Personism was born.

Plus ça change. The telephone apart, sonnets used to get written this way, or rather it became the convention that this was the way they were written. Convention, like the verbal code, crowds itself betwixt just when you might think you are catching life in the raw. Still, there are differences. Like Berryman, O'Hara has the throwaway humour of the moment, humour which if the poem is good enough becomes as imperishable as its fragments. 'Life, friends, is boring. We must not say so' . . . and that boredom so engagingly invoked by Berryman is boredom in poetry, not in life, as is the process of 'going to pieces'.

> Women, cigarettes, liquor, need need need
> until he went to pieces.
> The pieces sat up & wrote. They did not heed
> their piecedom but kept very quietly on
> among the chaos.

What is funny and moving about that is also what has always been
true: that the disintegrating poet cannot help but produce un-
disintegrating verbal patterns. Difference is never in the basic
philosophy of art but in the poet's attitude to consciousness and
experience, and thus to style:

> How strange, that all
> The terrors, pains, and early miseries,
> Regrets, vexations, lassitudes interfused
> Within my mind, should e'er have born a part,
> And that a needful part, in making up
> The calm existence that is mine when I
> Am worthy of myself.

Wordsworth assumes that the calm out of which the poem
eventually appears to proceed is the proper thing for the poetic
consciousness, just as it is equally proper to recognize the detritus in
which its constituents were born, and which made them possible. To
stay with the detritus produces a different kind of style, the style of a
Berryman or an O'Hara for instance, but nothing else has changed
very greatly. How could it?

Naturally a good American critic like Helen Vendler is more
interested in differences than resemblances and in analysing the
newness of today's American poetic sensibility. Of Frank O'Hara
she writes:

The wish *not* to impute significance has rarely been stronger in lyric poetry.
It happened, it went like this, it's over. Why is it worth recording? Because it
happened. Why is what happened worth recording? Because what else is
there to record. And why should we want to read it? Because what else is
there to know except what has happened to people? Such a radical and
dismissive logic flouts the whole male world and its relentless demand for
ideologies, causes, and systems of significance.

That is worth pondering, even if one cannot entirely agree with it.
The cultivation of impoverishment in American poetry certainly
takes many forms, from the clerkly visions and precisions of Wallace
Stevens to the self-absorption of Berryman and the concentration of
Sylvia Plath or Louise Gluck on elemental female awareness. The
implication is that gay people, like women, have no need for
anything in the creation of poetry but the simplest immediacies.

But everything Helen Vendler writes is worth producing. She is
certainly the most thoughtful and humane as she is the least system-
bound critic of poetry now writing – professionally writing one
might say – for her examination of a poet is always as absolutely

business-like and thorough as it is sympathetic, like that of a really good doctor. All the pieces were done originally as reviews, or in poetry magazines, but the effect of the book is to give a comprehensive and highly authoritative picture of the American poetry scene today. There is nothing bitty about the technique: the whole sweep of her survey is sure and purposive, and coming to the end of the book one feels that a number of really significant generalizations have been made about the nature of the American poetic phenomenon, and the way it relates to the American consciousness.

As one would expect of a critic who has written the best detailed study of Wallace Stevens's poetry, as well as one of the best on George Herbert's, her individual insights are unsurpassed in their power of showing something unexpected and underlying in a poetry's approach. Thus in her essay on Marianne Moore, which appeared in the *New Yorker*, she demolishes once and for all the image of a poet who likes to stand with her head on one side and imagine or contemplate a pattern, a fable, an animal. Marianne Moore's creatures are states of mind, and defences against the threats and the poses asserted by other people; they are both insight and weapon, and deadly serious. (All American poetry is deadly serious, even when it attempts or affects not to be. True lightness is an aspect of invention or feigning, of traditions of acceptance, and America's poets use various kinds of deadpan or ironic negation as a means of discovery, an exploratory tool.) Helen Vendler notes with compassion the touching irony that Moore's poetic persona, refusing enigma but availing itself of mannerism, finally hardened into a mask that could not be taken off. Her translation of La Fontaine's Fables is disastrous, for she could not escape there a ritualization of the quaintness which her own poems so suggestively undercut. By the time the Ford company asked her to christen the car that became the Edsel, she had become a sort of animal totem, and 'it may be true, as Yeats said, that "all great men are owls, scarecrows, by the time their fame has come" '. She turned into one of the fabled beasts who in a sense had protected her.

The same kind of insight distinguishes one of Helen Vendler's pieces on Robert Lowell, that relating to his last volume, about which she unexpectedly observes that it was not only his most Horatian but that Horace was – in the midst of all Lowell's other virtuosities and imitations – increasingly a kind of invisible model. Horace's extreme compactness, his power of being at once intimate, easy, and densely allusive, quotidian in a sense as well, were all the developing and mature aims of Lowell's great talent. It is true that Horace's elegant density is apt to become in him what Lowell calls 'the horrifying mortmain of ephemera', but Helen Vendler's insight does hold, for when the idea is there one perceives how much Lowell's later tone depends on a curious kind of sophisticated intercourse – rather un-American – as between poet and reader, a relation borrowed as it were from the intimacy of aristocrats, even though it is not confined to that social tone. Horace hobnobbed with the great and influential, to whom not so much culture itself as the atmosphere of culture was the natural air to breathe; and he manages to amplify and transmit the quality of that intercourse, while avoiding its exclusiveness. In this sense both Lowell and Berryman were socially innovatory poets, bringing a new kind of suavity and intellectual worldliness to the American tradition.

Ars longa vita brevis for Horace; but the extreme modern self-consciousness about the relation of the two would have meant nothing to him. Here too Lowell was perhaps finding inspiration for his need for a similar type of unselfconsciousness, for 'one life, one writing'.

> Conscience incurable
> convinces me I am not writing my life;
> life never assures which part of ourself is life.

The leisurely truth of the third line goes oddly with the reference to conscience, the New England legacy that admonishes that life is real, life is earnest. Lowell is right to imply that he does not 'cannibalize' his life, as a fellow-poet said he did, in the interest of his poetry. That Yeatsian dichotomy has been expunged with a particularly American thoroughness. Turn memory into tableaux, as in 'Life Studies', or turn the letters and words of the live today on to the page: for Lowell it is all one method of exploring and expanding poetry as the self, making the two (in Berryman's words)

> together lie at once, forever or
> as long as I happen.

Of course the structuralists repeat their tautology, which Helen Vendler puts in her more commonsensical way by a comment apropos the 'live' material in Lowell that 'we cannot go behind the art: the illusion that we can is art's most compelling hallucination'. She instances a recent Mary Cassatt exhibition at the Boston Museum of Fine Arts in which domestic objects from the painter's house were exhibited together with the paintings in which they figured. 'The good intentions of the exhibition – to bring art closer to biography and therefore closer to the viewer – begged, once again, the central question: what had the data become in the picture?' Cézanne's properties are preserved untransfigured in his studio, 'all light fled from them'. Their appeal is to the curiosity of the philistine. Conversely, as Harold Rosenberg has observed, if you put a spade in an exhibition it becomes 'art' because of its context, though for no other reason. 'Live' matter put into poetry is transformed even more completely by its context.

This American version of the question of the marriage of art and life, and the way in which American technological expertise and enterprise have made use of it, is the most important single factor in their modern art, and not only the art of poetry. The fact that the question is a non-question does not matter: what matters is what art thinks it can make of it, in terms of new effects and new directions. Where poetry is concerned it is also, bizarrely enough, responsible for the impression that it may give us that life, as I put it, is bad enough but not so bad as it can seem in the powerful focus of a strong poetry. Art intensifies the contingent and exaggerates in its own forceful way the unconsecrated vagueness of being, 'the horrifying mortmain of ephemera'. The process is analogous to that practised by Vermeer (an artist Lowell greatly admired and sought inspiration from) but of course its opposite. Vermeer's intensifications into pearly strangeness of domestic conditioning, domestic vacancy – why should they not be analogous to Lowell's meticulous life studies and his densely felt, close-written ramblings? It must be admitted though, I think, that they are *not* analogous – in no way – and the reason seems to lie in the lack of *otherness* in Lowell's poetic vision. We cannot go behind his art, but his art has certainly succeeded in not transforming his experience for us. As Helen Vendler puts it, 'If vision – even balked vision – is the end of art, then Lowell is inconsequential.' No doubt he meant to be.

If in his own way Lowell does have something of what he called Vermeer's 'grace of accuracy', it is accuracy that reduces experience to the thing itself. In the early poems – most notably in 'The Quaker Graveyard' – the poetical does its own thing; rhetoric goes through the motions, so effectively including all the expectable conventions that, as Helen Vendler says, 'it struck everyone as a true poem'. Lowell's great originality was to get rid of all that, and only a great poet could be so reductive, with a reductiveness – and of an

American kind – that leaves Yeats standing. Lowell came in time to be able to exclude every vestige of the poetical. Poetry could suffer too of course, as it does in the 'Notebook' – the baby sometimes went out with the bathwater – but every sentence in his last collection is in its unique way of the strongest fibre of poetry. The religion that has been an adjunct of the poetical in his early work has vanished completely. This is indeed a classic poetry: Lowell wanted it to be 'heart-breaking' and indeed it is, in the sense that some of Horace's Odes are. Not that it 'trivialises existence', as those who dislike it have claimed, but every word knows that there is nothing to life except the skills and appetencies of living, and the memory of what they have shown us.

Lowell's poems make us realize, as few other poems could do, the importance of otherness in most poetry, those elements of vision or visionary make-believe that create and sustain it. Lowell can be beautifully witty, but he has no more humour than Horace – what I understand by humour here is the queer companion of otherness, usually unrecognized by it. What a poet creates, or feigns in creation, is always slightly ridiculous, and this usually involuntary humour – the premises of humour one might say – is as much present in Milton or in Tennyson as it is in Wordsworth and Keats. Vermeer himself has this beautiful and mysterious hilarity lurking immanent in the poses and expressions of his world, in the very arrestment of his tranquillities. Such an otherness is laboriously catalogued and expatiated on by Wordsworth, in his Leech-gatherer and in the haunting figures of the Prelude, the blind man, the soldier, the 'female' seen in a desolate place, 'her garments vex'd and tossed by the strong wind'. The spots of time are those of romance, however much a poet such as Wordsworth may give them a philosophic status of his own, and all romantic otherness is accompanied in contemplation by a sense of incongruity which is a part of its saving power. A romantic poetry of today, such as Philip Larkin's, understands this very well. The brides of 'The Whitsun Weddings' are the brides of romance, 'smiling and recognising and going dark' even as their dozen marriages 'got under way'.

I have always wondered what Americans might make of the buried humour in 'The Whitsun Weddings', because the submerged but continuous tradition that produced it, and the poetic appetite it satisfies, is quite outside the really remarkable achievement – the renaissance one might almost say – of modern American poetry. Varied as it is, that achievement has in common the abandonment of the European romantic tradition of otherness, the exploration of new kinds of consciousness and feeling that do without the romantic perspective, that are in a sense both sparse and classical, however densely filled (as Lowell's poems are) by not only the detritus of living and thinking but by heraldic and symbolic presences and totems of all kinds. Successful American poetry can often be sentimental, extremely so, as E. E. Cummings was, and as (in a different way) Randall Jarrell and Jane Merrill, Elisabeth Bishop or Sylvia Plath can be, but such sentimentality is never an aspect of the poetry that creates otherness. The reason, at least in the case of the two women poets, seems to be not only trying too hard, but also the lack in their poetry of an area of creation in which humour can lead its intangible life. When Elisabeth Bishop writes of her Fish, or of the Moose glimpsed by night by the passengers on a bus, the invitation in these highly competent poems to take part in a magical experience is far too overt. The exactness is too earnest, too insistent on the adequate potency of the thing as it is.

Berryman thought Rilke a jerk (those goddammed angels for crissake) and he and his peers should by rights, one feels, have thought Wallace Stevens one too. For that sublimely eloquent comedy attending the inspiration of those Rilkean angels is also the summer lightning that illuminates the progress in being of a poem by Stevens – the only great American poet to produce his own remarkable American version of European otherness in poetry. Otherness with him is of course a form of absence, and a meticulousness in rendering the implications of absence for the consciousness of the poet.

> Yet the absence of the imagination had
> Itself to be imagined

as he puts it in 'The Plain Sense of Things'. With Stevens the old question of Life and Art, on which the American scene conferred so insistent an awareness, was a question of the false and the true sublime, of whether the American poet could fill in the picture blank with anything resembling traditional sublimity. 'Poetry is not a literary activity; it is a vital activity' Stevens wrote to Richard Eberhart. Here is the old tautology again, but Stevens presumably thought the point worth making because the 'vital' was for him the inside of the mind, the place where the visions and inventions of poetry used to be born, but which for that purpose is now 'The empty spirit / In vacant space'. However, that absence has itself to be imagined, and the process produces that curious 'unsponsored' and unstable eloquence which makes up Stevens's original and personal style, or styles, for as Helen Vendler points out there are many of them, and their angularity of relation is part of their effect. Harold Bloom explored the ways in which, in the context of his own theory of influence in art, Stevens is an obsessed romantic, with a visionary world no less rich than that of his predecessors, and no less opening on to otherness, though otherness here takes the form of negation:

> . . . the listener who listens in the snow
> and, nothing himself, beholds
>   nothing that is not there
> and the nothing that is.

Such things are as well-known to every American schoolperson as 'La Belle Dame sans Merci' or 'Break, Break, Break' used to be in an English classroom. The paradox is how much they proclaim, for all their apparent bleakness, a rich interior life and a close relation with otherness. Such a poem goes with the notes in Stevens's journals, which open eyes upon an oddly cosy and touching kind of inner fantasy. 'Sometimes, just before I go to sleep, I fancy myself on a green mountain – southward, I think. It's simply green, the grass – no trees, just an enormous, continental ridge.' And then a bit later: 'I'm going to come down from the green mountain tonight and imagine a warm sea booming on a tropical coast.' This Tennysonian dream is separate from but wholly at home with the American work ethic, the poet and dreamer of the evening sitting daily in his office at the Hartford Accident and Indemnity Company, where Stevens eventually became a vice-president. We learn from Helen Vendler's essays that he declined to give the Charles Eliot Norton lectures at Harvard in his old age because he could not have taken a year off from his office and still have been able to return. To explore the otherness of the poetry consciousness he needed the daily support of the toad, Work.

Stevens's Americanness is unmistakable; that of Eliot and Auden highly dubious, if indeed it can be said to be a relevant aspect of those two highly artificial makers and creators. Auden's imaginary world – 'the shops, the works, the whole green country / Where a cigarette comforts the guilty and a kiss the weak' – creates otherness by the sheer joyful irresponsibility of technique: otherness becomes comedy, and Helen Vendler writes of 'the critical appetite that still, unreasonably but unquellably, wishes that Auden's immense talent

had been spent on the high serious'. She is not in the least
unsympathetic about Auden or Eliot, whose *Waste Land* manuscript
she reviews, but she is perfunctory, implying in the kindliest manner
that they are in some sense outsiders. Even her penetrating sympathy
can make nothing of Eliot's theological and Anglican ruminations,
and she feels they ended 'in verse which stretched feebler and feebler
through the tracts of the *Quartets*': so unlike that superbly full-
flowing incomprehensibility which continued to pour from the
interior of the Stevens consciousness.

Sympathetic as she is Helen Vendler can be censorious about the
private lives of her poets – she is surprisingly stuffy about Lowell's
third marriage – but her level-headedness comes out most clearly in
her studies of black poets and women poets, poets, that is to say,
who make a particular point of their racial and sexual status. She
greatly admires Adrienne Rich's poetry, but has the strongest
reservations about the view of woman as poet – 'thinking through
the body' – which some of the poems express, and most notably the
Rich autobiography.

Once in a while someone used to ask me, 'Don't you ever write poems about
your children?' The male poets of my generation did write poems about
their children – especially their daughters. For me, poetry was where I lived
as no-one's mother, where I existed as myself.

'Especially their daughters' is clearly a crack at Yeats, whose
daughter would have fitted in the most natural way in the world into
his own mythology. For Adrienne Rich, children are not a possible
part of her consciousness as a poet: and hence, paradoxically, that
consciousness is an exclusively female affair. A previous generation
might have been puzzled by this oddity but not ours, accustomed as
we have become to the wish of the female to cut herself off from the
traditional appendages that in the past defined her femininity. The
child is father of the man, but to be 'no-one's mother' is not
necessarily a good begetter of the poet. Helen Vendler is doubtful
too.

Is it a delusion that writing mothers practise on themselves, a perpetuation
of a fantasy of intact girlhood? Rich does not say: 'Poetry was where I lived
as no-one's daughter, as no-one's wife.' Is there something about the
relation with children, in contrast to relations with adults, which makes it
unavailable to the writer? Is it simply that one can separate oneself from
other adults, but not from children?

Creatively speaking, Virginia Woolf could indeed be a daughter, but it is hard to imagine the consciousness of her books extending to that of her own child, though a childless writer like Elizabeth Bowen could marvellously imagine and write about having a son. Rich's point makes an odd twist to the life/art question: Can poetry not be made of something from which one cannot separate onself – a further evidence of what divides it from life?

Apropos the exclusively female consciousness, which such a poet wishes to own and to use, Helen Vendler remarks 'Why not tell women to imitate Keats or Shakespeare?' There are models for such 'thinking through the body: that they are men does not vitiate their usefulness'. She is not terribly enthusiastic either about the 1977 Yale Younger Poet, Olga Broumas, who has 'a schoolgirl catalogue of respect: she wants to say "Great spirits now on earth are sojourning", but the sentiment comes out as self-conscious attitudinising in a chapel full of niches: "Ann, Sylvia. Virginia. Adrienne, the last, magnificent last"'. Broumas's sex poems ('The Queen's own pearl at my fingertips) are certainly unbearably arch:

> my jester's bells on our four
> small steeples, as Sunday dawns
> clear in February, and God claps and claps
> her one hand.

Poetry, and language in good poetry, is sexy by nature; to make it go through these sort of antics is merely embarrassing. The influence of the 'magnificent last' does not seem a liberating one. Adrienne Rich praises a colleague, author of *The First Sex*, for trying 'to prime the imagination of women living today to conceive of other modes of existence'. Admirable: but those 'other modes' are apt to become one particular specialist outlook. Helen Vendler as usual makes a wise judgement: 'Freud, according to Rich, was "terribly limited both by his culture and his gender". What Rich finds true of Freud is of course true of herself.'

'Modern' poetry is in fact an affair of the past, for by the time it has been recognized as modern the poetry scene has changed or moved on, and nowhere is this truer than in America. 'Minimalism' replaces 'Personism'.

> What happened to her
> and what happened to her
> and what happened to her?

That little poem by Robert Creeley has something of the same charm as Ezra Pound had when he was being brief and modern. But

Ammons and Ashbery are more in keeping with the young American wish for a poetry that does not make up its mind or its words for good and all, but gives the illusion of finding its way along as provisionally as speech – art once again doing its best to defer to the rhythms of life. Charles Simic, by contrast, a 'minimalist' of sorts, seems happily old-fashioned, as in his poem on Charon which A. E. Housman would have seen the point of:

> With only his feeble lantern
> To tell him where he is
> And every time a mountain
> Of fresh corpses to load up
>
> Take them to the other side
> Where there are plenty more
> I'd say by now he must be confused
> As to which side is which
>
> I'd say it doesn't matter.

Poems of every moment show the old-fashioned and the up-to-date coexisting, as no doubt they always have. Helen Vendler leans to the side of uncertainty (Ashbery, Ammons) as being the coming, or at least the done, thing; for though her invariable charity approves Simic she deprecates his 'weakness for climax' and that his poems 'tend towards a known shape'. Were they 'less the captives of structure, the poems would gain an uncertainty of progress more suited to their blind exploring'. All poets have explored blindly, but now, like justice, they must be seen to be doing it. This book gives one a real sense of the flowering of American poetry, and of what may well be thought of as its greatest, or Golden, epoch. Most in any age will always fall by the way, but that cannot and should not be helped. I wonder if Helen Vendler has often perused Louis Untermeyer's massive anthology of the American poetry of the twenties and thirties, and meditated on the many voices to be found there that are now heard no more.

'A poet insufficiently himself?': Bloom on Stevens

In his now famous essay. 'The anxiety of influence', Harold Bloom coined the term 'misprision', signifying the process by which 'strong poets make poetic history misreading one another, so as to clear imaginative space for themselves'. The influences on him may make a poet 'not less but more original'. Could the same go for critics? Under the influence of the same anxieties they rearrange the rhetorical tableaux of their predecessors, swerve their arguments down perspectives that look less familiar. Bloom observed that 'the best critics of our time remain Empson and Wilson Knight, for they have misinterpreted more antithetically than all the others'. His own ambition is to work by the same dialectic.

There is a difference however. Empson needed when young to impress the sophisticated, in literary London and Cambridge. Bloom began his ministry, so to speak, among the savages, the braves in bare feet and jeans who squat on the campus around the tribal shaman. To spellbind them needs no less talent but a different technique: the sophisticated are caught by simplicity, and slangy untechnical surprises; the naive, by conjurations of power and the magic of mumbo-jumbo. Introduced to the modes of misprision and 'synechdochal rhetoricity', to *clinamen* and *askesis*, they are speedily converted to the new sect.

Bloom is very much aware of the American tradition, once religious, then transcendental, now secularized into sociological self-scrutiny which for historic and geographic reasons has never felt at home in English empiricism, with its instinct for common sense and the use of Occam's razor. American intellectuals have usually aspired to join the continental set. The wide open spaces are more at home with German metaphysics, or even with 'pataphysics', as Jarry ironically termed that peculiarly French pursuit of 'imaginary conclusions', with its elegant linguistic round dance.

There is a revealing passage in *A Map of Misreading*, the book of practical criticism which followed the theoretical essay:

Without willing the change, critics have become negative theologians. I do not believe that I am talking about an ideology, nor am I acknowledging any shade whatever of the recent Marxist critiques of our profession. Whatever the academic profession now is on the continent (shall we say an anthropology half-Marxist, half-Buddhist?) or in Britain (shall we say a middle-class amateurism displacing an aristocratic amateurism?), it is currently in America a wholly Emersonian phenomenon. Emerson abandoned his church to become a secular orator, rightly trusting that the lecture, rather than the sermon, was the proper and luminous melody for Americans. We have institutionalised Emerson's procedures.

And Wallace Stevens reinterpreted them into a poetry that has now become 'the proper and luminous melody for Americans'. Though Emerson may seem an oddly square cult-figure for our times, Bloom has always energetically justified his importance in the living tradition of American romanticism, a visionary company in which Stevens, the brightest star, is now joined in the heavens by such poets as Ammons and John Ashbery. It may seem odd to find those two English amateurs, Empson and Wilson Knight, in the same pantheon, but Bloom's idea of romantic 'misprision' is nothing if not eclectic. When he quotes Scholem on the Kabbalists – 'everything not only *is* in everything else but also *acts upon* everything else' – it seems all part of Emersonian togetherness. 'I am the batsman and the bat, I am the bowler and the ball', as the English parodist put it. Bloom seeks to institutionalize the togetherness into what he called in 'The anxiety of influence', 'a wholly different practical criticism'.

Let us give up the failed enterprise of seeking to 'understand' any single poem as an entity in itself. Let us . . . read any poem as its poet's deliberate misinterpretation, *as a poet*, of a precursor poem or of poetry in general.

Poetic ignition as a solid state affair: the whole enterprise sealed off? Bloom is of course well aware that this is the logical and, oddly enough, also the *romantic* finale to Eliot's classic and symmetric adage that 'the conscious present is an awareness of the past in a way that the past's awareness of itself cannot show'. Poet and precursor 'fade into the continuum', not of classic tradition but of the world of romantic poetry, in which a 'new poem's achievement' may make us feel not that a precursor has influenced it, but that 'the later poet has himself written the precursor's characteristic work', so that the world of Stevens is at one with that of Shelley, Whitman and Emerson. No wonder Gore Vidal has recently observed that 'selves are hard to come by in America'. For Bloom it is un-American to possess one, especially for an American poet.

The apotheosis of Wallace Stevens is the logical climax of Bloom's theorization about the nature of romantic poetry. There is in Stevens a remarkably pure horror of all European-type influence, together naturally with a total dependence upon it, which makes him for Bloom the perfect case. And this has real interest and importance, much more so, to my mind, than the way Bloom has become a campus shaman by combining evangelical ardour with schoolman's rhetoric, like Puttenham shaking hands with General Booth. Perhaps one should always ask the simplest question of the critic of poetry: what sort does he really like and why does he like it? If the question is worth asking one is really learning something from the critic, and one always learns a great deal from Bloom. In his case he is fascinated by the sort of poetry that is *not really there*, and – even better – the kind that knows it never can be. In a letter, Stevens stated what he thought to be his theme: 'We live in the description of a place and not in the place itself.' This is virtually the language of Derrida, and as Bloom points out it is also that of Emerson – 'our poetry, our language itself, are not satisfactions, but suggestions . . .'

It is certainly the point of Stevens's longer poems that they are not about 'the place itself', and Bloom suggests, subtly and continuously, that this romantic homelessness, lamented or feared by the early romantic poets, has been made use of by the later ones, after more than a century of anxious misprision and reworking, until it has become the proper and the only subject for a poet in our time. I will suggest here simplifications and examples which he might not accept, but which outline, I think, the real significance of his views, and the objections to them. Romantic poetry is fragmentary because it can never find reality, can never discover what it's all about, and the desire to do so becomes obsessional, both in terms of epistemology and of the linguistic medium. Moreover each poet has to reject with force the previous search for 'truth', while necessarily availing himself of the same worlds of metaphor and metonymy. Keats's 'Hyperion' and Shelley's 'Triumph of Life' give up in despair, because the poets feel and realize that their poetry is *poetical*, that it is lying on the outside of Milton and Dante, as it were, and failing to create a new local habitation and a name. It is using 'poetry' to try and talk about 'life'. *'Then what is life? I cried'* – and at that moment it can only be appropriate for the poem to break off.

It is in this appropriateness, which to Shelley no doubt was an absolute dissatisfaction, even despair, that the later romantic technique sees its hope. Let us make a positive virtue of not being able to be more than approximately poetic. To do so as effectively as he has done is the ground of Stevens's success and his achievement. Not to be in life, not to be in the language, not to be in 'the place': out of these disabilities, consciously nurtured, he makes his poetry; it succeeds by failing to be or become any of the three realities, but by making its own kind of attempt on them. Bloom's sub-title – 'The poems of our climate' – shows how much he considers this to be the only thing nowadays, the logical result of our multiple awareness of alienation.

But objections remain, and there are distinctions to be made. Bloom's primal error, I should have thought, is to assume, with other moderns, that since poetry is all the same stuff, and outside existence, it can have for us and for the poets themselves no separate realities of its own; and that good poets realize this more and more comprehensively. I think he is wrong. Keats must have despaired when he realized that 'Hyperion' was an abstract poem, a thought poem, that 'made the visible a little hard to see', and not a poem 'exactly itself', like 'The Eve of St Agnes'. Shelley drowned shortly after giving up on 'The Triumph of Life'. It does not sound as if they thought the same way as Bloom, or Stevens, about the nature of the poetic as enquiry into the possibilities of the poetic. Their attempt on poetry as life was a doomed exploration, not a strategy for enabling them to write poetry.

Doomed, in their case, because their sense of poetic absoluteness was itself so unconsciously absolute. Nor is the absolute as poetry just an illusion of their time: it always accompanies the kind of poetic genius in which Bloom cannot afford to be interested. For all its arbitrariness and scrappiness *The Waste Land* is such an absolute poem, a poem 'exactly itself'. The phrases in quotes are from Stevens's poem, 'The Creations of Sound', in which he attacks Eliot, as 'X', on the ground that he is 'an obstruction, a man too exactly himself', and that his poems 'do not make the visible a little hard to see'. The criticism is as acute as we should expect. A poet like Eliot *is* a solid object, as his poems are – themselves and not another thing, in Bishop Butler's phrase – and their reality makes total visibility in their world, the world of Phlebas the Phoenician, and the 'small house agent's clerk, with one bold stare'. The deep patient animosity which Stevens nourished for Eliot (*Harmonium* came out nine months after the success of *The Waste Land* and attracted little attention) is that of a man who cannot afford to acknowledge the fact of a millionaire while he himself is looking for ways of making the largest possible income out of a modest poetic capital.

This is an invidious metaphor of course: it suggests both that the two poets can be compared, and that Eliot possesses an absolute superiority. The second may be true – I should say it was – but neither is relevant to my argument, which is that Bloom has to ignore the kind of poetry that Eliot wrote, and that was being written long before, and is still being written today. In *A Map of Misreading* he observed that Shakespeare had no part in his thesis that poets succeed by deliberately modifying their predecessors, because Shakespeare was not influenced by Marlowe but swallowed him whole. Very true, but he implied that Shakespeare was the great exception: in fact the same is true of all authentic poetic genius which becomes 'exactly itself'. Keats with Spenser, Eliot with Laforgue, equally take or steal what they want. Eliot knew that the bad poet imitates and the good poet steals.

But it is not a question of goodness and badness, and both Bloom and Stevens score a point against Eliot, Bloom by pointing out that Eliot set up a defensive doctrine of 'impersonality' when he is himself the most wholly personal of poets. It is, none the less, a question of two different categories, however much they may merge and overlap. Poets in the Bloomian category are never themselves because they swim in the poetical as if in water, and, as poets, poetry is for them the whole world, which exists 'pour aboutir à une autre poème', as Mallarmé might have said. This is certainly true of the poem sequences of Stevens, or of Ashbery and Ammons and others. Bloom may well be right that historically this is the most significant tendency of romanticism, a kind of depersonalized co-possession of the whole medium, as evident today in social living as in art, and physically present in certain kinds of abstract painting, as in the sculptures that invite or move into the audience, or the theatre actors who do the same thing. The most important thing about Wallace Stevens's poetry is that it seems fastidious, deeply pondered, idiosyncratically exclusive; but that it is really co-operative, communal, impressionistic and sketchy, a mild show-off before persons who, like those in local church or lecture-hall, are already *au fait* with the preacher's tone.

As preachers used to talk about God, so this kind of poetry has

come to talk about 'reality'. 'I am the poet of reality', said Whitman
in an early poem, and Stevens wrote in a letter about his poem 'Angel
Surrounded by Paysans': 'The question of how to represent the angel
of reality is not an easy question.' The tone of that is amazingly like
the opening of a certain kind of sermon, and it merges into its own
literary criticism and that of the critics who have become, as Bloom
says, 'negative theologians'. One of the signs of 'reality' poetry is to
mingle easily with the style of those discussing it, while my category
of 'exactly itself' poetry (for want of a better descriptive term) is
simply a different thing altogether. It would be tempting, though
perhaps excessively Eliotian, to compare the first with the sermon
and the second with the lesson and the rubric.

But more important, the poetry that is exactly itself has no need to
evade its provenance, because the objects in it and the story in it have
their own selves which can be like nothing else. The armour of
Achilles refuses to dwindle on the road towards meaning and
'reality', any more than the kidney which that other Bloom bought
to eat for his breakfast, or the exquisite backside which Alisoun
projected from the shop-window. The critics' poets, as Viereck
called them, cannot provide such objects, or the words which call
them into being. The poet of 'reality' is not the poet of real things.
Even Whitman has none, though Whitman's marvellous powers
prevent his lines ever being merged into criticism – when he is
quoted the words move straight past what is said about them, as
Stevens's have neither the power nor the wish to do, and Whitman's
wonderful – and often wonderfully funny – rhetorical exploitations
and evasions of being himself are a part of the natural *drama* of his
work, not of its expression of 'reality'.

Bloom's theory of influence tends to run together romantic
poetry, about which he has many real insights, with a larger theory
of influence, extending to Spenser and Milton, Wordsworth and
Shelley, and now down to Stevens. In the proof of influence here one
can concur, as much as the late C. S. Lewis would have done, but the
fact remains that Spenser and Milton, even Wordsworth and Shelley
too, are a very different matter from Bloom's modern poetry. Clear
and evident as the line of influence may be, it says nothing of the
autonomous and convincing *stories* which are the real selves of
Spenser and Milton, and which show, it seems to me, what
Coleridge – that early and most sensitive of romantic reality-seekers
– had in mind when he stressed in our relation to poetical art the
'willing suspension of disbelief'. Coleridge perceived that as poetry
became more transparent, more involved in fables of the mind, it

would lose its habitual sense of reality and the visible, in possession of which the poetical imagination can do as it pleases, acting by what he termed 'double touch'. The great quest poems of Milton and Spenser are at once familiar and strange, ethos and theology far less important than their exactness in themselves, the exactness of *literal importance*. The world of Eliot's religious poetry has the same kind of validity, a created world in which our lack of belief is fully suspended.

Bloom, though, assumes what, following Simone Weil, it is now fashionable to think of it as 'decreations', by which the test of a poem's authenticity is fully internalized: we are no longer called on to suspend disbelief but to concentrate on a tropal geometry in which that question does not arise. Quest poems are read as poems not about actual journeys but about states of mind. Frank Kermode's admittedly delicate and persuasive reading turns the meaning of 'Resolution and Independence' into a property of the poem, instead of the result of an encounter with an actual leech-gatherer. Bloom's great instance of the totally 'influenced' romantic quest, which he also has admirably analysed in more than one book, is 'Childe Roland to the Dark Tower Came', in which Browning did indeed convert – and with an ingenuity that demands our continual homage and attention – an old story into an existential state of mind.

Bloom is of course far too clever to be merely formalistic in his approach; and in this, as he has already told us, he is at one in spirit with a theorist like Geoffrey Hartman, and his book with its tautological title, *Beyond Formalism*. But here again he need only speak with the tones of Stevens himself in order to show us he is 'moved', and to 'move' us, as well as demonstrating to us the tropal geometry. Of the phrase 'Exquisite in poverty', in 'Esthétique du Mal', he observes it

is the formula meant to defend this chant against the critical accusation that it is too sentimental a consolation. I do not think that the judgment of any critic here can be purely cognitive in its determinations, and I for one am very moved.

What on earth is 'moved' supposed to mean in this context, either for us or for him? It seems ritualistic obligation, rather than the response to experience into which a poetry that is 'exactly itself' rushes us the nearest way. When Wordsworth writes

> As high as we have mounted in delight
> In our dejection do we sink as low,
> To me that morning did it happen so

the third line moves us before we know it, in the exact rapidity with which it registers an experience outside the poetic.

This is the last thing we should expect of Stevens's longer poems, and why should they give it to us? By talking in this way Bloom demonstrates an extraordinary awkwardness, a musclebound quality in his criticism, which seems the result of having it all ways, making the batsman equal the bat and the bowler the ball, bringing us all, and in his poem, into the same comprehensive area. There does seem something rather indecent in this intimacy – tropes in closest commonalty spread, as it were – although it has the effect of suggesting to us something unexpected and true about the nature of Stevens's poetry: that its fastidiousness is really a sort of wistful familiarity. Bloom emphasizes the close debt to Wordsworth; and in the longer poems, as in the *Prelude* and 'Tintern Abbey', there is the same effect of an imitation style, by turns soothing or rotund, never quite justifying its existence and yet insisting on that existence in a manner ultimately wearisome to many readers. It is significant that Stevens as poetic master, wholly self-justifying and 'himself', is like Wordsworth in appearing only in short poems – 'Girl in A Nightgown', or the more famous 'The Snowman', 'Dry Loaf', or 'The Death of A Soldier'. This phenomenon would surely be worth examining, would be in fact *the* important thing to examine, for nothing is more fundamental or more worth investigation in the nature of long romantic poems than their tendency for the poetical to be maintained as a film on the surface of abstraction, like petrol on a puddle. It seems to me arguable that Stevens's longer poems are no more ultimately successful in this respect than are such obvious failures as Browning's 'La Saisiaz' or Conrad Aiken's 'Senlin'.

But Bloom's pursuit of influence and its tropes never gets around to the simpler technical questions of what actually constitutes goodness and badness in this poetry. Frank Kermode's short book seems to me vastly more helpful in this respect, though it is true that all Stevens buffs are apt to take for granted the distinction of everything in him, as experts no doubt find all chess games beautiful. There seems again a point to be made about Stevens's fear of a poetry 'exactly itself', a fear whose verbal symptoms constitute 'Stevensishness' so to speak. In 'The Idea of Order at Key West', 'Esthétique du Mal', and most notably 'Sunday Morning', the rhetoric often rings with a peculiar and as if deliberate falsity, a device it might be for excluding the old confident European 'story in it' kind of poem: the influence of real rhetoric is kept at bay by means of a false equivalent.

I remember reading 'Sunday Morning', a poem I still consider
much over-praised, for the first time, and feeling that lines like

> Supple and turbulent, a ring of men
> Shall chant in orgy on a summer morn
> Their boisterous devotion to the sun
> Not as a god, but as a god might be

had strayed in from a different sort of poetry, for a reason the poet
might be unable to give. Such an impression about romantic rhetoric
is not uncommon – one finds it in the *Prelude*, in 'Hyperion' and in
poems of Tennyson – and it shows how cogent Bloom's basic ideas
about romantic influences can be. Eliot comparison is again
revealing. *The Waste Land* is full of stolen quotations which, just
because they are stolen, have become wholly a part of Eliot's
invented world and attendants upon its history. The romantic effect
on Stevens is quite different but perhaps equally deliberate, an
attempt to make a virtue out of writing a poem 'not as a poem, but as
a poem might be', somewhat as Browning deliberately fights off the
quest properties and suspenses in 'Childe Roland'.

The evasion would then be radical; an evasion by poetic means of
poetry itself. Stevens might be saying: to write good poetry now, one
must pretend that it resembles good poetry. The trope would be too
ingenious by half, but it is unfortunate that Bloom's emphasis on his
own mechanistic view of tropal influence obscures so important an
issue. He comes close to it, though, I think in this sentence: 'the
language of British and American poetry, from at least Wordsworth
to the present, is overdetermined in its patternings and so necessarily
is underdetermined in its meanings'.

This goes with an earlier pronouncement, about 'Childe Roland':
'Roland's consciousness is grounded in the realisation that meaning
has wandered already, and in a despair of ever bringing it back.'
Stevens, too, seems afraid of meaning, as something 'exactly itself',
and located in the achievement of a style. Avoid style by pretending
it, and meaning can be guaranteed to slip away into the proper limbo
of uncertainty and 'blankness' (a favourite Stevens word). The stress
of 'reality', and the apparent search for the feel of meaning, will do
the same job.

This seems to me the basic trope of Stevens – maybe one inherited
from American vacancies and making use of them – but it is the only
one Bloom overlooks. Its use by Stevens joins the intimate with the
evasive as if the two were the same thing – a highly Jamesian ploy.
Yet Bloom is still in a strong position, for if 'underdetermination' is

indeed the point in Stevens, a basic weakness turned into a strength, that is all the more reason why poet and critic are so close together. Meaning 'wanders', can wander, has wandered, into the *critics*, as part of the process of the poet's tropal overdetermination. Stevens is indeed the perfect critic's poet, as Bloom amply demonstrates in his elaborations on the possibilities of meaning, which is also buried influence, in the poems. But here the real originality of Stevens does escape him. Ultimately it is not possible to say much about the poetry because its effectiveness consists in saying so little itself. Bloom glosses that little very well: 'The crucial revelation is that life itself . . . is imaginative need . . . in the larger context of the space of life. Life too lives in a place that is not its own and, much more, not itself.' We get the message, as most readers and critics of Stevens have done. But Bloom goes on to clutter the situation with sentences like this: '*Chocorua* begins with a hushed stanza of definition and division that declares its own synechdochal rhetoricity, and that says what it is to be an Emersonian mountain in New Hampshire.'

No doubt the two are much the same. Such shadow-boxing is on a level with Stevens's own 'Yea-saying', praised by Bloom, but surely not much more than ritual affirmation as artificial as the ritual compassion, a suitably muted American version of the jaunty rhetoric of Valéry's *Il faut tenter de vivre*. 'Under every no / Lay a passion for yes that had never been broken' is no doubt a true saying and a needful one, but it shares the same defect with Wordsworthian affirmation. In poems 'exactly themselves' it is the poem that says 'Yes', and not the poet.

Bloom seems to think no other kind of poetry than the romantic and 'approximately poetic' can or should exist for America's poets. And it may be that only by living in New Haven, figuratively speaking, can one understand the need for New Haven's poet to be what he is, and focus the image of reality that he does. Reality is in this sense a very American thing – however much Stevens has managed to universalize it as an aspect of all human consciousness – a product of vacancy and of the nothing in particular, a very *natural* thing. Hardy apprehended this in his poem on refusing an invitation to America, and to compare New Haven to Wessex is to see why poetic 'reality' means nothing in the poetry of the Englishman. Wessex is a geographical story which Hardy could invent almost without knowing it, as Eliot more consciously invented the London of *The Waste Land*: both are real, because 'themselves', in exactly the same sense as, say, the castle and the country which Keats invented for 'The Eve of St Agnes'.

The decreative poetry that is not itself but approximately and romantically poetic, may none the less be a more specifically local affair than it claims, situated in American experience, and copied in a European context rather than felt. Auden seems to hint something like this when he refers to Stevens in 'In Praise of Limestone'.

> The poet
> Admired for his earnest habit of calling
> The sun the sun, his mind Puzzle, is made uneasy
> By these solid statues which so obviously doubt
> His antimythological myth.

The solid European object, as well as artefact, is too much with us to believe in American blankness. Bloom revenges himself on 'In Praise of Limestone' by calling it 'one of the most overrated poems of the century'; it is certainly antithetical to Stevens, and not in the Bloomian sense in which poets defend themselves from each other by new antitheses. It, and its poet, are indeed exactly themselves, not in the pejorative sense in which Stevens uses that description, but in a manner more loose, confident, baggy, free-flowing, than the description can bear to admit.

Finally, I doubt whether Bloom is even necessarily right in suggesting that good and real American poetry is now all of the romantic type that attracts him. Berryman and Lowell seem the obvious exceptions, good poets by any standards, indisputably American, but trained by themselves on European lines. Both have followed Yeats in seeking consciously to *make* themselves, in the sense in which other poets, such as Eliot, *are* themselves. It might indeed be argued that this making of the poetic self is the opposing response to those forces in romanticism which tended in the nineteenth century to deprive the poet of his identity, forces with which the spirit of American transcendentalism was so much in sympathy. Bloom played this down in his study of Yeats, stressing the influence of Shelley, but Yeats would not have sunk his identity in the great Shelleyan poem: he was the first to realize that if the modern poet's subject had to be 'reality', the self and its drama offered the best and perhaps the only available reality to be manufactured. *Life Studies* and *Dream Songs* are in the direct successors of Yeats, and inevitably opposed to that other tradition of Stevens, Carlos Williams, and their successors.

The process of self-making becomes a joke in Berryman, but a joke all the more in earnest for that:

> I didn't want my next poem to be *exactly* like Yeats
> or exactly like Auden

> since in that case where the hell was *I*?
> but what instead *did* I want it to sound like?

Quite properly Bloom is against Berryman, and presumably against Lowell too. Like Yeats and Eliot they have the instincts of aristocracy, the instincts that make 'the story in it', despite Lowell's efforts in *Notebook* to spill out his art in a fashionably contingent manner. Bloom's view is probably sound here: after their great initial success it seems unlikely that Lowell and Berryman will continue to appeal to the young in the way that Stevens, or Ashbery, do.

By contrast Stevens's 'world without imagination' does have an impressive durability, something 'permanent, obscure and dark', and the reductiveness that appeals in our time, perhaps increasingly. One paradox – an involuntary one – of Bloom's long book is that the 'difficult rightness' of Stevens does not call for his cultivated and comparative kind of literary appreciation. It is more like the complexity of sport forms, football and such, unsuited to Bloom's insouciant learning and warmth of erudite reference (I particularly enjoyed the ways in which he singled out his own favourite poem from *Harmonium*).

In the end a shadow falls. An alert and discerning censor in a totalitarian state, who would block the publication of Eliot or Lowell, Auden or Larkin, and other individualist poets, would have no qualms in allowing the continued appearance of Stevens. This may seem an unfair point, but it suggests something of the faceless side of Stevens, and his identification with that undifferentiated communal America which still resembles something in the future, in its indifference to, or denial of, Apollonian individuality, its lack of any need to evade

> the strict austerity
> One vast, subjugating, final tone

which *The Comedian as the Letter C* is himself determined *not* to evade. Whoever seeks to evade and to create his own individuality, as James did, as Eliot and Lowell and Berryman have done, is thereby debarred from participation in the true romance of American poverty. Bloom implies this with almost fanatical vigour, and shows his case to be a formidable one. Reading between the lines (which are not always easy to read) one finds his book to be an extended social and cultural commentary on a whole century of American self-consciousness, and the logic of its cherished and intransigent blankness.

The poetry of John Ashbery

The poet's mind used to make up stories: now it investigates the reasons why it is no longer able to do so. Consciousness picks its way in words through a meagre indeterminate area which it seems to try to render in exact terms. Most contemporary American poetry wants only to offer what Helen Vendler has called 'an interior state clarified in language'. 'Clarified' is an ambiguous word here, meaning the poetry's effort to achieve the effect of being clear on the page. In John Ashbery's case the wordage trembles with a perpetual delicacy that suggests meaning without doing anything so banal as to seem to attempt it. Poetic syntax is constructed to express with a certain intensity a notion of the meaningful that does not convey meaning.

Or does not do so by the normal linguistic route. Inventive poetry, that makes up stories, does so by emphasizing the usual ability of language to embody them, makes that ability into a positive power. 'Jabberwocky' emphasizes it by inventing its own words as it goes along, to demonstrate how completely and finally they then make up the tale. It parodies the charged language of poetry – particularly romantic poetry – in which the force of denotation itself produces connotation.

> St Agnes' Eve – Ah, bitter chill it was!
> The owl, for all his feathers, was a-cold . . .
>
> . . . And they are gone: aye, ages long ago
> These lovers fled away into the storm . . .

The poetry of the Romantics shows consciousness in two kinds, the kind that uses words to tell stories to and about itself, and the kind that knows words cannot express its intuitional being, even though that being can only become aware of itself by using them. Wordsworth, like Keats, can tell stories, stories about himself, but his poetry is also beginning to investigate the power of language in poetry to deny explicit meaning, to be precise about nothing more than itself, 'and something ever more about to be'.

The language of the *Prelude*, or of Shelley's 'Mont Blanc', seeks a mode for the inexpressible. Its clarity is a way of abdicating from the inexpressible mode of being that it also sustains. The clarity may be illusory, but the Romantic dawn and the Age of Reason unite to give it a great and naive confidence, so that the reader feels it is trembling on the verge of some great revelation, some breakthrough about the state of the universe and man's nature. As this kind of poetry develops and survives throughout the nineteenth century and into our own day, it learns how to use the effect without any expectation of getting beyond the effect. Most, though by no means all, of Wallace Stevens's poetry works on this principle. In Wordsworth the language of much of the *Prelude* is very different from that of a narrative poem like 'Resolution and Independence'.

Criticism of poetry in American universities, dominated as it is by the writings on romantic effect of Bloom, Hartman, de Man and others, seems to have brought to an abrupt end the fashion for narrative poetry. Berryman and Lowell were the great contemporary narrators, compulsive tellers of stories about the self, and their style was sharply and wholly comprehensive, perfectly expressing what Berryman's mentor R.P. Blackmur called 'the matter in hand', as well as 'adding to the stock of available reality'. Such poetry invented the self as Keats invented his lovers in their winter castle, or Hopkins the wreck of the *Deutschland*, or Milton the loss of Paradise: it was indeed a comparable feat of inventive artifice. By contrast, Ashbery's poetry, warmly admired by Bloom, perfectly illustrates Bloom's own thesis that 'the meaning of a poem is another poem'.

No question of adding to the stock of 'available reality'. The poem succeeds if it creates the image of another poem, and so on *ad infinitum*, like the advertisement picture that contains a picture of itself. Clearly, the poem in my eye and mind is not the poem that Keats or Lowell or Ted Hughes wrote, however absolute and real an artefact it may seem to be: but this is like saying that I am not really seeing a coloured surface but only a refraction of atoms that gives the appearance of colour, etc. The truth of art is the truth of appearance, and its invention is like that of the eye inventing the object it sees. That, at least, is the art of inventive and narrational poetry. The ghost or shadow poetry of Stevens and Ashbery and others can equally claim the title of art, but it is based upon a different premise: that we can never see the object or the poem as it really is, never quite know what we see or see what we know. Such art is born from a uniquely American mixture of influences. The metaphysical climate of Coleridge's, of Wordsworth's and Shelley's poetry is transmuted by Thoreau and Emerson. On the other hand, the scientific climate of physics and semantics destabilizes the confidences of art: the American poet knows that nothing exists in its own self and that Heisenberg's electrons cannot be objectively observed because the art of observation changes their nature. Such mental attitudes produce their own techniques, which rapidly become as conventionalized as any others in the history of poetry.

Ashbery has great skill in these conventions and something that can only be called charm, which has increased with each volume he has produced. The monochrome sixteen-line poems of *Shadow Train* have a great deal of charm, and an elegance of diction which can be heard by the inner ear reciting itself at poetry meetings on campuses, an elegance that mimes the act of evanescence, swooping on the sixteenth line to a vanishing point which echoes the dying fall in the alexandrines at the end of some of the stanzas of *The Faerie Queene*.

> In the time it takes for nothing to happen
> The places, the chairs, the tables, the branches,
>   were yours then.

> I mean
> He can pass with me in the meaning and we still
>   not see ourselves.

> young people and their sweet names falling,
>   almost too many of these.

Some of these sonnet-like poems have a deftly suggested 'inside' to them, as in a Mannerist picture. Ashbery's long poem 'Self-Portrait in a Convex Mirror' dealt in great apparent detail with the Parmigianino self-portrait in Vienna, described with admiration by Vasari.

> Francesco one day set himself
> To take his own portrait, looking at himself for that purpose
> In a convex mirror, such as is used by barbers . . .
> He accordingly caused a ball of wood to be made
> By a turner, and having divided it in half and
> Brought it to the size of the mirror, he set himself
> With great art to copy all that he saw in the glass.

The implications of this, for space and time, absorbed Ashbery; and he spent hundreds of delicate lines apparently talking about them.

> The words are only speculation
> (From the Latin *speculum*, mirror):
> They seek and cannot find the meaning of the music.
> We see only postures of the dream,
> Riders of the motion that swings the face
> Into view under evening skies, with no
> False disarray as proof of authenticity.

The tone is of a pastel Stevens, a mildly camp Eliot, yet it has a sureness and confidence of its own, however much we seem to have heard before what it seems to say. The artist's eyes in the mirror proclaim

> That everything is surface. The surface is what's there.
> And nothing can exist except what's there.

The poetry gently nibbles at an old paradox. Art is appearance, but while inventive, story-telling art ignores this and gets on with its invention and story, Mannerist art pauses, circles and remains, enchanted by the beauty of the paradox itself, 'the pure / Affirmation that doesn't affirm anything'. This kind of art is intent on the detritus of living that takes place beyond the enchanted glass, as if Keats, having launched the owl huddled in its cold feathers, and the hare limping through the frozen grass, had gone on to talk about the ordinary evening he was having in Chichester, Sussex. The paradox gives way to another. The strange thing about 'The Eve of St Agnes' is that the more we become absorbed in its tale, its invented truth, the more conscious we are of Keats leading his ordinary life in and around the poem. A very vivid inventive art, in fact, has it both ways: leading us into the story, and also into the being of the story-teller. By dwelling on the precariousness of its existence in the midst of life a Mannerist art such as Ashbery's causes both to fade into nothing on every instant and at every word, like the grin of the Cheshire cat.

But that is the point of the business. The art of fading in this way is a perfectly genuine one, like Sylvia Plath's attribution to her poetry of the art of dying. It is an art to suggest that 'Tomorrow is easy but today is uncharted', that the people who come into the studio, like the words that come from the poet's mind, influence the portrait and the poetry, filter into it

> until no part
> Remains that is surely you.

Everything, says the poet, merges into 'one neutral band', surrounding him on all sides 'everywhere I look'.

> And I cannot explain the action of levelling,
> Why it should all boil down to one
> Uniform substance, a magma of interiors.
> My guide in these matters is yourself.

Parmigianino, that is. The poet cannot explain, but he can suggest how poetry can now be made, not of course out of the things themselves, but by speaking of

> The small accidents and pleasures
> Of the day as it moved gracelessly on,

and of how

> What should be the vacuum of a dream
> Becomes continually replete as the source of dreams.

In one of the most satisfying moments of the poem the consciousness both of life and of art is seen as in the 'Ode on a Grecian Urn'.

> Like a wave breaking on a rock, giving up
> Its shape in a gesture which expresses that shape.

And the poet concludes:

> Why be unhappy with this arrangement, since
> Dreams prolong us as they are absorbed?
> Something like living occurs, a movement
> Out of the dream into its codification.

Something like living occurs; something like art occurs. Although his range is wider than all this might suggest, Ashbery founds the substance of his verse on the ideas explored in 'Self-Portrait in a Convex Mirror', and this is particularly true of the sequence of poems in *Shadow Train*. But a further dimension has been added: the 'magma of interiors' now proffers the notion of drama, the shadow of a story. We write it ourselves, of course, according to the Bloomian recipe that the meaning of a poem is itself another poem, the recipe that is both entailed on the Deconstructionists and repudiated by them.

Not that Ashbery is in any true sense related to or influenced by these still contemporary intellectual fashions, although their leading exponents admire his work. His other 'ideas', as embodied in his extended prose poems (*Three Poems*, 1970), some of the pieces in *The Double Dream of Spring*, in his elegant little plays and in *A Nest of Ninnies*, the novel he wrote with James Schuyler, have more in common with those of the French aesthetes Bachelard and Blanchot. One of the good things about Ashbery is that he never seems in the forefront of the fashion. *Three Poems*, not one of his more successful works – prose poems are not his forte – has the rather *passé* air which is both deft and comfortable in his best poetry but somehow not right in prose.

You know that emptiness that was the only way you could express a thing? The awkwardness around what were necessary topics of discussion, amounting to total silence on all the most important issues. This was our way of doing.

Maybe it was, but Ashbery's presentation of experience does not lend itself to manifesto. The important issue for a poet like Larkin is what he has to say, and if he has nothing to say he is silent. Ashbery, on the contrary, gets going when he has nothing to say. The absence of a theme is what he both starts with and describes. 'The poetry talks about itself. That is mainly what it does.'

Poets who say such things are usually in fact evangelists who want their poetry to change our lives. Like any other *bien pensant* of the game, Ashbery has given interviews and spoken of the 'pleasure of poetry that forces you back into life'. Such protesting too much means very little, although there is an odd kind of truth involved. Certainly this poetry is not a substitute for life, offering, as the magic of inventive poetry must do, an alternative drama. When Ashbery begins a poem with the line 'A pleasant smell of frying sausages' or (in inverted commas) 'Once I let a guy blow me. I kind of backed away from the experience', we know that an anecdote or drama, with Auden's or Larkin's narrative punch, will not follow. And yet the absence of a drama in some of the poems of *Shadow Train* is also its presence. A good example is the poem called 'Drunken Americans'. Like Wallace Stevens, Ashbery uses rather chunky, bizarre or coy titles, laid-on-the-line invented positives that seem not to connect with the negatives of the poem but to offer a kind of jaunty fiction for its dumb metaphysics. These titles 'see through' the inventions of living day by day, in which this moment is life but so was the last one. The two moments connect: Ashbery says he likes the 'English' spelling 'connexions'. In 'Drunken Americans' the poet sees a reflection in the mirror, a man's image

> fabricating itself
> Out of the old, average light of a college town;

and after a bus trip sees the same 'he' 'arguing behind steamed glass,
/ With an invisible proprietor'. These glimpses and moments have
some importance to the poet that is unknown to the reader: it
appears to prompt the reflections of the second two quatrains.

> What if you can't own
>
> This one either? For it seems that all
> Moments are like this: thin, unsatisfactory
> As gruel, worn away more each time you return to them.
> Until one day you rip the canvas from its frame
>
> And take it home with you. You think the god-given
> Assertiveness in you has triumphed
> Over the stingy scenario: these objects are real as meat,
> As tears. We are all soiled with this desire, at the last
>   moment, the last.

Something obscurely moves in the poem, and perhaps moves us, but
what is it exactly? The intensity of vision in an alcoholic moment,
which is yet not intense but merely watery and distasteful until the
will and the ego assert themselves in an act of artifice which is also an
act of destruction? 'Tears' mutely and significantly represents the
will to believe that something has happened; the ego lives by meat
and tears, and desires its moments to seem as real as they are. What
the 'something' is may be suggested in the next poem, entitled
'Something Similar', in which the poet gives a colour photo, 'to be
sweet with you / As the times allow'.

It is a very oblique way of suggesting romance. But then this
poetry seems not to wish to own anything, not even the words for
the moments of which it is made up. The sonnet-like form recalls,
perhaps intentionally, the mysterious drama in the Shakespearean
sequence. But there is a difference, apart from the obvious one. No
one would claim that our lack of knowledge is Shakespeare's actual
specification in what he is writing. There is something 'true' in there,
even if – particularly if – it is being invented. But Ashbery is a poet
who stylizes into apparent existence the non-events of consciousness, sometimes contrasting them in a rather witty way with the
perpetual work of art that consciousness has to make up as it goes
along. As he wrote in a poem called 'No Way of Knowing',

> It has worked
> And will go on working. All attempts to influence
> The working are parallelism, undulation, writhing

Sometimes but kept to the domain of metaphor.
There is no way of knowing whether these are
Our neighbours or friendly savages trapped in the distance
By the red tape of a mirage. The fact that
We drawled 'hallo' just lazily enough this morning
Doesn't mean that a style was inaugurated.

The feel of the poetry is compulsive enough for us to see life for a moment the Ashbery way, as the young Auden once made us see it his way. Auden's world of spies and significances, solitary women and derelict works, distilled from its excitingness in the thirties the absolute authority of a new fashion. Much more muted, Ashbery's manner has some claim to be the new voice of the late seventies and today, replacing the old-fashioned directness of life-studies and confessions. He depresses the properties of early Auden to give his own version of a new sense of, and employment of, time, of alienation as amiability.

Someone is coming to get you:
The mailman or butler enters with a letter on a tray
Whose message is to change everything, but in the meantime
One is to worry about one's smell or dandruff or lost glasses –
If only the curtain-raiser would end, but it is interminable.
But there is this consolation:
If it turns out to be not worth doing I haven't done it;
If the sight appals me, I have seen nothing.

Those lines from 'Grand Galop' skilfully synthesize the minatory style of Auden with Larkin's stylization of the non-life that we are vaguely conscious of mostly leading. Ashbery has since slowed down into more elegant and friendly kinds of pseudo-precision, somehow reminiscent of a campus art-shop, Virginia Woolf's shadow features on a clean tee-shirt, like the Turin shroud.

Yes, but – there are no 'yes, buts'.
The body is what all this is about and it dispenses
In sheeted fragments, all somewhere around
But difficult to read correctly since there is
No common vantage point, no point of view
Like the 'I' in a novel. And in truth
No one never saw the point of any.

Tell that to Henry James. The sonnet poems of *Shadow Train* have something of the Jamesian absence of specification, of events suggested which, as in *The Turn of the Screw*, are not intended by the author to have taken place either one way or another. But

James's absence of solution is not the absence of a story. Ashbery's popularity, like that of Virginia Woolf, which has proved so durable throughout the fashion changes in America, is connected with the air of being too helpless to organize a story.

> It connects up,
> Not *to* anything, but kind of like
> Closing the ranks so as to leave them open.

Helplessness is a pose: the real thing is hard to turn into an art that makes it seem authentic. What is more impressive about Ashbery's poems is their tactile urbanity, the spruce craft of their diction, which, like James's prose, becomes more enjoyable and revealing, in and for itself, each time one makes one's way through it.

Moreover, a typically modern kind of intimacy grows out of the very absence of what one conventionally understands by that quality. It is an odd paradox that Ashbery as an American poet is more 'shy', more distant in his manner, than any English equivalent of comparable talent writing today. This kind of good taste, a poetic version of 'Wasp' characteristics, is a comparatively recent phenomenon in American poetry. Nothing could be more different, for example, from the gamy, compulsively readable anecdotage of late Berryman, in *Love and Fame*. Robert Creeley (much derided by Berryman), Richard Wilbur, Robert Bly and A. R. Ammons share something of this verbal stand-offishness, but Ashbery is better at it than they are and uses it in more diverse and interesting ways.

The question remains whether it is not in some respects a way of escape from the reader, a means of teasing him or amusing him in order to avoid saying anything of real interest. Wasps have good manners, but not necessarily that completely personal perception and utterance – the two fused together – which in the context of modern poetry produces something really interesting. The point is of some significance, for English poets today tend to be braver than Americans in fashioning their view of 'the matter in hand', even though usually without thereby adding to 'the stock of available reality'. I take this at random from a recent review:

> On Saturday morning a drove of joggers
> Plods round the park's periphery
> Like startled cattle fleeing
> The gad-fly specture of cholesterol.

That is the poet actually speaking to us, in an old-fashioned, mildly witty manner, in a way that Ashbery, for all his colloquial ease ('Yes, but – there are no "yes, buts" '), would never dream of doing. The quotation above makes it clear, rather depressingly so, that the poet lives in just the same world that we do. Though Wordsworth called himself 'a man speaking to men', his experiences and the words he put them in are unique, by definition quite different from ours: no one else has had them or could utter them. And by that criterion Ashbery is a very genuine poet.

Yet there remains a discrepancy between his expression and what is personal to his vision: the first is wholly his own; the second – if he inadvertently lets us catch sight of it – can seem very second-hand. Larkin never writes a poem in which the two do not coincide, and that gives his vision its compelling directness. It is possible to get the impression that Ashbery may take some little shared cliché – the loneliness of urban America, or the contingency of its appearances – and very carefully work this up until the poem stands unique and upright by virtue of its own indistinct distinction. '*Märchenbilder*' shows how successful the process can be.

> How shall I put it?
> 'The rain thundered on the uneven red flagstones.
>
> The steadfast tin soldier gazed beyond the drops
> Remembering the hat-shaped paper boat that soon . . .'
> That's not it either.
> Think about the long summer evenings of the past, the queen
> anne's lace.

The poet's own vision enters and transforms the fairy-tale but is too homeless to reside within its pat invention.

> *Es war einmal* . . . No, it's too heavy
> To be said.

Saying, for Ashbery, requires the lightest and most evasive of touches. His poems hate to be held down; his style seems to have trouble sometimes with its own simplicity. This is shown by the opening of 'City Afternoon', a poem that ties itself to a famous photograph which shocked American sensibilities in the thirties, a snap of pedestrians waiting for the lights to change, their features significantly empty of the American dream.

> A veil of haze protects this
> Long-ago afternoon forgotten by everybody
> In this photograph, most of them now
> Sucked screaming through old age and death.

But the poem disappears into the photograph. It is instructive to compare it with that masterpiece of invention, Larkin's poem on looking at a young girl's photograph album.

Shadow Train is composed of poems that repeat with an appropriately greater faintness Ashbery's gift of his own version of this negative capability. There is something soothing about poems that do not assert themselves, but vanish in performance into what they appear to be about. Since the days of *The Tennis Court Oath* (1957) and *Rivers and Mountains*, the poems have become steadily clearer and more simple, more effective at distancing themselves from the self-conciousness of the 'poetry scene'. And that means much in terms of their originality and their quality. Like other good modern American poets, Ashbery has been careful to keep Englishness out of his voice: instead of it one can hear the French tone (he spent ten years studying in France), the Italian of Montale, something, too, of the later Mandelstam in translation and of more recent Westernized Russian poets, such as Brodsky. But these international overtones have produced a voice that can be heard reading itself in a purely and distinctively American context.

The point is of some significance in terms of the contrast between Englishness and Americanness in the contemporary poetic voice. The usually positive and robust reality of what the English voice is saying is often let down (as in the four lines I quoted above) by a fatal over-presence. The poem has exposed itself, and is caught there on the page in all its unavoidability of being. Keats, most English of English poets, has this kind of reality at its best, but the permanence can be embarrassing if the poem has failed quite to make it (in the nature of things, not many can) and has to stand for ever on the magazine page or in the collection, all its shortcomings honestly revealed. Still more revealed, on the radio or at a reading, by the exposed and exposing tones of the English poetry voice. That could never happen to Ashbery. He avoids definition as America does, in the 'No Way of Knowing' which is one of his titles. In a poem he once made a joke of it, referring to English writers:

> They're so clever about some things
> Probably smarter generally than we are
> Although there is supposed to be something
> We have that they don't – don't ask me
> What it is.

Ashbery's poetry, the later poetry especially, shows what it is with a singular felicity. What his poetry does is finely told in a sentence from 'A Man of Words':

> Behind the mask
> Is still a continental appreciation
> Of what is fine, rarely appears and when it does is already
> Dying on the breeze that brought it to the threshold
> Of speech.

Moment after moment: *Day by Day* by Robert Lowell

Poets who make their poems and their readers a part of their daily lives are a feature of our time. Strange if Shelley, for instance, had been so familiar; had cast and recast for us anecdotes of his childhood, his school-friends, his marriages, his sensations and thoughts. Like most Western poets before us his creative consciousness was a sword to be used for and against the world, in the service of God or learning, atheism, progress, hope or despair. Now, to a poet, his consciousness seems all there is: nothing else has much sense any more.

This is not necessarily because we live in a nightmare age – on the contrary; our age may be too settled and cosy for external effort to seem worthwhile. Perhaps we have entered on a cycle of Cathay. Certainly, much of Lowell's late poetry – and *Day by Day* is his final collection – has the beautifully crafted unstrained intimacy of the Chinese classics. The ancient glittering eyes are gay because desperation is taken for granted and there is no need for their glance to convey it.

> Where is Hart Crane,
> the disinherited, the fly by night,
> who gave
> the drunken Dionysus firmer feet?
>
> To each the rotting natural to his age.
>
> Dividing the minute we cannot prolong,
> I stand swaying at the end of the party,
> A half-filled glass in each hand –

Li Po might also have raised a glass in each hand and drunk to another drunken poet. In the earlier part of the poem Lowell contemplates the friendly dereliction of his own house in Kent, which reminds him of Longfellow's house on Brattle Street, and 'the long face of his wife who burnt to death', of 'the New England Augustans' who

> lived so long one thought
> the snow of their hair would never melt

and so via Hart Crane to the end of the party, the present moment. In the hands of a master like Lowell it is easy to forget how much sheer effort, how much manic will-power and ambition has gone into this leisurely and beautiful commonplace.

Though both Lowell and Berryman fit naturally in the tradition of the unfenced American consciousness, it is arguable that the way they craft that consciousness in verse did not originate in America. It is not compatible with the undifferentiated response of Wallace Stevens and his disciples, the 'latest free men' who homogenize experience in order to be and do the same as everyone else. That 'self' of Lowell and Berryman seems to have been inspired by Yeats out of Hardy, a dazzling hybrid of Hardy's musing day-by-day poetic being, and Yeats's highly conscious self-creating and recreating. Like Berryman's, Lowell's poetry seems designed to offer an absolute self even before Mallarmé's eternity has had a chance 'to change it into what it really is'. In the process one could say that the example of Hardy could supply the day-by-day continualness, that sense of the hundrum which liked to write about even the 'dullest of dull-hued days': Yeats supplied the drama and the exclusiveness.

Lowell's connections were of course far grander than anything Yeats could manage – there would have been no need for him to record of the parish of Drumcliff 'An ancestor was rector here' instead of 'my grandfather was the curate' – and it is a nice question in what ways Lowell's position at the top of the American social tree affects his self-presentation. Certainly it gives it a kind of aristocratic gossipy ease and confidence; people with such connections assume the response of others, in their own class and outside it, and yet Lowell is far too confident ever to sound even faintly snobbish, as Yeats undoubtedly was. There is something spacious and seigneurial in his self-absorption, but its extraordinary appeal, as a 'Life Study', is neither social nor diagnostic.

Given that amount of talent feeling its way towards originality, any sort of poet might do it, and indeed Berryman is the other big instance of the fascination to be got out of the poet's day-to-dayness. 'Life, friends, is boring', he wrote in *Dream Songs*: 'we must not say so'. And he went on to speak of his mother's dictum that the bored

have no 'inner resources'. This indeed is a poetry without inner
resources, which in a curious way makes it so compulsive. In a poem
called 'The Shell', about another *alter ego* poet, Lowell says that he
was not

> comfortably himself
> when he made
> his verse the echo of his conscious mind.

The art is in holding the reader with a glittering eye by being all too
uncomfortably yourself. Consciousness is what Berryman called
'irreversible loss'; both for him and Lowell, as Lowell writes in 'Art
of the Possible'.

> Your profession of making what can't be done
> the one thing you can do

doesn't apply to living –

> the art of the possible
> that art abhors.

For Hardy, as indeed for Tennyson, writing helped you to live; and
in this sense Lowell and Berryman are scions of quite another
tradition, the continental one of the lost poet, the damned and the
dandy. In this volume Lowell has recovered from the excess and
inertia of *Notebook* and *History*, and moved very close to
Berryman. He writes a poem for him headed 'after reading his last
Dream Song'.

> Yet really we had the same life,
> the generic one
> our generation offered
> (*Les Maudits* – the compliment
> each American generation
> pays itself in passing . . .)
> We asked to be obsessed with writing,
> and we were.

The odd contemporary conjunction is that the *poète maudit* does
not now reject life as something for the valets, but claims to *be* it.

> In the old New York we said,
> 'If life could write,
> it would have written like us.'

The poetry does indeed give a powerful illusion to that effect, for us
at this moment, but for how long?

Mothers of course continue to play a big part. Lowell's is an old friend since the day when her body was shipped back from Italy, 'wrapped in foil like panettone'. She and her psychoanalyst's practice – shared, it seems, with Merrill Moore – appear a good deal in *Day by Day*, no longer as the figure in *Life Studies*, caught expertly by Lowell's terrible camera, but as a presence to be pondered in a no less deadly but more comradely fashion:

> It has taken me the time since you died
> to discover you are as human as I am . . .
> if I am

In the poem 'Unwanted' she is compared with another of the same kind:

> I read an article on a friend
> as if recognising my obituary:
> 'Though his mother loved her son consumingly,
> she lacked a really affectionate nature;
> so he always loved what he missed.'
> This was John Berryman's mother,
> not mine.

As he says in another poem: 'this is not the directness that catches / everything on the run and then expires.' The stylishness that was typical of *Life Studies* – the poem arrested by its own finality, like a suicide hitting the pavement – has developed through *Notebook* and *The Dolphin* into a style almost too relaxed and judicious, but such a poem as 'Unwanted', the moving masterpiece of this book, is a complete justification.

> Is the one unpardonable sin
> our fear of not being wanted?
> For this, will mother go on cleaning house
> for eternity, and making it unlivable?
> Is getting well ever an art,
> or art a way to get well?

For a poet so wholly identified with difficulties in living there is something heroically natural in rising to the challenge of knowing one is on the way out. Yet as any *New Yorker* poem today shows us, the tone of true desperation can also be imitated. Even Lowell, like Larkin, is sometimes caught in his own manner, but Larkin's poems can turn this sardonically to account by sending up their own awareness of it, as in 'I work all day, and get half drunk at night.' The Lowell equivalent – 'I cannot sleep solo, / I loathe age with

terror' – is unresonant, for in poetry, as in other affairs of life,
American know-how cannot take that wryly complacent English
pleasure in things going and being wrong. Lowell deals with
desperation, as with the way it repeats itself, in a manner quite
different from that of Empson or Larkin. On other subjects than self
and family he is apt to beat the air or be too smart, as in 'Since 1939',
which refers to Auden and by implication to his poem on that 'low
dishonest decade', and ends:

> if we see a light at the end of the tunnel,
> it's the light of an oncoming train.

Some curious exclusiveness in Lowellian honesty makes it impossible for him to achieve the public or the epigrammatic note; but
the opening poem, 'Ulysses and Circe', is a tender conjugal allegory
of the most effective kind, which treats the figures of the myth as if
they were self and father, wife and friends.

So is 'Marriage', a meditation on Van Eyck's picture of the young
Arnolfini couple, and also on his own poetry and current domesticity. 'The picture is too much like their life' is an odd commentary
on his own life studies, which pull off the triumphant paradox of
such art – being of absorbing and almost magical interest while at
the same time conveying that there is nothing really very interesting
about them or about the poet himself. Another and more moving
paradox of the poetry is that its restlessness is a real progress:

> we learn the spirit is very willing to give up
> but the body is not weak and will not die.

Trying to be nothing but itself, it still grows and develops, always on
the move outwards and never settling for good in a well-known area
– 'no dog knows my smell'. 'The Downlook' speaks of 'an anthology
of the unredeemable world', but

> There's no greater happiness in days of the downlook
> than to turn back to recapture former joy.

That is a splendid denial of Dante's famous commonplace about the
greatest misery being to remember happiness in time of misfortune,
and it is followed by other lines which affirm and share the happiness
of art.

> others have been lost like this,
> yet found foothold
> by winning the dolphin from the humming water.

Since it matured, Lowell's poetry was always a kind of diary ('we are designed for the moment') and now it is over it still seems to continue like one, holding triumphantly at bay the truth enunciated by the 'dead master' of *Little Gidding*.

> For last year's words belong to last year's language
> And next year's words await another voice.

Confidences: *Delusions, etc.* by John Berryman

The publicity of a suicide, and the fashionable notion that to live on the edge of one – eventually falling over – is the modern sensibility's most authentic stance, should not deter us from recognizing that Berryman's poetry has 'added to the stock of available reality' by creating for consciousness a new shape and voice. His *Dream Songs* are as wholly absorbing as *Hours of Idleness* must once have been. Berryman, like Lowell, has demonstrated that verses, old-fashioned 'numbers', are still capable of being a 'form that's large enough to swim in and talk on any subject that I choose', and capable of focusing a sprawl of experience more intensely than any prose.

This is a portent in itself for prose today starts with all the confidence. But that leads to confidences. And in their fashioning of poetry, Lowell and Berryman have solved the problem of how not to be the great American bore. Compare their talking verse, dense as lead one moment and light as feathers the next, with the brutal monotony of that talking prose which Hemingway evolved and which Miller, Mailer, Burroughs and others have practised in their various ways. In *Dream Songs* and *Love and Fame* Berryman makes that kind of prose appear, beside his verse, not only doltish and limited but incapable even of straight talking.

It is not much good quoting him because the effect, the 'imperial sway', is built up over a long period. This does not mean that his poetry is like *Paterson* or Pound's *Cantos*: in fact, it works in a quite opposite manner. Yeats and Auden were his masters, with all that such a relationship implies of 'making', as he recognizes in 'Two Organs'.

> I didn't want my next poem to be exactly like Yeats
> or exactly like Auden
> since in that case where the hell was *I*?
> but what instead *did* I want it to sound like?

The anguish of making it sound like it sounds is present in it in a very direct way, much more directly than in Yeats. In *Dream Songs* Berryman seems to have managed to hold in opposed tension and full view the poet at his desk as he was putting down the words, and the words themselves as they appear on the page – the poet wrestling in his flesh and his 'huddle of needs' while the poetry engraves itself for ever. Our attention is kept by a vivid sense of the pain of the process and our pleasure in its product.

Certain sorts of judgement become irrelevant in consequence. The poet is not asking us to pity his racked state or to understand the shameless, obsessed and exhibitonist behaviour it goes with. When Yeats ('hard-headed Willie', as Berryman calls him) writes, 'I walk through a long schoolroom questioning', or,

> I count those feathered balls of soot
> The moorhen guides upon the stream
> To silence the envy in my thought,

it is well understood he is doing no such thing. Experience and poetry do not coincide: this is the rhetoric of the moment, not its actuality: the thought he is silencing and the questions he asks have been cooked up in the study. His air of immediate imperiousness is a bit of a fraud, which we see through and enjoy him all the more for: all the same, we do judge.

And with Berryman we don't, for how judge someone who while talking and tormenting himself is also writing a deathless poem about the talk and the torment? Except that deeper down we know this combination to be a formalistic device and Berryman's control of it to be total: the abundant humour is an index of that certainty of control. This knowledge makes us watch the taut spring vibrate with an even rapter attention. There is a parallel with the formalism so brilliantly used by Lowell in *Life Studies*, where the poetry seems itself the act of expiation and cancellation, as if poet and subject had died the instant the words hit the paper. Lowell's emblem might be a speech cut off at the moment of death: Berryman's, the Word condemned eternally to the torture of composing itself at its desk.

This posthumous collection is disappointing, perhaps inevitably so. Berryman had become himself in his poetry well before he died: indeed, he died partly of that fact. Compared to the great arch of experience of his main collections, an arch wherethrough

> Gleams that untravell'd world, whose margin fades
> For ever and for ever when I move,

the last poems are uncertain and repetitious, failing to achieve what is so essential for his spell, a total correlation of mood and meaning. Here we have to start again at the beginning of each poem and the 'imperial sway', as Berryman defined it for himself, struggling for it with such concentration (he observes in a poem that it was not the achievement and perhaps not the aspiration of Pound), is never built up. Tennyson's 'untravelled world' is visited by this poet in the act of movement, but in *Delusions, etc* it is thrown away in affected starts and jumps. Strangely enough, the trouble seems to be that these poems are not sufficiently about Berryman: Berryman has already been brought to being in the big collections and there is nowhere else for him to go. The 'Henry' whom we came to know so well in *Dream Songs* returns for a poem or two, but in a painfully disembodied state: having survived his book, he cannot – like Sherlock Holmes after the Reichenbach Falls – ever be quite the same man again.

For although Berryman brings the world and its denizens under his imperial sway, and on a scale remarkable in any poetry, he cannot let them operate on their own. The poems in *Love and Fame* which described his Cambridge experiences before the war brought in other persons, famous or anonymous, of an intense reality because they were all a part of his prolonged and arduous nightmare, as are God, and various wives and other ladies, and of course the father who shot himself. But when he wrote of other people in hospital, willing them to possess and exist in their own problems, the tension cracked and the sway collapsed. Virtues themselves must be subdued to the mad concentration of this poetry, like vices: they cannot function at the side in a blessed or even in an amiable contingency – indeed the contingency which seems to be the very stuff of the poems' texture has been raised to the heights of formal apotheosis. Hardy also wrote about himself, and small or large things happening to him, in collections of a great many short poems, but these are truly random: so unformal is Hardy's presentation of the self that we can meet it afresh in each poem as if we had never known it before, and feel curiosity about its doings, as in life. Curiosity is not precisely the word for our reception of the Berryman experience. In spite of all the loose ends of talk, the name-dropping and the allusions, we have no urge to find out with whom, when, why and what. 'I perfect my metres', he wrote, 'until no mosquito can get through.'

We can see the process beginning in *Homage to Mistress Bradstreet*, Berryman's early and determined breakthrough into the big league. Mistress Bradstreet, the seventeenth-century New England poetess who turned out 'proportioned spiritless' poems in the manner of Quarles and Sylvester ('her favourite poets unfortunately'), is subsumed into the author by his fascination with the difference between what she was and what she wrote: in his evocation of her he forces the two into coincidence as he forced them when making his own poetry. She is imagined as him, writing of herself then as he of himself now, and thus the absorbing interest and beauty of the poem is not historically or objectively enlightening. Berryman suggests the process in his preface to *Dream Songs*: 'Many opinions and errors in the songs are to be referred not to the character Henry, still less to the author, but to the title of the work. The poem, then, whatever its wide cast of characters, is essentially about an imaginary character (not the poet, not me) named Henry.' Which means the poet and me.

In *Dream Songs* Delmore Schwarz and many another entered in the same way, very eerily, but when in *Delusions, etc* we are given a poem called 'In Memoriam Dylan Thomas' it is sadly about nothing in particular. A first section describes in suitable detail the death in coma, then:

> So much for the age's prodigy, born one day
> before I surfaced – when this fact emerged
> Dylan grew stuffy and would puff all up
>   rearing his head back and roar
>
> 'A little more – more – *respect* there, Berryman!'
> Ah he had that, – so far ahead of me,
> I half-adored him for his intricate booms & indecent tales
>   almost entirely untrue.

In his anecdotage in *Love and Fame* Berryman was superb, but here something has pulled him off the peak of his mastery; reminiscence, neither interesting nor revealing for its own sake, turns too simply true to work. There is something moving about the bald way in which the two poets become exactly themselves in that fatigued report. And yet at such moments the traveller whose tale is only of himself is on the verge of becoming what his whole oeuvre has striven so cunningly and so triumphantly against, the man of confidences that Wallace Stevens found 'an obstruction, a man too exactly himself'. Fatigue or despair, supposedly, overcame at last Berryman's marvellous resistance to that self as it was, his determination to make it what in the prologue to his *Sonnets* he called 'soluble in art'. In spite of every apparent difference, Berryman shared most of Stevens's aesthetic premises, and so his private *besoin de la fatalité* becomes a great public monument, 'to terrify and comfort'.

To fulfil Blackmur's desideratum of a language

> so twisted and posed in a form
> that it not only expresses the matter in hand
> but adds to the stock of available reality

had been the great ambition: 'I was never altogether the same man after *that*.' For the 'supernatural crafter' the materials available to make reality came to an end, but not the heroism that Berryman learnt from 'hard-headed Willie' and made the goal of his art.

> I had, from my beginning, to adore heroes
> & I elected that they witness to,
> show forth, transfigure . . .

E. E. Cummings: *Complete Poems, 1910–1962*; and *Dreams in the Mirror. A biography of E. E. Cummings* by Richard S. Kennedy

American poetry has two traditions: open and closed. The first may well be the mutated offspring of the styles of poetry shipped over wholesale, at one time or another, from England; the second represents the more or less systematic repudiation of those ready-made poetics by the developing American consciousness. 'Closed' poetry is in fact usually much more original in technique and tone than 'open' poetry, and it reveals its ancestry only in its degree of encapsulation. Its idiom is self-defining: it does not merge with or enter other poetic areas; it cannot breed, and can hardly even metamorphose.

The immense and various achievements of American poetry owe much to the difference between these two traditions, and to their possible modes of combination. Robert Frost might be said to write a closed sort of poetry that looks as if it were open: the style of the first deviously and beautifully works to give the impression of the second. Something altogether more complex but not wholly dissimilar seems to be taking place in the poetry of Wallace Stevens and John Berryman. But the boldness of American poetry is towards the previously undefined and unexpressed, although poets of the open tradition – Robinson Jeffers, Robert Lowell (who at moments can sound so strangely like him), William Carlos Williams, A. R. Ammons, John Ashbery – are not only obvious heirs of Whitman but are all, as it were, on the best of terms with the laborious traditions and hermetic practices of closed poetry; they are as familiar with Emily Dickinson as they are with Ezra Pound, and with Edwin Arlington Robinson, John Crowe Ransom, Marianne Moore and E. E. Cummings as well.

What do not pass from one tradition to the other are the sense and the uses of time. 'Closed' poets may have long careers – some of the longest, steadiest and most prolific – but time seems to stand still for them (and so for their readers). They do not, like the two spectral poets in the waning dusk of *Little Gidding*, 'urge the mind to aftersight and foresight'. Again, the cause may be essentially historical. In 1867 Henry Timrod composed an 'Ode for the Commemoration of the Fallen':

> Stoop, angels, hither from the skies!
>   There is no holier spot of ground
> Than where defeated valor lies,
>   By mourning beauty crowned!

The homely 'spot' does not prevent the poetry from slipping effortlessly, and very movingly, into the English idiom of more than a hundred years earlier, the commemorative idiom of Collins. But there is nothing derivative or old-fashioned about the sound of it: it ignores times, standing in its own enclosure outside it. The Timrod syndrome, as we might call it, is surprisingly endemic in closed American poetry; an idiom, once fixed (and no matter where it comes from), has its own special place. English and European poetry, by contrast, is a great deal more corporate and collective, moving all together when it moves at all. And Cummings offers a striking example of the Timrod syndrome in a very different guise; he too can tranquilly ignore what is going on outside his own self-occupied enclosure, impervious to fate and history, of which contemporaries like his friend Allen Tate, and the younger generation of Robert Lowell, were so wonderfully aware. No poetry could be less closed than the 'Ode to the Confederate Dead':

> Turn your eyes to the immoderate past,
> Turn to the inscrutable infantry rising
> Demons out of the earth – they will not last.

It is the implicit claim of American open poetry not 'to last', but to be in just that state of instability and turmoil which, as it does also in Lowell's 'For the Union Dead', joins the personal to the public chimera, the predicament of now to that of the past.

Such poetry is its own continuing drama, and also an index of changing awareness. Inside their own closed idiom a John Crowe Ransom or an E. E. Cummings can do almost anything, provided they do not reveal themselves to be sensitive to outside possibilities. The poems they make must not show signs of wanting to be 'understood'. Ransom perceived this very well: 'little helpless', as Cummings's first wife called him, did not. The wife, Elaine Thayer, also made the memorable comment: 'I don't like people who want to be understood.' A perpetual child, Cummings did like to be understood, and his charm made his friends eager to help and protect him. But in his best poems he is absorbed, like a good child in its toys, and isn't in the least concerned with understanding. The analogy is exact, for the reader must get down with the poet among the building blocks on the floor; it is no good meeting him when he is charming the grown-ups – especially the more sentimental ones – with his cute ways. Auden once wrote that 'to grow up does not mean to outgrow either childhood or adolescence but to make use of them in an adult way'. By this criterion Cummings's poetic techniques are designed to perpetuate adolescence, both in the poetry and the poet.

Most good poets suffer for their gift and use it to make such suffering visible – to write out the nature of it is to enhance its reality. Cummings uses the gift to retain and maximize the insulation of a happy childhood. Poetry is his toy, but not 'his toy, his dream, his rest', as it was for Berryman and Lowell, the plotted and cultivated scenario of an otherwise distracted existence. It is a paradox that although Cummings's typographical dodges seem to be drawing attention to themselves they in fact come off best when they are at their least self-conscious. The poems that are admirable in *Tulips and Chimneys* (published in 1922, a memorable year in literary annals) are the series of 'Actualities' and 'Post Impressions'. Sexual experience with ladies like Marj and Lil provided Cummings with the perfect subject for his format: detachment in comic physical involvement; the agilely precarious recording of experience and appearances, even as the poet lies passive in the sleazy, clumsy, but not hostile machine which he is laboriously manipulating. Experience, particularly sexual experience, is like a new American mechanism to be spryly mastered (as in that splendid poem 'she being Brand') and the poet in the happiest way is both operator and passive recorder.

All his life Cummings was able to write such poems, but they alternate with the winsome and folksy type which became more common as time went on. Here his best technique goes bad on him; artful verbalization emphasizes rather than remakes cliché, as it often does in the poetry of Dylan Thomas, with which Cummings's has many affinities. But what suits the rhymed sentences of Patience Strong sounds worse than banal in the arrangement of such virtuosos:

> the trick of finding what you didn't lose
> (existing's tricky: but to live's a gift)

> the teachable imposture of always
> arriving at the place you never left

A poem from Cummings's juvenilia borrows Keats's thrush:

> Music is sweet from the thrush's thoat!
>   Oh little thrush
>   With the holy note,
> Like a footstep of God in a sick-room's hush
>   my soul you crush.

That is engaging, but the note is still being struck fifty years later.

>   o purple finch
>   please tell me why
>   this summer world (and you and i
>   who love so much to live)
>   must die

Finches, unlike thrushes, do not in fact sing; but this special bird, 'eagerly sweet carolling', informs the poet that it would not be able to do so if it had anything to tell him. The early thrush poem seems an honest effort, but the purple finch has acquired a style quite incongruous with what it is required to say.

The young Cummings was clearly very bright and quick to learn, but unlike his master Pound he has no real intellectual curiosity, and little wish to understand other sorts of art than the ones he could make use of. Unlike most good poets he was inarticulate in a critical context. His attempt in the 1920s to write about T. S. Eliot's poetry for the *Dial* had to be rejected after he had produced a few comments on the level of 'this is one of the few huge fragilities before which comment is disgusting'. His prefaces to his collections make embarrassing reading, and are not unlike Dylan Thomas's comments on his own verse. In the 1950s Cummings too became a great draw on the poetry-reading circuit, his Peter Pan charm making a special appeal to girl students. But he was happiest whittling away in the Wendy house at Patchin Place, Greenwich Village, or at Joy Farm, the New Hampshire holiday home of his parents.

In a political sense he was equally naive. He had met and admired Aragon in Europe, and in 1931 translated his laborious (and unpunctuated) long poem *Front Rouge*: it is hard to say whether the translation or the original is the more *ennuyant* today. Cummings's own visit to the Soviet Union where he had no one to look after him, was such a chapter of minor accidents and misfortunes that he does not seem to have had time for any of the larger statements of retrospective admiration or disillusion customary among writers at the time: he was too busy recording the minutiae of what happened to him. Late in life, in 1956, he produced a little poem about the martyrdom of Hungary which must have brought a blush for poetry to the cheek of W. H. Auden, if he ever read it (it is instructive to compare Auden's own succinct poetic comment on the event: 'The ogre does what ogres can . . .'). On the other hand the poem beginning:

> 16 heures
> L'Étoile
> the communists have fine eyes

is highly memorable because it uniquely and effectively registers a chaotic, child's-eye impression of the genuine Cummings sort. It is the difference between the private and public face, the public and private comment. Poets march against the Bomb and make their own protests, but Cummings's public announcement that he could 'never forgive' President Truman for dropping the bombs was merely absurd. It sounds like a small boy who says he will never forgive you for sneaking off with his pencil sharpener. After which he would soon recover what Cummings artlessly referred to as his 'natural buoyancy of spirits'.

Not unnaturally, father-figures were important to Cummings. His own father was a remarkable man, a self-made Baptist minister who became influential in cultural circles in Cambridge and Boston and well known throughout the United States for his writings and the causes he sponsored. He also made a fair amount of money. He was obsessively devoted to his son, to whose interests as an artist, writer and erratic husband he devoted himself tirelessly; but he was also anxious to keep Cummings permanently captive in the family on a regular allowance. Cummings had to escape from this overpowering solicitude, but he never escaped very far, and he always hero-worshipped his father ('He is a famous man whereas I am a small eye poet') and ran for help to him in crises. He was also very close to a warm and sympathetic mother, the closer after his father, motoring up to New Hampshire, was killed by a train on a level-crossing in a snowstorm: his mother survived with a fractured skull.

The oedipal experience finally liberated Cummings, and significantly stabilized his own private life. Of his three beautiful wives the only one who responded to and got on with his mother was the third,

Marion Morehouse, an ex-model and failed actress, and she and Cummings remained happily married until his death in 1962. Elaine Thayer, his first wife, was also socially the grandest, a demurely dazzling little rich girl, married to the young millionaire dilettante Scofield Thayer, who admired Cummings's verses at Harvard, became his first patron, and sent a cheque for a thousand dollars for the epithalamion Cummings wrote for his wedding. (Cummings senior was greatly displeased.) Thayer took an emancipated view of marriage, lived in a bachelor penthouse and neglected his wife, who inveigled Cummings into a kind of Peter Pan and Wendy affair, as a result of which a daughter was born. After divorce and remarriage to Cummings Elaine reverted to type and became disenchantedly toughminded, soon going off with an Irish banker. For many years Cummings was denied access to his daughter, who grew up not knowing he was her father. Cummings went from frying pan to fire: his second wife was a demonic lady who when in liquor, as she usually was, complained loudly and publicly about the small size of his penis.

These facts about Cummings's life are not unusual, given the time and the milieu he moved in, but they have no relation to the poet and his poetry. We cannot feel, as we do with most imaginative writers, that the life helps us to see more deeply into the art, to understand it better. This might be a sign that the art itself is inferior, but in Cummings's case we can hardly say that. Most bad art is an involuntary pastiche of what was going at the time: his is certainly not. He was a genuine original, like John Crowe Ransom, who has also recently been the subject of a big biography, Thomas Daniel Young's *Gentleman in a Dustcoat*. The charm of both books is that they could in a sense have been written about anybody, and their accumulation of careful, often pedestrian detail is interesting in itself rather than for the light it throws upon the subjects. They are 'pure' biographies, like an old-time Bradshaw. Ransom was of course different, a Southern gentleman, a scholar, golfer, and quietly devoted family man. A hood seems to cover his personality; nothing can be flushed out from the darkness under it, and – as in the case of Cummings's more conventionally rackety life – there was probably nothing much there. The main interest of Ransom's biography is in the group of critics and poets with whom he was associated.

With both, the talent for composing a 'closed' kind of poetry seems independent of the nature of the poet, even seems to act as a substitute for it. Both live in the ponderous past, encased in solid

Victorian three-decker jobs which might have been composed about
the time George Eliot died and bespoken by the family of an
influential bishop. As we move on from winter engagements to
summer vacations ('there was some talk of their going again to
Bangor that year but in the event they did not'), we marvel at the
meticulousness of the research (Cummings's Aunt Jane left him
seventeen thousand, four hundred and twenty three dollars and sixty
four cents) and come to love it for its own sake. The tone, a little
owlish in its reverence for the past, seems as appropriate to the
vanished 1930s as art deco. It is with this sort of decorum that
Richard S. Kennedy discovers for us that the Cummingses sometimes stayed in the summer with Max Eastman and his wife at
Martha's Vineyard, and that the Eastmans 'had a private beach that
allowed nude bathing. Marion especially enjoyed it, for, proud of
the beauty of her body, she liked to share it with intimate friends.' A
grainy photograph shows nice faces, teeth and smiles, but discreetly
cuts out anything below them.

Even Cummings's experience in France in the First World War –
experiences that led to the writing of *The Enormous Room* –
become part of the family archive. His duties were limited to
washing down ambulances behind the lines, and even there he
behaved so irresponsibly that he and a fellow delinquent were sent to
a detention centre for dubious foreigners and minor offenders. This
was like a mad school, which suited Cummings exactly. He loved
the misfits there – 'delectable mountains' as he calls them – and his
lively account of the place is still highly readable. Despite the
occasional tedium of the macaronic style, its vision of excremental
innocence still survives while *Three Soldiers*, the more painstaking
war novel by Cummings's friend Dos Passos, has become hardly
more than a curiosity.

At its best, *The Enormous Room* has the clear ebullient vividness
which Cummings got from his hero Joyce: in 1918 bits of *Ulysses*
were appearing in *The Little Review* where he found them shortly
after he had also discovered Pound. The poem which came as a
revelation to him was *The Return* ('Slow on the leash, pallid the
leash-men!') and he wrote soon afterwards a poem which, however
much it owes to the classical aura of Pound, H. D. and Imagism, is
unmistakably his own.

      Tumbling-hair
        picker of buttercups
          violets

dandelions
And the big bullying daisies
   through the field wonderful
with eyes a little sorry
Another comes
   also picking flowers.

The iconography of the Dis and Persephone story ('herself a fairer
flower') is compressed into a new and successful form. From his
Harvard days Cummings had a grounding in the classics – a
considerably better one than Pound – and a good teacher had
encouraged him to attempt translations, both free and exact. His
technical breakthrough, which still owed much to Pound and was
probably not consciously arrived at, was the discovery that the same
idiom would fit any situation. Joyce's grand style adapted itself
deliberately to the meanest context, and Cummings's miniatures
learned to do the same. A simple example is one of the 'Portraits' in
Tulips and Chimneys, 'i walked the boulevard':

i saw a dirty child
skating on noisy wheels of joy

pathetic dress fluttering

behind her a mothermonster
with red grumbling face

cluttered in pursuit

pleasantly elephantine

while nearby the father

a thick cheerful man

with majestic bulbous lips
and forlorn piggish hands

joked to a girlish whore

with busy rhythmic mouth
and silly purple eyelids

of how she was with child.

There is here the same dependence on a neat 'point' which marks all
Cummings's successful poetic contraptions, though the point may
build up in the poem's shape and not be sprung in the last line. There
are contexts, like the 'war' poems and the semi-political squibs
where such a point will not work, and where Cummings's cute
cursory innocence does not answer. But point can come in the form of

an excellent descriptive conceit, like the sky in 'Impressions II', first resolved 'by the correct fingers of April' into 'a clutter of trite jewels',

> now like a moth with stumbling
>
> wings flutters and flops along the
> grass collides with trees and
> houses and finally
> butts into the river.

Himself a painter and draughtsman, though of no great originality or power, Cummings at his verbal best often suggests the painterly techniques of the Impressionists and post-Impressionists and their admiration for Japanese art. His verse in fact is at its best when it draws attention not to its own words but to the picture they are bringing into existence. That is the kind of observation that would mean nothing in connection with most poetry, but with Cummings there can be a real sense of space between the words on the page and the mental images evoked. In the best poems, and the ones that best stand rereading, we seem to slip straight into the mental images. The zestful verbal capers, anthology pieces such as 'anyone lived in a pretty how town', have a short reading life: their verbal substance is not of the kind that survives prolonged acquaintance. The poetry is at its worst when the verbal and sentimental are made to play engaging games together, as in 'my father moved through dooms of love' or 'sons of unless and children of almost'.

This indicates a matter of great importance in relation to Joyce's verbal art. *Finnegans Wake* not only remains wholly and eerily alive but it can move us deeply in the simplest way. Joyce has in a sense found the modern way of doing what Dickens did in relation to crossing-sweepers and the deaths of children and Barkis going out with the tide and David Copperfield's vision of his mother holding up her baby in her arms. Cummings often seems to be looking for the modern way of doing such things, and not finding it. It is of course invidious to compare a great writer with a minor verbal artist, but the point is none the less a valid one. Cummings almost never moves us: he is his own child, too self-absorbed.

Almost never, but he approaches tenderness sometimes, as in the 'etcetera' poem, in which the word falls through successive slots of meaning – a way of dismissing sentiment, of pushing detail impatiently aside, evading parental exhortation, shrugging off oneself and one's dreams – until it falls into its final and tenderly intimate meaning, all the more tender and intimate for being a euphemism and earning a capital letter.

> (dreaming,
> et
>   cetera, of
> Your smile
> eyes knees and of your Etcetera).

In general, though, Cummings has none of the artist's sensitivity to the outside world and to the reality of other people and their responses. Nothing shows this more clearly than a small poem which must upset friends and fellow artists, the non-Jews, as is the way with such things, more than the Jews themselves.

> a kike is the most dangerous
> machine as yet invented
> by even yankee ingenu
> ity (out of a jew, a few
> dead dollars and some twisted laws)
> it comes both prigged and canted

– 'pricked and cunted' in the original version, which had to be bowdlerized when submitted to the *Quarterly Review of Literature*. It appeared in 1950 in the collection *Xaipe*, published by OUP after Cummings's American publishers had declined to continue making losses on his work.

Despite remonstrances Cummings insisted on including it, whipping out his smallboy reaction and protesting that a kike was not a Jew but an American hybrid, which was the point of the poem, and citing his recent experiences in Hollywood ('a wailing wall for Christians') where he had endeared himself to no one and failed to obtain employment. Many Cummings poems, especially in the *Xaipe* volume, are wishfully satirical, but to be effectively bitter a satirist must be involved. Memorable open poetry is subversive in its very nature, but a closed poetry cannot go out to subvert. Shock words like 'kike' and 'nigger' do not quite seem quaint, however, even in our unshockable era; liberal America minded them very much, and perhaps would still do so. The real trouble is that they point to something mean – in both the American and the English sense – in the poet's satiric impulse. As his biographer shrewdly observes, Cummings could only see the world as directed at him and 'emblematic' of his situation. So does everyone at times, poets particularly, but while poets like Yeats and Lowell return by this very process to the universal, Cummings remains in his own area of smallness.

Out of it come his own special effects, which are certainly like no one else's. He is a poet for do-it-yourself readers, and the best criticism of his poetry, like Norman Friedman's *E. E. Cummings: The Art of His Poetry*, takes a technical and structural line and gets down to close analysis of the typography. This collected edition is austerely and beautifully produced, without notes or introduction, but these are not missed. There are felicities every few pages and once in a while a whole poem that succeeds. Cummings's own way of treating the mythological flourished and persisted: one of the best of the poems that he wrote towards the end of his career, harking back to the Persephone piece, recounts the tale of Venus, Vulcan, and Mars, and the laughter of the gods when the lovers are taken in the artificer husband's web:

> my tragic tale concludes herewith:
> soldier, beware of mrs smith.

Halcyon structures: *City without Walls* by W. H. Auden

W. H. Auden is the rarest kind of poet in a post-romantic age: interested not in himself but in the plural aspects and manifestations of the world which he turns into his art; interested in people and animals as in ideas and landscapes, rivers, buildings, metres, histories, coigns and quirks. In his poetry, as in Renaissance rhetoric and the diagrams of Vitruvian man, the human being can take on the impersonal contours of nature or art without ceasing to be human: one poem in this book is called 'Profile', another, 'River Profile'. All this is rare in an age in which even reportage can become a sort of self-caress (witness Norman Mailer's pieces on the Moonshot) and in which most good poetry embodies 'My Sense of Myself, cast as Aged Endymion' (Robert Graves), 'The Child who Died' (Robert Lowell), 'The Child about to Die' (Sylvia Plath) – an age in which the Poet as Poem seems not so much the answer to, as the only possible formulation of, the increasingly baffled and plaintive question: how can language accommodate me?

Whatever its virtues and powers, such poetry is claustrophobic; beside it, even the world of the Symbolists, in which towers, swans, lakes or schoolchildren are properties of the poetic mind, seems to give us some elbow-room on life in common. Much poetry today gets more and more trapped in its box, like television, and by comparison the 'halcyon structures' which Auden continues to erect appear like the Baroque theatre of the old-fashioned cinema.

The converse of claustrophobia in modern poetry (and not only poetry) is what reviewers call 'profound seriousness'. The phrase has been applied with proper respect both to Auden's poems and essays, but however well-intentioned an obeisance to a large figure in literature, it has not the smallest relevance. Profoundly serious writers today are those who for various reasons – they may be urgent and worthy ones – distrust the power of art to say things for them, and suppose that the artificial, the carefully fashioned and inge-niously crafted, is capable only of being itself.

It is true that Auden has drawn a distinction between the poetry of Ariel, the poetry of delight, and that of Prospero, the poetry of wisdom, but it works only as a helpful and commonsensical diagram. The two cannot be separated: but delight calls for more experience in the reader – something corresponding to the craft that has brought it into being – in order to reveal its wisdom. Shakespeare in 'Venus and Adonis' is as *wise* as Fulke Greville (whom it would be meaningful to call a 'profoundly serious' poet) once we have learnt to understand and participate in the rich idioms of the art that does not conceal art but revels in it. The poetry that begins in 'contraption' (to use another Auden term) may none the less end in revelation; but it will not get there by way of seriousness, profound or otherwise.

Auden's early poetry often employed portentousness as an engaging device of rhetoric and artificiality, but never seriousness (insofar as 'Spain' was a 'serious' poem it was a bad one). 'Consider this, and in our time' (*Poems*, 1930) was a superb bit of rhetoric since discarded – for example, a threateningly ellipsed and telegraphic syntax dotted with anacolutha – to create a mood that was commonplace in intellectual circles at the time but was never so successfully caught in poetic language.

In *City without Walls* he meditates on equally commonplace topics of our time – the vistas of boredom and neurosis, compulsory leisure and compelled privacy; the cult of sport and violence instead of work and war, the possibility of the Bomb and its aftermath – and in the hands of his idiom and metre (a cunning fusion of rhymeless classical measures with the stressed alliterations of Old English poetry) these ordinary fears and foretellings become a sort of magic compound delighting the eye and yet engaging the mind. Rhetoric and meditation combine – Ulysses summoning up the terrors of time and anarchy in *Troilus and Cressida*, on the one hand, and on the other, Tennyson's honey-tongued flirtation in *In Memoriam* with the gropings of Victorian science.

> What they view may be vulgar rubbish,
> what they listen to witless noise,
> but it gives shelter, shields them from
> Sunday's Bane, the basilisking
> glare of Nothing, our pernicious foe.
>
> For what to Nothing shall nobodies answer?
> Still super-physiques are socially there,

frequently photographed, feel at home,
but ordinary flesh is unwanted:
engines do better what biceps did.

Quite soon computers may expel from the world
all but the top intelligent few,
the egos they leisure be left to dig
value and virtue from an invisible realm
of hobbies, sex, consumption, vague

tussles with ghosts. Against Whom
shall the Sons band to rebel there,
where Troll-Father, Tusked-Mother,
are dream-monsters like dinosaurs
with a built-in obsolescence?

A Gadgeted Age, but as unwordly
as when the faint light filtered down
on the first men in Mirkwood,
waiting their turn at the water-hole
with the magic beasts who made the paths.

Small marvel, then, if many adopt
cancer as the only offered career
worth while, if wards are full of
gents who believe they are Jesus Christ
or guilty of the Unforgivable Sin.

Yet another rhetorician, Langland, is played on as a mute variable in
the withdrawal sequence:

Thus I was thinking at three a.m.
In mid-Manhattan till interrupted,
cut short by a sharp voice.

It tells the poet not to play 'Jeremiah-cum-Juvenal', and he retorts:
'So what, if my words are true.'

Thereupon, bored, a third voice:
'Go to sleep now for God's sake!
You both will feel better by breakfast time.'

Evading without deprecation 'the preacher's loose immodest
tone', Auden secures for himself the last reward of the picking and
unpicking scald – to be most simply himself when his verse is at its
most entrancingly mannered. Accuracy and affection, the proper
way to observe both animals and men, is present in his 'Mosaic for

Marianne Moore', in which the animals she describes get a voice for
their acknowledgements:

> For poems, dolphin-graceful as carts from Sweden,
> our thank-you should be a right
> good salvo of barks . . .

And in the 'Eulogy' for Professor Nevill Coghill:

> you countenanced all species,
> the alphas, the bone-
> idle, the obstreperous
> and the really rum . . .

A penetrating familiarity comprehends in its glance the animal in us
all that yawns and scratches and lusts as a part of our angelic faculty
and our god-like apprehension. Auden is singularly and excellently
lacking in the modern dualism that is obsessed with the flesh and its
mechanic achievements ('Run smoothly by Jaguar farmers') and yet
cannot see itself performing the act. For him the flesh is spiritual
because comic, more accurately and lyrically mimed in the copu-
lations of the zoo than in those of the modern screen, and a *gestalt*
for ever out of reach of the ludicrous *Selbstlichkeit* of a Henry
Miller, whose pudenda tick like parts of his typewriter.

> For a while
> we talked by the fire,
> then, carrying candles, climbed
> steep stairs. Love was made
> then and there: so halcyoned,
> soon we fell asleep
> to the sound of a river
> swabbling through a gorge.

'Love was made' – the casual passive tells us much about the poet's
ability not to be himself when doing what everyone else does, and
'Song of the Devil' shows him still retaining (as in 'City without
Walls') an affection for Groddeck's theories, which have stood the
test of time better than most others of their epoch.

> Ever since observation taught me temptation
> Is a matter of timing, I've tried
> To clothe my fiction in up-to-date diction,
> The contemporary jargon of Pride.
> > I can recall when, to win the more
> > > Obstinate round,
> > The best bet was to say to them: 'Sin the more
> > > That Grace may abound.'

If you pass up a dame, you've yourself to blame,
For shame is neurotic, so snatch!
All rules are too formal, in fact they're abnormal,
For any desire is natch.
    So take your proper share, man, of
      Dope and drink:
    Aren't you the Chairman of
      Ego, Inc?

The most remarkable *tour de force* in this collection are the eight songs from *Mother Courage*, metrically the most subtle ballads Auden has given us. Their air of simplicity conceals a degree of technical experience and sophistication that makes the point a great deal better than does the 'war equals capitalism' insistence of their originals. 'Song of Fraternisation' –

That May the days were bright,
And starry every night.
The regiment stood on parade:
They gave their drums the usual thwack,
They led us then behind a stack,
Where they fraternised with us

– 'Song of Unconditional Surrender', and 'Song of the Soldier before the Inn' –

No sermon, now, Rev! It's a crime.
The cavalry have no time,
Dying for King and Country

– seem to me as superior to Brecht as the songs in Pushkin's *Feast in Time of Plague* are superior to their prototypes in John Wilson's *City of the Plague*. But then Brecht, unlike Auden or Pushkin, is undoubtedly a 'profoundly serious' writer.

The flight of the disenchanter: *Early Auden* by Edward Mendelson

Both Humphrey Carpenter in his recent biography and now Edward Mendelson in this very illuminating critical study emphasize the vulnerability of the younger Auden, and perhaps the Auden of any age. A secure childhood, but accompanied by a sense of failure and inadequacy at school and in relation to others; a fear of appearing dull and anxious and uncouth, compensated for by making himself the legendary figure who seems to understand everyone and everything – 'Hunt the lion, climb the peak, / No one guesses you are weak' – this dualism is commonplace among the gifted of all ages, particularly the gifted young. Most such persons, though, have a secure place, a secret wholeness of self-satisfaction into which they can withdraw. We can detect it, even enter it to our own corresponding satisfaction, in the poems of Edward Thomas, of Hardy, of Eliot. But not in Auden's. He is not even on terms of intimacy with the 'Wound' to which he writes the letter.

The act of working – and Auden became a workaholic as well as a heavy drinker – obscures most effectively the question of who one is. 'The soul doubtless is immortal where a soul can be discerned.' The poem's immortality, in Auden's case, does not depend on the survival in it of a self. It is interesting that he instinctively sought one, at the time of his juvenilia, in the poems of Hardy and Edward Thomas, twin voices to be imitated. A special favourite was one of Thomas's most characteristic poems, 'Lights Out': 'I have come to the borders of sleep . . .'

> The tall forest towers;
> Its cloudly foliage lowers
> Ahead, shelf above shelf;
> In silence I hear and obey
> That I may lose my way
> And myself.

The poet's desire to get lost in sleep reveals his actual presence in the poem more subtly and strongly than anything else could do, as it does in Philip Larkin's poem with the repeated line: 'Beneath it all, desire of oblivion runs.' Those negations disclose an individuality as nothing in Auden does. His sort of equivalent would be to write, as he does in 'Oxford', 'Here too the knowledge of death / Is a consuming love' – and the tone of that could be paraphrased from a guidebook or a work of psychology.

'All I have is a voice', he wrote, in his early work, and its potency depended on its impersonal authority. Charles Madge's reaction – 'There waited for me in the summer morning, / Auden, fiercely, I read, shuddered and knew' – was common among those at the time who understood the nature of new utterance in poetry and were unconsciously awaiting it. That it was not the voice of an individual was, in terms of the Zeitgeist, so much the better: a bleak impersonal severity was in fashion, as was the idea of communal enterprise, in poetry as in society. But Auden never did develop his individuality. The cosy mannerisms of his latter period are no more personal than the youthful tones, but are just as much something in the air, the sound of the leader of a group or fashion, though no longer one that was minatory and exhilarating.

Not infrequently it happens that the tone was not altered at all between the early and the late periods. As soon as the undergraduate of 1926 was introduced by his friend Tom Driberg to *The Waste Land* he took to writing stanzas like

> In Spring we waited. Princes felt
> Through darkness for unwoken queens;
> The itching lover weighed himself
> At stations on august machines

which has not only ceased to be Eliot and become Auden but is the same Auden – although not as accomplished – as the one who around 1950 was to write for Cyril Connolly that most plummy of camp poems, 'The Fall of Rome'.

> Fantastic grow the evening gowns;
> Agents of the Fisc pursue
> Absconding tax-defaulters through
> The sewers of provincial towns.

The always questionable relation between self and group is characteristic of this poetry, the sign of a duality both accepted and exploited by the poet. Mendelson observes that as he began his career Auden wanted 'both absolute isolation and absolute community, one for the mind, the other for the flesh', and 'in his poems he had no need for a dramatic mask; he was invisible without one'. This may be a way of saying that the poems do not necessarily believe in their own air of complete confidence, of assertiveness over and rapport with the reader. They seem to be in personal charge but disappear into the isolation of art. Barbara Everett comments that 'it is the sound of a man who knows that he sounds like this, assents to sounding like this, but is not like this'. Then what is he like? Nothing else. The art is all, as it is in Mozart or Shakespeare: it is the art (as Auden put it in 'The Age of Anxiety') of 'the sane who know they are acting', rather than 'the mad who do not'. Sanity for this poet is keeping the show on the road.

The poet is what the poetry seems; part of the art of the contraption is to make up an impression – a disconcerting or alluring one – of the man inside it. The uniqueness of Auden's poetry lies in its being the result of an act of will. A similar act of will might have made him a doctor, a geologist, a brilliant teacher. That he turned out to be a brilliant poet does not alter the essential arbitrariness of his decision to become one. And his attitude to his art ('we *may* write, we *must* live') remained permanently affected by that decision. The paradox is that other poets who have, as it were, found themselves in their poetry, take their dedication to it for granted: their art is for them the most important *human* activity, proclaiming poet as man and man as poet, paired in harmony. Gabriel Josipovici blames Auden for his attitude to art, rightly seeing in it a rejection of the slow, painful exploratory process which results in the organic creation of a Mallarmé, a Joyce, an Eliot, a Wallace Stevens or a Montale. Auden's act was that of scald or court poet, lead man in a team, the analogy again being with modern activities likes physics or film-making. For such an act, art must be highly decorated but untrustworthy, halcyon but bogus, beautifully made to be true to nothing else. Auden is the 'half-witted Swedish deckhand' whom Basil Wright and Harry Watt, the directors of *Night Mail*, saw scribbling 'the most beautiful verse' for them on an old GPO table and telling them to 'just roll it up and throw it away' when its profuseness had to be checked. *Night Mail* is the strongest magic ever brewed by Auden, a magic that completely enchants and dispossesses what it celebrates.

The brilliant creature who looks like a Swedish deckhand is also an image of the Mozart who so affronted the serious Salieri, a legend dramatized with elegant intensity by Pushkin and vulgarized in the play *Amadeus*. Artists dedicated as and for themselves recognize such genius but secretly, almost unconsciously, hate and envy it, for it discredits their labours to bring their own special gifts to fruition. 'Negative capability' takes on a special meaning in Auden's case. He comes as close as any poet in the post-Romantic age to what Coleridge said of Shakespeare – 'a very Proteus of the fire and flood' – naming and inhabiting people and things, entering into being while having no being of his own. In our time this primary activity of the naive poet is no longer possible. Auden could not get into things and people, but he got instead into the spirits and sense of the age, into its moods and dreams, its fears and neuroses, its fashions and crazes, from Homer Lane to Sheldon, from the yo-yo to the carbon date. He turned into hard magic everything in the consciousness of the time that was questioning and uncertain, muddled and ap-prehensive, everything that was reaching out, as the poetry itself seemed to be doing, for new devices and solutions, new images of wholeness and salvation.

Poetry eternalizes these things, but also embodies in the process the very weakness its transforms, its 'flat ephermeal' nature. Poetry only survives 'in the valley of its making'. That marvellous poem 'Spain', which chastened liberals disapprove of today, gets its power from its accurate conjuration of the illusions of a special moment, its fidelity to that moment's sense of 'Today, the struggle', and tomorrow (which never comes in poem or history) the idyllic social utopia. Auden, as he told Isherwood, knew they could only live among lunatics, and the same is true of his poems. Unlike most great poetry they do not beckon to another world but make one out of the absurdities of the present.

Of course, if that had been the poet's intention the magic would not have worked: the young Auden wrestled with real problems as other intellectuals were doing. Mendelson is not only his most perceptive critic but executor, guardian and scholar-chief of Auden studies, and this study tells us more than any other about the background of his early work and the scaffolding and ideas behind his poetry, particularly of the big stuff, ambitious raids on significance like *The Orators* and *The Ascent of F6*. Mendelson's tone is humourous and humane, and he never tries to impose a paraphrase of an interpretation, but he is up against the problem that all Auden critics face. Since his art was not evolved and explored but magical and ephemeral, Auden's poems lose their point in the focus of commentary, just as they frequently did when he himself revised them at a much later date ('Oxford' lost everything when its syntax was made more plausive). I recall the sensible and humanitarian glosses made by Richard Hoggart in his early study, and my own feeling when I was working on Auden that they were in a frustrating way both true and not true; that one could neither take the poems as magic anecdotes and incantations nor as (what for instance 'Just as his dream foretold' or 'Our hunting fathers' seemed to be) coherent meditations on social and personal states.

The success of an Auden poem, especially an early one, depends on its simplicity. When he pursues a complex argument as in 'Meiosis', which Mendelson analyses, the poem sustains the complexity by making a special thing of it, like an ingenious pump or gear, but calls in magic too as an insurance (the Dantesque last line) and ends up with all its bits and pieces seeming strewn on the page around it. Mendelson picks them up, observing that the poem explores a heterosexual conceit, the progress of the seed into the womb, with all the consciousness this must imply of imperfections passed on and inspissated traumas perpetuated; yet because love is the universal and functional instinct the seed-giver is not depressed by this knowledge. The poem is an impressive, even satisfying contraption, but there is no life in it. In his maturity Auden would have been more genial, more cunning and more clear, but it is doubtful if he would have been more inspiring. The poem lacks sex and its excitement of the group, the excitement that is so extraordinary and has such controlled success in 'Consider':

> Then, ready, start your rumour, soft
> But horrifying in its capacity to disgust
> Which, spreading magnified, shall come to be
> A polar peril, a prodigious alarm,
> Scattering the people, as torn-up paper
> Rags and utensils in a sudden gust,
> Seized with immeasurable neurotic dread.

As the Airman would say: 'Much more research needed into the crucial problem – group organization.' Mendelson feels that energy like this is 'a projection of the Airman's (Auden's) contradictory desire for order and no order at once'. But where do we find Auden at all in such a poem? Granted his near-obsession with organization and meaning, and with the importance, which he often stressed, of a subject, the fact remains that the personality and behaviour of the Airman exist only as a secret excitement or glee. In 'Consider' it seems likely that the rumour 'horrifying in its capacity to disgust' is in fact connected with homosexuality, and the secret group knowledge that goes with it. But this again is a case of Auden's talent for disappearing not only into the overwhelming atmosphere of the poem but into the general sense of apprehension and impending disaster ('It is later than you think') which the poem has conjured up.

The ideal Auden poem of this date always moves outwards into a public scene imagined in its significant details and observed as if from the air or by radio ('Supplied elsewhere to farmers and their dogs / Sitting in kitchens in the stormy fens'). The torn-up paper is reminiscent of the famous shot in *Things to Come*, where the camera focuses on a ragged scrap of newsprint caught on wire, giving news of ultimate war-horrors. The image of the helmeted airman, with his lordly perspective, is superb but farcical, too, just as his exhortation is also a spell of comfort against the horrors that a demoralized society imagines are awaiting it. Auden's poetry is deeply aware that the group want both to be thrilled by their bard and to joke with him, and that the ideal shaman is both a power and a figure of fun. The Airman is related to the curious persona of 'Mother' which Auden adopted socially in his late maturity, when in addition to the role defined in 'Your mother knows best' he would present mother as a clown figure, reciting the first line of Spender's poem as 'Your old mother thinks continually of them that are truly great.' Reading Benedict and Malinowski, the young Auden was no doubt well aware of the function of this kind of thing in group anthropology: the fear of mothers or bears was negated by the shaman taking on their role.

Mendelson quotes a letter written in 1932 in which Auden revealed the source of *The Orators*, probably with a touch of parody of Eliot's notes to *The Waste Land*:

The genesis of the book was a paper written by an anthropologist friend of mine about ritual epilepsy among the Trobriand Islanders, linking it up with the flying powers of witches, sexual abnormalities etc.

The friend was John Layard, who had shot himself through the head in Berlin two years before, out of jealousy over a boy Auden was also interested in. Amazingly he failed to kill himself and was taken to hospital by Auden, after which he made a full recovery. Despite his depressions and instability he was a remarkable theorist and original thinker, and the papers he wrote for the *Journal of the Royal Anthropological Institute* – 'Flying Tricksters, Ghosts, Gods and

Epileptics', and 'Shamanism: an Analysis Based on the Flying Tricksters of Malekula' – are the specific influences, behind *The Orators*, mixed with the doctrines of D. H. and the personality of T. E. Lawrence, and with the image of a revolutionary hero that came from Lenin and the early romance of Nazism and *Fuehrerprinzip*.

Together with the charade *Paid on Both Sides*, *The Orators* developed the Auden technique later adopted in the plays he wrote with Isherwood: exotic and mythical matter from the past and present and transposed into the group life of English schools and homes. Such a transposition was standard practice among the modernists – Eliot had used it in *The Waste Land* – but Auden gave it not only the special emphasis of a game among initiates but a corresponding and disarming frivolity (though *Paid on Both Sides* is significantly more serious, and more moving, than *The Orators*). As usual there is a discrepancy, particularly grotesque in the latter case, between the impact of the work of art and what the artist and his critics have said about it. Auden wrote to Naomi Mitchison that 'the theme was the failure of the romantic conception of personality'; and expressing dissatisfaction to another correspondent he said the result was 'far too obscure and equivocal' – what was intended as a critique of the Fascist outlook 'might be interpreted as a favourable exposition'. That, indeed, is one reason why *The Orators* comes off as well as it does, for Mendelson emphasizes that however much the early Auden wanted to respond 'positively' to the challenge of the time and become the young poet spokesman for enlightenment and left-wing ideals, his art would not oblige. The group was essential to it, the cause was not. And neither was the Message. However much he tinkered with *The Ascent of F6*, the end remained a muddle, though the individual speeches and poems are so effective; and compared with its group liveliness the satire of *The Dog Beneath the Skin* operates on the most elementary level.

The most significant comment on *The Orators* was made by Auden himself in a preface to a new edition in 1966. He cannot, he says, 'think myself back into the frame of mind in which I wrote it. My name on the title page seems a pseydonym for someone else, someone talented but near the border of sanity, who might well in a year or two become a Nazi.' Its central theme, he then felt, was hero-worship, but had he ever been a hero-worshipper? Had he in fact, before he went to America and fell in love with Chester Kallman, ever been anybody, except a brilliant and dispossessed talent? The later Auden does not recognize the earlier, just as the writer of the early poems seems wholly different from the anxious and wretched being of his Journal and Diaries. Keats is Keats in letters as in poems, but Auden is not Auden. No wonder his early work and his manifestos to friends are so obsessed with 'wholeness'; and it is highly ironical that Madge and other readers ('My states of mind were broken. It was untrue / The easy doctrine which separated things') should have been so struck by the force of the new doctrine. Mendelson comments: 'Madge had it backward. Auden implied connections and relations only to announce their absence or failure.' It is rather, perhaps, that Auden's early poetry is always having the opposite effect to the one proclaimed, delighting when it threatens, reassuring when it warns, relaxing when it sets out to brace. No wonder Leavis, the apostle of true wholeness, was so disillusioned.

With great acuteness, Mendelson traces the wholeness of the problem to an early essay called 'Writing' which Auden did for Naomi Mitchison who was editing a collection called *An Outline for Boys and Girls and Their Parents*. Written in a simple family style, it discusses the connection of words with isolation and self-consciousness. In trying to bridge a gulf and restore wholeness, language in fact connives at the disjunction it tries to overcome. A hunting group learns to talk when it tries to recreate the communal excitement of the hunt (was Auden recalling Tolstoy's theory of art, here?) but words are naturally antagonistic both to user and referent. In reconstituting experience they separate us from it and from the wholeness we seek to attain. Mendelson suggests that Auden's account of language's origin in a sense of absence, its ineffectual efforts to bridge a gap, comes close to structuralist theory 'a generation before Derrida and Lacan', although the poet's schoolroom style in the essay is at the furthest possible remove from the opacity of later theoreticians. Be that as it may, the piece certainly sheds light on the way Auden's diction gets its characteristic effects, and the gap his poems make between subject and response, a gap that becomes virtually an aesthetic weapon. Mendelson's nose for what is relevant in unlikely places – critics, as he says, have written off this essay because of the book it came out in – is typical of the sensitive and detailed scholarship he brings to this period of Auden's life.

One might add that the even more effective weapon with which the poetry both underlines and combats the alienation of language is what might be termed the Saving Personification. Direct appeals fail: it seems merely out of place when at the end of that ambitious poem

'The Malverns' Auden invokes the words of Wilfred Owen and Katherine Mansfield ('Kathy in her journal') to rub the message home; as out of place as when in *1929* ('It was Easter as I walked in the public gardens') he introduces us to an actual drop-out on a bench. It is true that 'The Malverns' is a superlatively absorbing poem, and also the first poem in which Auden's settled maturity is forecast, with its caressing verbal catalogues and its simplistic ingenuities of appeal. It humanizes the helmeted airman and introduces us for the first time to that totally unintimate intimacy which from now on will be the tone of a poet 'assuming to sound like this', as he does in the Byron pastiche in *Letters from Iceland*.

The reader's feeling of intimacy with most poets takes two forms. First, that the poet is revealing to him, quite naturally and by the act of composition, something he could not reveal to anyone else; second, and conversely, that the poet 'in touching our hearts by revealing his own', as Hardy puts it, also reveals that he has a self to keep back. The second does not apply to later confessional poetry, like Lowell's and Berryman's, whose convention is a complete avowal to the reader; and neither applies to Auden. His early intimacy of threats and promises is like the disclosures of an older and dazzling schoolboy prodigy to the reader as younger child; and this changes to the reader being accepted as one of a group of comrades and initiates, the poet forthcoming and unbuttoned but retaining his powers of fascination and omniscience. The poems written in Brussels in 1938–9, 'Musée des Beaux Arts', 'Gare du Midi', 'The Capital' and 'Epitaph on a Tyrant' – are good examples of this, and the success of such a style of communication reveals the hollowness, embarrassment even, when the group seems to have disappeared, and the poet of 'Lay your sleeping head' and 'I sit in one of the dives / On Fifty-Second street' is talking to us on our own. The residue of discomfort and unreality in such poems is produced by a suggestion of contrived aloneness, a person-to-person relation does not come naturally.

It is here that the Saving Personification comes to the rescue. These feats have an air of the unintentional, of inadventure, of something the poet does not bother about and the reader can carry away with him.

> And, gentle, do not care to know,
> Where Poland draws her eastern bow,
>   What violence is done,
> Nor ask what doubtful act allows

> Our freedom in this English house
>   Our picnics in the sun.

The simple reference to Poland holds considerable complexity. Poland under Pilsudski is a tyrant appropriately armed. But the bow is also that a violin and musician, the vulnerable instrument of peace, while the pictorial referrent in the personification is Rembrandt's Polish Rider, the taut and soldierly masculine figure with the features of a girl; more generically, Poland plays the part in history of both victim and rebel. The beauty of the image seems serenely independent of the pushy insistence of the poet as leader and lecturer. It is the same with the green heraldic glimpses of English landscape that Auden lifted from Anthony Collett's *The Changing Face of England*:

> Calm at this moment the Dutch sea so shallow
> That sunk St Paul's would ever show its golden cross
> And still the deep water that divides us still from Norway.

Perhaps the plunge into what seems a limpid imagination is the effect of true secrecy, not elsewhere found in Auden, the poet concealing his simple debt in Eliot's remembered dictum that 'the bad poet imitates, the good poet steals'. I think that John Fuller, the doyen in England of Auden minutiae, has also pointed out Auden's extraordinary debt to Collett's handbook, whose barely altered phrases none the less suffer a seachange, calming and stabilizing the compositional alembic. All the personifications do that.

> As Fahrenheit in an odd corner of great Celsius' kingdom
> Might mumble of the summers measured once by him.

– this might be borrowed too, but the effect of all Auden's borrowing – whether of phrases, ideas, or doctrines – is to emphasize the immense spread and richness of his achievement, and the retreat, too, by personification into a kind of shyness.

> To find those clearings where the shy humiliations
> Gambol on sunny afternoons, the waterhole to which
> The scarred rogue sorrow comes quietly in the small hours.

The most pellucid and complete of all such things in Auden's poetry is probably the madrigal 'O lurcher-loving collier', set to music by Benjamin Britten, which Auden wrote to ornament the last moments of *Coal Face*, a short documentary film about mining.

Everything that the young Auden wrote has a bottom of good sense. His poetry's hospitality towards crazes of every kind, crackpot or otherwise, carries into its art one of the most universal of human tendencies, and corrects it with a faith and a scepticism that, again as with most human beings, are almost identical. 'You cannot have poetry unless you have a certain amount of faith in something, but faith is never unalloyed with doubts.' A true magic is its own antidote. For Auden as for Nabokov, 'art is a game of intricate enchantment and deception', but Auden also wrote that 'in so far as poetry, or any of the arts, can be said to have an ulterior purpose, it is, by telling the truth, to disenchant and disintoxicate'. It was by his genius for resolving this paradox that Auden became, as Mendelson justly claims, 'the most inclusive poet of the twentieth century, its most technically skilled, and its most truthful'.

The best of Betjeman: *John Betjeman's Collected Poems* compiled by the Earl of Birkenhead; and *Church Poems* by John Betjeman

In Anthony Burgess's latest novel, *Earthly Powers*, there is a parody of a Betjeman poem.

> Thus kneeling at the altar rail
> We ate the word's white papery wafer.
> Here, so I thought, desire must fail,
> My chastity be never safer.
> But then I saw your tongue protrude
> To catch the wisp of angel's food.

In a brilliant piece of word play the angel food cake of the children's tea-party becomes the Host: sex, worship and childhood come together on the tip of the darting tongue that demurely holds it. Essence of Betjeman, it would seem, compressed in a few workman-like lines. But not so. Betjeman himself is never so explicit in his real poetry. It escapes, in fact, from its always apparently so intrusive subject-matter.

How this happens is itself a comment on the way a lot of poetry works, and the kind of world it creates and at times departs from. Burgess's parody shows what Betjeman is *not* like, because he singles points and ideas out for treatment in the same way that his own prose makes points, is chatty, ingenious, witty, informative. Burgess, one might say, turns art into non-art, fascinating, energetic, even suspenseful non-art, rather as his novel about Shakespeare sought to turn the art into the man. In this, he is not unlike those actual Elizabethan writers – Hall, Nashe, Greene – who created a whole great literary Elizabethan world of non-art, hardly read today but still well worth reading. In any fertile age there is a great deal of it, and our own is no exception.

But Betjeman's poetry is a particularly clear case of a poetry that does not contain its subject-matter. Never 'of its time', it has turned itself into a separate space–time continuum in which there is nothing but the poetry. This may seem so grotesque a point to make about the churchy, snobby, peopled, artlessly confiding and revealing world of Betjeman that it requires some clarification. Take the early poem 'Death in Leamington' – Betjeman's 'Lake Isle of Innisfree', as it has been called. The source of its amazing new reality is not at all easy to find. It is certainly not about death in any sense, though death and the fear of death are frequently emphasized in Betjeman's poetry, offered us as a theme with a too insistent abandon. It is not even about architecture ('From those yellow Italianate arches / Do you hear the plaster drop?'), or the sense of place, or all three things coming together. Its effectiveness, going with the new and awkward life put into the simple metre, is an entirely new way of seeing things, an abandonment so unlike anything else as to become impersonal, disconnected with the poet.

> She died in the upstairs bedroom
>   By the light of the ev'ning star
> That shone through the plate glass window
>   From over Leamington Spa

The unexpectedness of plate glass in this context goes with the archaizing laboriousness of the dropped trisyllable in 'evening'. But neither is emphasized in a pantomimic or hammed-up way, as things so often are in less successful Betjeman, and in the Burgess parody. The thing is completely rapt and self-absorbed.

We meet the window again and learn something else about it.

> She bolted the big round window,
>   She let the blinds unroll . . .

The nurse's activities, soothingly purposive, ungracefully habitual, dominate the poem, sinking to a conscious hush in the last two lines.

> And tiptoeing gently over the stairs
>   Turned down the gas in the hall.

Before, she had moved into the room – 'Breast high 'mid the stands and chairs' – another line of deeply penetrative awkwardness, 'breast high' suggesting, among other things, the dense growth in some creature's native haunt, which is being explored. And who but Betjeman would have written 'over the stairs' instead of 'down the stairs'? Sensible laced black shoes are carefully picked up for the quiet negotiation of each riser.

The impact of the poem depends on the unseen but felt working of these actions – inter-relations of actions and things – with the bald

vulgar lines of nudging statement or exclamation, obviously
arranged to be somehow offensive.

> But the fingers that would have work'd it
> > [the crochet]
> Were dead as the spoken word,

and

> But nurse was alone with her own little soul
> And the things were alone with theirs,

and

> Oh! Chintzy, chintzy cheeriness,
> Half dead and half alive!

Even as the poem takes him in, the reader notes and objects to the
juvenile getting-above-himself of those comments, but their feebleness as comments does none the less mingle with the deep singular
art of the poem's tone and movement. In depriving it of seriousness,
they confirm its effectiveness as art. If the poem was what the
American poetess Aline Kilmer, earnest disciple of Emily Dickinson,
meant when she said in a poem that 'things have a terrible
permanence when people die,' it would be banal. The world of the
poem is so unusual that the platitude of death has no part in it.

Platitudes are, in fact, used instead as a way of pointing to the
poem's originality. And that is the only true function of comment in
Betjeman's poetry. A poem in which Betjeman imagines his own
death – a much later poem – again acquires its chilling force from the
way in which cliché and detail combine without having anything in
common.

> Say in what cottage hospital
> Whose pale-green walls resound
> To the tap-tap-tap on the parquet
> Of inflexible nurses' feet
> Shall I myself be lying
> When they range the screens around?

The imitation of poetic language ('Say in what . . .') and of popular
trench humour ('When "They" range the screens . . .') does nothing
to detract from the fact that this is a real nightmare place. Death, and
the deaths of others, is a platitude, but one's own death is something
unique, singular with the same perfect singularity achieved by the
poem.

No doubt the modish thing today would be to give Betjeman the same label that has been stuck on Gavin Ewart: 'a deeply serious poet'. That is the mechanical accolade, the last infirmity of contemporary clichés. Its irrelevance consists in the fact that no good poetry can be other than serious, whereas poetry written to be serious today is seldom good. The word has been deeply tainted by post-Arnoldian use, and should be retired indefinitely. Seriousness in nineteenth-century poetry hangs out self-consciously, as even Keats's does in 'Hyperion' and Tennyson's in 'Morte d'Arthur' ('Lest one good custom should corrupt the world'). Betjeman's poetry is founded on these nineteenth-century models and on the atmosphere of the Victorian age, and he makes as idiosyncratic a use of its gravity as of its rhythms and metres.

The difficulty, of course, is that he cannot 'hang out' from his world: it is too much its own place for that. At times, this very fact can be used against itself, and to accentuate the note of Betjemanic comedy. In 'Beside the Seaside', a relaxed and rambling account of Cornish childhood holidays, the central 'event', which might have been got up in prose by almost any indifferent short-story writer, is the disillusion of Jennifer, aged twelve or so, when she finds that this summer she is no longer the little favourite on the beach.

> And here it was the tragedy began,
> That life-long tragedy of Jennifer
> Which ate into her soul and made her take
> To secretarial work in later life
> In a department of the Board of Trade.

This parodies, and deliberately crudely, the pregnant psychological episode favoured not only by such stories, but by sombre or sentimental Victorian narratives as well, where the 'blighted life' is a favourite theme. The parody is of course 'unserious', and to find its frivolity gratuitous would be to make heavy weather. None the less, the tone *is* irritating just because it does 'hang out', presenting a deliberate challenge to the serious. The tone is too much one of interior understanding, of a joke shared with the reader. It is precisely because good poetry is never 'serious' that when here it deliberately chooses not to be so it brings up the whole irritating question and rubs it the wrong way.

Jennifer and her family are first presented in the poem with the same rapt attention and delight that looks into the Betjeman world and sees church interiors and Pams and Joan Hunter-Dunns. But metre and manner preclude those bursts of lyric magnificence: Betjeman essays the mock-sententious. He becomes knowing, over-conscious, collusive with the reader; the local and parodic tone invites a mockery of its own world, and of course the people inside it.

> A single topic occupies our minds.

> 'Tis hinted at or boldly blazoned in
> Our accents, clothes and ways of eating fish,
> and being introduced and taking leave,
> 'Farewell', 'So long', 'Bunghosky', 'Cherribye' –
> That topic all-absorbing, as it was,
> Is now and ever shall be, to us – CLASS.

Very true no doubt, or at least very likely. But the lines make a point of being pleased with the effect of their own complacency, and ask us too winningly to share the pleasure. Perhaps it is churlish not to join in, but the summons to togetherness is not the most attractive feature of Betjeman's poetry. The really great poems – 'A Subaltern's Love-Song', 'Indoor Games near Newbury', 'Upper Lambourne', 'Spring Morning in North Oxford', 'Youth and Age on Beaulieu River', and most of all, 'Love in A Valley', are outbursts of erotic pleasure in the people that go with places. The adoration is classless, and the pleasure not only erotic but solipsistic. No togetherness there.

In these poems, Betjeman is a complete original: no other poet had perceived or expressed these things before, although the poetry is not concerned with being itself but is quite happy to be poetical and to borrow indiscriminately from poetic convention. In that, as in much else, Betjeman is like Wordsworth. The genuineness does not depend on a new style but on a new kind of perception, and in both poets there are 'two voices'. Wordsworth enjoying and Wordsworth expatiating are very different things, and the same is true with Betjeman. He is versatile; he has many tones; but only the passion rings true. His satire, his erudition and descriptive passages, even his enthusiasm and his humour, have something not quite right about them. I suppose this is part of the camp effect, which his fans revel in as much as they revel in everything else about him, but at his best Betjeman is emphatically not a camp poet. He is, though, when in 'Beside the Seaside' he strikes the warm-hearted line about the holiday pursuits (this was in the 1930s) of the vulgar Brown family:

> with allowances
> For this and that and little income tax,

They probably earn seven times as much
As poor old Grosvenor-Smith. But who will grudge
Them this, their wild spontaneous holiday?
The morning paddle, then the mystery tour
By motor-coach inland this afternoon.
For that old mother what a happy time!

This can be taken as either straight or not straight, but either way it is no more satisfactory than the end of 'Margate 1940':

And I think, as these fairy-lit sights I recall,
It is these we are fighting for, foremost of all.

The Poet Laureate would have no bother writing in the Soviet Union, because his fervent celebration of the Gleaming Heights of Socialism or kind hearts at the Kolkhoz could be taken according to taste. But banality in 'Leamington Spa' and other masterpieces is doing a real job, no hanging out, but integral with the intensity of the perception. Betjeman at his best ('The Best of Betjeman', as we learn from *Summoned by Bells*, was a work the author dreamed up at school in Highgate and submitted to one of the temporary masters, T. S. Eliot, who made no comment) has the totality of childhood, or rather of adolescence, when emotional ecstasies find their consummation in the sight of a packet of Weights pressed in the Surrey sand, in the makes of Rovers and Austins and Lagondas, in rhododendrons ('Lucky the rhododendrons') casually swiped at by the tennis racquet of a girl with an arm 'as firm and as hairy as Hendren's'. Surprised by these joys, the reader is swept into them as if with Kubla Khan in Xanadu, or in Keats's castle on the Eve of St Agnes.

Betjeman's joys and sorrows go straight back to the early Romantics. He is not a bit like Hardy and Philip Larkin, who are often associated with him. No comparison could be more misleading. Their idiom is one of deprivation, of that pleasure in things going wrong, or never having been right, which has become so much a part of English culture and consciousness. But Betjeman's gaiety, like his sense of glory, is the most genuine thing about him. Hardy and Philip Larkin cheer us up, and themselves, by the tender scrupulousness with which they couple the unshapely ills of existence with noticings and perceptions that reconcile us to those ills. Deprivation is associated in them with the hiding-places of comfort. Their poems are not out to please or to exhibit pleasure, and they have no social sense at all. Betjeman's poems are not exactly *about*

'How to get on in Society' (the title of the famous one that starts
'Phone for the fish-knives, Norman'), but they reflect the personality
of someone who is obviously getting on very well indeed.

Laugh the Betjeman way and the best people will laugh with you.
D. H. Lawrence had a comparable power, the jester's vitality that
attracts the upper crust, and the social 'feel' in his verse has odd
affinities with Betjeman's: both are obviously – in their works and
out of them – the life and soul of a 'set'. There is of course no more to
it than that – Betjeman's preoccupations having nothing of
Lawrence in them – but the butterfly moods and the inspired
mimicry have a curious relation: Betjeman's world of things is as
authentic as Lawrence's beasts, birds and flowers. There is a sharp
distinction in both writers, too, between the solitary and the social
personality, and the real poet in each is the solitary one.

In such cases, no doubt, the social comes in the end wholly to
preponderate. To be in Betjeman's 'set' now, and for the last twenty
years or so, is to enjoy the things he enjoys, the churches, the
architecture, the nostalgically or exuberantly self-mocking Anglican
emotions.

> Dear old, bloody old England
> Of telegraph poles and tin . . .

That struck the right note, but anything graver and more satirical is
apt to fall flat. Larkin has, rather oddly, referred to Betjeman as a
'committed writer', an adjective which might seem as beside the
point as 'serious' would be. And yet perhaps not. A committed
writer is more concerned with what he says than how he says it, and
that, oddly enough, is both what impresses about the bulk of
Betjeman's work, and what goes wrong. It takes a committed poet to
express his convictions and feelings with such forcible flatness.
That, after all, is an aspect of Betjeman's Wordsworthian side, and
Wordsworth wrote a hundred or so 'Ecclesiastical Sonnets' which
are pretty unreadable today.

Readable Betjeman always is, though his Anglican ditties and
'Poems in the Porch', now reprinted with others as *Church Poems*,
do not go very far back in terms of Anglican tradition. There is
nothing Elizabethan about them, nothing of the sharpness of Donne
or the mysterious sweetness of Herbert. He does not think in his
poems, as they did or seem to do; he does not even ruminate, as
Philip Larkin so impressively does in his poem 'Church Going'. But
why should he? His faith is in the ongoing power of Church –

necessities, restorations and revampings of prayer-book not-withstanding.

> The Church's restoration
> In eighteen-eighty-three
> Has left for contemplation
> Not what there used to be.

No, where Betjeman is concerned it has left more, much more. He is identified with a new sort of revival, unserious but certainly committed in its own way, done with all the fervour of the nineteenth-century hymns but sending itself up at the same time. The dual response is important: it is because the hymn is so robustly absurd that we sing it with the delight that we do. A mutual admiration society perhaps, a 'set' again, but what else has the social side of religion, in its vitality and in its complex utilities, ever been? Betjeman relishes and reveres every historic and contemporary aspect, from 'Undenominational / But still the church of God' –

> Revival ran along the hedge
> And made my spirit whole
> When steam was on the window panes
> And glory in my soul –

to the elaborate Art Nouveau of Holy Trinity, Sloane Street:

> The tall red house soars upward to the stars,
> The doors are chased with sardonyx and gold,
> And in the long white room
> Thin drapery draws backward to unfold
> Cadogan Square between the window-bars
> And Whistler's mother knitting in the gloom.

Church poems, like poems of plain works of art with a sub-clerical interest and flavour, could hardly have occurred without Betjeman's preparation of the ground.

In their poems Hardy and Larkin are natural dramatists. They intensify anonymous moods, invent situations; only the settings and the noticings are immediately and personally 'true'. With Betjeman it is different. Although his imagination is so Victorian, he does entirely without the odd Victorian gift for disingenuousness, for pretence and concealment. Like a certain sort of church he fancies, with carved pilasters and gilt commandment boards, where

> pre-Tractarian sermons roll'd
> Doctrinal, sound and dry,

his natural voice is that of the late eighteenth-century poets whose
tones converge in the spacious decorum of Wordsworth's *Prelude*
and *Excursion*. Betjeman has no persona: he is simply himself. That
explains the immense popularity of *Summoned by Bells*, the verse
autobiography with real names in it, real parents and reactions to
them, all the youthful experiences and impressions complete, up to
the age of leaving Oxford without a degree and taking perforce a
prep-school job where

> Harsh hand-bells harried me from sleep
> For thirty pounds a year and keep.

As in all the best autobiographies, from Edmund Gosse to Jocelyn
Brooke, the flavour of personal experience is exactly caught.

> All silvery on frosty Sunday nights
> Were City steeples white against the stars.
> And narrowly the chasms wound between
> Italianate counting-houses, Roman banks,
> To this church and to that. Huge office-doors,
> Their granite thresholds worn by weekday feet
> (Now far away in slippered ease at Penge),
> Stood locked. St Botolph this, St Mary that,
> Alone shone out resplendent in the dark.
> I used to stand by intersecting lanes
> Among the silent offices, and wait,
> Choosing which bell to follow: not a peal,
> For that meant somewhere active; not St Paul's,
> For that was too well-known. I liked things dim –
> Some lazy rector living in Bexhill
> Who most unwillingly on Sunday came
> To take the statutory services,
> A single bell would tinkle down a lane:
> My echoing steps would track the source of sound . . .

Such things are as authentic as the skating or climbing episodes in
the *Prelude*, the singularity of the poet's taste being substituted for
the shock of recognition which surprises the reader of Wordsworth.
Betjeman's emotions are both intense and narcissistically self-aware.

> 'Twas not, I think, a conscious search for God
> That brought me to these dim forgotten fanes.
> Largely it was a longing for the past,
> With a slight sense of something unfulfilled;
> And yet another feeling drew me there,
> A sense of guilt increasing with the years –
> 'When I am dead you will be sorry, John' –

> Here I could pray my mother would not die.
> Thus were my London Sundays incomplete
> If unaccompanied by Evening Prayer.
> How trivial used to seem the Underground,
> How worldly looked the over-lighted west,
> How different and smug and wise I felt
> When from the east I made my journey home!

It has the same flat accuracy of tone, however effectively crafted, that will later tell us, after the author has been sent down from Oxford for failing in Divinity (of all things!), that

> Maurice Bowra's company
> Taught me far more than all my tutors did.

The personal Betjeman is compulsive, but the rare impersonal one – the one who has disappeared wholly into ecstasies of subalterns and their girlfriends, and the fir-dry alleys round Camberley bungalows, and the waste water running out into the dark – is even better. That is what I meant by the two voices in his poetry, and how one of them escapes from the humour and the in-jokes, from the idiosyncratic subject-matter, escapes beyond parody into a world no longer its own, one for which no reader of poetry could feel the incomprehension or distaste which might legitimately be felt for the personal Betjeman, the in-Betjeman. That world belongs to the ages.

The last Romantic: Philip Larkin

Why is Larkin so different from other poets of today? The simple question is not easy to answer, although every appreciative critic and lover of poetry has his own solution and his own diagnosis of Larkin's virtues. Long ago the Poet Laureate referred to him as 'the John Clare of the building estates', a decidedly quaint though no doubt heartfelt compliment, in line with Eric Homberger's later summing-up of Larkin as 'the saddest heart in the post-war supermarket', or the more magisterial pronouncement that his poetry is 'representative of the modern English condition: a poetry of lowered sights and diminishing expectations'. These judgements suggest his glum accuracy about places and emotions – particularly his own – an unillusioned accuracy beautifully, and in a very English way, satisfying both the poet and ourselves with what another critic has called 'a central dread of satisfaction'. As Larkin has himself wryly remarked: 'Deprivation for me is what daffodils were for Wordsworth.' What is perfect as a poem is what is imperfect in life.

More recently the Larkin effect has been defined in terms of his own peculiar use of symbolism, the symbolism that Yeats got from the French poets, especially Mallarmé. In her essay 'Philip Larkin: after Symbolism' Barbara Everett has pointed out these French echoes; the fact that, for example, 'Sympathy in White Major' is a kind of symbolist parody of Gautier's 'Symphonie en blanc majeur', and 'Arrivals, Departures' echoes Baudelaire's 'Le Port'. It is quite true that Larkin's brand of rhetoric, as it suddenly flowers at the end of poems like 'Absences' ('Such attics cleared of me! Such absences.'), 'Next Please', and 'High Windows', has the sound of French eloquence, or rather a uniquely effective English adaptation of it. Larkin is also adept at the Baudelairean device of dislocating the pulse and rhythm of lines from the actual things they are speaking of – Baudelaire's decaying corpses or *affreuses juives*, Larkin's trains and hospitals and bed-sitters and death-fears – so

93

that a different and disembodied image is created, something that is nowhere and endless, forever 'out of reach', like the landscape of 'Here'.

A more direct borrowing can be found at the end of 'An Arundel Tomb'. Of the stone effigies of the earl and countess we are told in the last stanza that 'Time has transfigured them into / Untruth'. The reference must be to Mallarmé's lines on the tomb of Poe: *'Tel qu'en lui-même enfin L'éternité change.'* The reversal is not ironic. Untruth is the home of poetry, the only place of transfiguration. Time, for Mallarmé, takes away what is irrelevant in Poe's life: for Larkin, it removes actuality from the history of the stone figures and their touching hand-in-hand pose (including the detail that the pose itself was added by a Victorian restorer, a fact presumably not known to Larkin, though it would have given him pleasure). Transfiguration is into a kind of poetic absence which includes only the idea of love, not its quotidian betrayals or fulfilments. 'What remains of us is love' in the sense that love equates with self-extinction. I think Larkin here gives his own entombed precision to the Symbol, which for the Symbolists gave out nothing but its own powers of suggestion. To Larkin it suggests the comfort of disappearance, selflessness, away-ness, and in the universe this is no doubt the true comfort of love.

The Symbol can deepen and reverse the familiarity of a poem, changing its nature like a symphony. For Hardy the nature of a poem on a tomb would be its fidelity in a homely historical way. Larkin in a radio talk said he wanted to write different sorts of poems. 'Someone once said that the great thing is not to be different from other people but different from yourself.' He wished he could write more often like the last line of 'Absences' ('Such attics cleared of me . . .') A highly personal poet, he uses Symbolism as a mode of the impersonal, to liberate the poem from its own world.

Barbara Everett in her essay looked at Larkin from a new angle, and in his short book on Larkin in the Methuen Contemporary Writers series Andrew Motion emphasizes even more the Symbolist side of Larkin. Although what he has to say is always perceptive it brings out once again, as every critic has done, the seeming capacity of Larkin to escape from his poems, not to be pinned down in them. The critic is not wrong or misguided, and yet Larkin is not there any more. Like the brides in 'The Whitsun Weddings' we travel with him on the same train, bound for the same destination, but when our procedures and projects get under way he has already departed elsewhere. Indeed that word, as I shall hope to show, stands for something very important in his poetry.

That absence from the critic, even from the reader, is unusual in the poetry of today, which in general is distinguished by togetherness and communality, a complex and clever intimacy with the reader. Poets understand each other because they write for each other. It is not a new phenomenon; it has happened with all collective poetry, with the metaphysicals and with the poets of the 'Tribe of Ben'. But Larkin is not like that. He seems to be present in his poetry historically, and as it were histrionically, as a nineteenth-century poet might now seem to us present in his poetry. His seeming intimacy can be startling and yet he is both shameless and reticent, confidential and yet invulnerably refined, wholly unselfconscious and yet inevitably withdrawn, unavailable to us and yet totally forthcoming, absent in presence. His presence is its own style of 'elsewhere'. The interior of his poetry, like a Vermeer interior, is both wholly accessible and completely mysterious.

As a student Larkin adored Yeats, feeding upon his music and his mystery, though disliking his ideas. After his influence was worked out there still lurked in Larkin's verse that riddling transition from loftiness to intimacy – those 'magnanimities of sound' as Yeats called them – which the old wizard could modulate so well. Yeats is eloquent about a great creator like himself being 'forced to choose / Perfection of the life or of the work'. In Larkin this high destiny undergoes a characteristic shift, though it is equally insistent. Now it is a domestic choice, presented with comic drabness. Yeats compared himself with the soldiers of the civil war, and Larkin ponders the active life of Arnold, the married man.

> To compare his life and mine
> Makes me feel a swine . . .

Comedy with Larkin never dis-elevates decorum, the eloquence of rhythm and tone.

Nor does it affect the role in his poetry of 'elsewhere', as it appears in that deceptively simple short poem, 'The Importance of Elsewhere'. Elsewhere is a fairy place, but it is not insubstantial.

> You can see how it was:
> Look at the picture and the cutlery.
> The music in the piano stool. That vase.

It is also sex. Sex can only be its real self in the other world, in the imagination, in the head. Where have we come across this before?

Not in any place as recondite as Symbolist poetry, but in one of the most famous of romantic poems.

> And this is why I sojourn here
> Alone and palely loitering,
> Though the sedge is withered from the lake,
> And no birds sing.

For Keats, as for many other nineteenth-century imaginations, sex was a fairy world that vanished in consummation. Larkin in his own way inherits the tradition, inherits, too, its legacy of disillusion. The erotic is elsewhere. 'Dry Point', in *The Less Deceived*, is a more explicit and more metaphysical poem than 'La Belle Dame Sans Merci', but it makes the same point with the same kind of intensity. When the erotic is trapped in the one-way street of sex, 'the wet spark comes, the bright blown walls collapse',

> But what sad scapes we cannot turn from then:
> What ashen hills! What salted, shrunken lakes!

'Elsewhere' is an avoidance of what in the poem 'Deceptions', a central poem in *The Less Deceived*, is 'fulfilment's desolate attic'. The two forms contrast in the plot of Larkin's first novel, *Jill*, whose hero, a young undergraduate, has his own private romance of elsewhere, based on the invention of a girl called Jill. Keats found himself losing in company any sense of identity, and John Kemp has the same experience with fellow-students and their girl-friends; his real being is invested in Jill, and all the details of her life, details set up in the manner of one of Larkin's own poems. When Kemp first sees and then actually meets the 'double' of Jill, a real girl called Gillian, who turns out to be the cousin of his room-mate's girl, he begins to go completely to pieces. His personality, already meagre, seems to take leave of the reader, and after a symbolic consummation when he embraces Gillian and kisses her, he is thrown into a fountain by her friends, catches a severe chill, and collapses in the college sickbay into delirium and disillusionment.

As gripping in its way as a Larkin poem, the novel tells a tale very similar to Keats's 'Lamia'. The hero of that poem invents, as it were, a wonderful woman, with whom he becomes so enamoured that he insists on marrying her at a public festival, though she warns him of the dire consequences. She changes back into a serpent, and he swoons into death ('in its marriage robe, the heavy body wound'). In both poem and novel the man who creates and contemplates romance is extinguished by its realization or fulfilment. ('To me it was dilution', as the narrating 'I' says of propagation, in 'Dockery and Son'.)

Both Larkin's novels vanished into the past, as is the way of the best fiction that is not followed up, and have only been revived recently by his solid fame as a poet. A third novel, begun as soon as Larkin had finished the second, was never completed. Surprisingly Andrew Motion considers the first, *Jill*, the more successful. For me its successor, *A Girl In Winter*, is far more subtle in its handling of the same theme and the girl, Katherine, far more effective than Kemp, both as a character in her own right and as a focus of consciousness. It is 'The Eve of St Agnes' to Jill's 'Lamia', though I doubt that the author was conscious of any affinity with either of Keats's poems. But the plot resemblance is as striking with the one as is the magic atmosphere – the kingdom of cold, the kingdom of warmth – is in the case of the other. In fact the novel was first called *The Kingdom of Winter*, and Larkin changed the title at the publisher's request. (A girl is always a good thing in a title: Kingsley Amis claims to have found *Jill* in a Soho bookstore, next to *High-heeled Yvonne*. That would have delighted Keats.)

Wallace Stevens said that 'a poet looks at the world as a man looks at a woman'. Stevens and Larkin are romantics of a very different colour – in any case what about poets who *are* women? – but as regards both Keats and Larkin the remark is certainly suggestive, almost literal. As the sight of almost any woman may be a fantasy for a man, so their world of looking and language is to them. In revising 'The Eve of St Agnes' Keats was very conscious of the contrast between poetic daydream and the physical reality of a seduction. He wouldn't think much of his hero, he said, if he left the heroine in the virgin state in which he found her. The ribald comment is not a part of the poem, as Keats knew very well, and yet the poem makes its own solution between romantic fantasy and undeceived awareness, a solution that seems to leave the poet out. Larkin it leaves very much in: there is no gap for him between romantic vision, 'ever eager-eyed', and boring bleak reality. Disillusion is a working part of the dream. With its own kind of beauty, as the last words of the novel tell us, and 'not saddening'. As it ends, his couple have no further interest in or desire for each other; nothing to look forward to but sleep. Like icefloes, 'in slow orderly procession', their 'unsatisfied dreams' move 'from darkness further into darkness'; and the girl's watch ticks persistently in the man's ears, counting the time till death.

For Larkin disillusionment intensifies the enchanted comforts of elsewhere and becomes a part of them. So even, at least from the view of art, does social vapidity and commonplace. In a poem from *High Windows*, 'Vers de Societé', Larkin converts social chit-chat ('Canted / Over to catch the drivel of some bitch / Who's read nothing but "Which" ') into elsewhere. Would he shun an invitation, preferring the solitude of dreams, as Madeline leaves the baronial party on St Agnes' Eve? Or would he hasten to accept and attend?

> In a pig's arse, friend.
> Day comes to an end.
> The gas fire breathes, the trees are darkly swayed.

But he goes to the party, for the world of elsewhere is also the acceptance world. Who but Larkin would juxtapose the exotic obscenity and the romantic line in such a way that instead of their making a brisk, glib contrast between real 'undeceived' life and deceptive dream, as they would do in the work of most moderns, they come quietly together in their own secret, consolatory meaning? Change of key in Larkin is never for contrast but obscurely rich enhancement, as in the consoling grandeur that rises out of the witty levity of 'Next Please'.

> Only one ship is seeking us, a black-
> Sailed unfamiliar, towing at her back
> A huge and birdless silence. In her wake
> No waters breed or break.

Symbolist technique marries in Larkin with the no-nonsense manner of 'the Movement', represented in sex terms by Kingsley Amis's Dai Evans and his earthy perky view of appetites and needs. Romance there is a silly cow with someone's hand up her skirt. In Larkin, so to speak, the hand is there but is part of the inviolable dream of 'Sunny Prestatyn'.

> *Come to sunny Prestatyn*
> Laughed the girl on the poster,
> Kneeling up on the sand . . .

Whatever disfigurement is inflicted on her image by the travelling public, culminating when 'a great transverse tear / Left only a hand and some blue. / Now *Fight Cancer* is there' – the girl in the poem remains inviolable, a Virgin with ballpoint moustaches offering herself to the odium which does not alter her transcendent nature. 'She was too good for this life'; but living, as seen in Larkin's poems, always is.

The critics who have seen the importance there of latter-day Symbolist technique would seize on the phrase 'some blue' – Mallarméan *Azur* – as highly significant. The poems are indeed full of such cunning pointers. In the last stanza of 'Next Please' that memorable adjective 'birdless' is no doubt carrying two senses; in colloquial and especially northern English bird can mean girl. But in Larkin's, as opposed to more contemporary poetry, such things don't want to be noticed, any more than does the deft adaptation of 'Movement' style, or the beautiful rhyme and stanza patterns, often modified from Spenser or Yeats or Donne. Such influences give his poetry no trace of anxiety; it has no obligations to them, disappearing into its own elsewhere, the romantic premise of simultaneous expectancy and disillusion, and Larkin's own proclaimed if unemphasized version of romantic solitude, the corsair's freedom,

> Drafting a world where no such road will run
> From you to me;
> To watch that world come up like a cold sun,
> Rewarding others, is my liberty.

The romantic has no possessions or commitments, and a secret sorrow. In a world of sexual and material acquisitiveness his elsewhere can never be possessed, least of all by the poet himself. Larkin's main difference is in this build-up of absence. It makes him pleasurably unpredictable, each poem unfamiliar. There is no place today where his poetry obviously lives, as there is, say, a Ted Hughes county and a Seamus Heaney land, a place domesticated by poets. Keats said that Hampstead had been 'damned' by Leigh Hunt, and the Lakes by Wordsworth. For Larkin elsewhere can only be completely authentic ('a real girl in a real place / In every sense empirically true!') if

> I have never found
> The place where I could say
> *This is my proper ground,*
> *Here I shall stay . . .*

The absolute reality of elsewhere only 'underwrites my existence' – the end of 'The Importance of Elsewhere' is, as one might expect, both downright and mysterious – if that existence is almost aggressively humdrum. Of reviewers who once wondered at this existence Larkin said: 'I'd like to know how they spend their time . . . do they kill a lot of dragons for instance?'

The tone is a Larkinian updating of the tone of Keats's letters, the refusal to be romantic which – kidding on the level – conceals a consciousness wholly devoted to romance. Yes, Larkin in his poems does in a sense kill dragons, just as he writes his own versions of the Nightingale Ode in such poems as 'Here', 'The Large Cool Store', 'Essential Beauty', 'Days'. In their deft, immaculate way these poems wonder at the quotidian realities they turn into fairy-lands forlorn, provided the beholder does not possess them but remains an equivalent of the figure parodied by Yeats's idea of Keats. ('I see a schoolboy when I think of him / With face and nose pressed to a sweet-shop window'.) Often, as in 'Essential Beauty', Larkin parodies them himself, his art finding the ways in which all true romance is intensified by parody. 'Our live imperfect eyes / That stare beyond this world . . . seeking the home / All such inhabit' may find in advertisement

> that unfocused she
> No match lit up, nor drag ever brought near

but the silent, poignant joke in the poem is that its art is itself an advertisement for elsewhere, feeding our 'bad habits of expectancy' that depend on non-fulfilment. 'Where can we live but days?' – but that question conjures up a vision as memorable as Keats's 'perilous seas' – 'the priest and the doctor / In their long coats / Running over the fields'.

The most famous of all Larkin's poems presents the 'I' as voyeur at Endymion-like rites of initiation and fulfilment. Hardy might well have written about finding himself on a trainful of brides about to start their married lives, and he would have taken his usual grimly compassionate pleasure in imagining their lives-to-be. His musings would certainly have been erotic, but nothing like so erotic as Larkin contrives to be in 'The Whitsun Weddings'. Everything in that poem is charged with the peculiar potency of Larkinian sexual arrest.

> and for
> Some fifty minutes, that in time would seem
> Just long enough to settle hats and say
> *I nearly died*,
> A dozen marriages got under way.

The fascinated concentration is on the fact of change which takes the form of stasis, like the lovers on St Agnes' Eve.

> ' They glide, like phantoms, into the wide hall;
> Like phantoms, to the iron porch, they glide . . .

The just-married couples 'watched the landscape, sitting side by side', for this moment voyeurs themselves, watched by a voyeur. Just the same double tactic is used throughout *A Girl in Winter*, a marvellous and sustained erotic prose poem, in which the girl Katherine, a foreigner without a surname, watches the English in what seems their elsewhere, and is herself watched by the author and his readers. So Madeline attends a vision of her future lover while he is gazing on her from hiding, and the reader of the poem on both. In the focus of this sort of poetry everything can be sexier than sex, for everything is seen as if in the sweet-shop window. Having her first meal in an English train Katherine is fascinated by clear soup joggling in white plates; when she has to take a colleague to the dentist she watches him drop into a glass of water a pink tablet which 'sank furiously to the bottom'. Through the poet's eyes the wedded couples watch train details of mesmeric significance and exactitude, and are then themselves plunged forward into an unending metaphor of Arthurian power and mystery, 'an arrow-shower / Sent out of sight, somewhere becoming rain'. The paradox of elsewhere, as glimpsed in this 'travelling coincidence', is that the unchanging human progress through sex to birth and death can be seen out of time, in the right words.

And they are not knowing words. Larkin's deepest romanticism is neither knowing nor overtly symbolic, but concentrated solely on its own vision and its own frankness. The double self and the dual vision are fixed counters which give the vision and the personality behind it an unexpected variety, as well as a kind of instant grip. He is the only sophisticated poet today who needs no sophisticated response from the reader; apparently not interested in art, its cosy responses and communal strategies, the poetry knows every sense of the difference between living in the world and looking in on it. Both activities are necessary to each other, but their interchange produces instant fiction in depth inside every poem. He is the only poet since Hardy really to use the novel, and the way he does it, inside an apparently limited poetic field, makes the 'confessional' poetry of the last twenty years, as well as the 'communal' poetry of today, seem one-dimensional.

The brevity of his poems, as of Hardy's, is an aspect of their robust variety. The personal and the fictional join hands in them, and with the novels, which are also in Larkin's case long poems. Hardy said the poet 'touches our hearts by revealing his own', and the simple sentiment fits Larkin as well as himself, all the more so because both in their own way express simple and forceful sentiments with which we may disagree. They share the essential simplicities of romanticism, and neither (in Hardy's case over a very long span) could be said to 'grow up' or mature. A kind of arrest becomes poetry in Larkin as it does in Keats, and has the same direct power to move us, partly by seeming ever young, undiminished, fixed in essential concentration. Keats might have stopped being a poet as Larkin, in one sense, stopped being a novelist.

Keats wrote that poetry 'simply tells the most heart-easing things'. The heart can be eased by unexpected things, as Larkin's poetry knows. It never seems to want to move us, or ease our hearts, but they escape into comfort none the less. Today nobody uses the word 'escapism', a common term of disapproval in the days when romanticism was being consciously reacted against. Larkin's poetry profoundly understands it, and the popular need for it, its increasing if unfashionable importance in a religionless age. He is a connoisseur of its most paradoxical instincts and of its place in the romantic tradition.

The man who is 'not deceived' is also the true escapist. Keats wrote to Reynolds: 'Until we are sick we understand not.' As an 'old-type natural fouled-up guy' Larkin makes a joke of it, but it means much for the stance of his art. Escapists make good novelists, and Larkin observed that he had found 'how to make poems readable as novels'. Like the tip of an iceberg his poems imply depths of lives and selves, a mass of material not written, or not revealed. In understanding the importance of elsewhere the undeceived also know that it 'tolls me back from thee to my sole self', and Larkin's poems are made from this relationship. His kind of romanticism is out of fashion today, and his curious version of 'escapism' would be frowned on if it were more widely recognized for what it is. His popularity, like that of many great idiosyncratic artists, rests on various sorts of misconception where the critics are concerned, and on the sound unexamined instincts of a more general public. It is none the less remarkable for that, and none the less deserved.

Looking in on Pushkin

One should start with a naive question: 'Is poetic genius universally recognized?' That is to say, when educated people who like and understand poetry and have read it widely over a number of years discover a 'great' poet who is new to them, do they perceive at once how great he is? Do they have something like Keats's experience on first looking into Chapman's Homer? If so, how and why?

The experience involves two kinds of recognition. Of a whole new world, with its own characteristics and curiosities, its own style in the largest sense. And also of something profoundly familiar, intimate; something that enlarges our experience even as we feel we have always known it. In the case of a foreign poet the mediating factor is important, though not necessarily decisive. Omar Khayyam wrote in the form of the short stanzaic epigram called the *rubai*, to which FitzGerald added an English dimension by linking the stanzas consecutively together. But though he changed and adapted he does not conceal the nature of Omar's *rubai*, the things it says and how it says them. It is to these the general bosom responds. And although there is no English version of Goethe's *Faust* which manages to add to it any sort of native dimension the reader of any translation can at least perceive why this is one of the great poems of the world. With Dante or Virgil the case is more obvious still.

So that when a great poet is called untranslatable we are entitled to feel a certain scepticism. If he does not come over at all can he be all that good, except to the taste of his fellow-countrymen, in the way that the Tibetans prefer their butter rancid or the Japanese their fish raw? When Robert Frost said: 'Poetry is what gets left out in translation' he might have been speaking of such a poet as Pushkin. But Frost meant poetry in a special sense, the sense of a bloom or distillation, the same sense that A. E. Housman had in mind when he said that the presence of poetry could be detected only by the tears it brought to the eyes or the prickles to the skin. It was the sort of view that Mallarmé and Maurice Blanchot have also held in their more elevated intellectual way, and it is not so far from the critics of today who hold that the business of criticism is not with literature as a human activity but with 'literariness', not with poetry but with 'poeticity'. The *fin de siècle* view of poetry as a special essence has turned into that of the poem as a piece of untransferable sign-language, as seen by semiologists and structuralists like Jakobson and Riffaterre.

But poetry can be a bulky discrete substance with a great deal inside it, and when a poem undergoes transformation into another language what is inside it is still there, hardly altered. Pope's *Iliad* is not the same as Homer's but it has the same story, the same characters, the same moving moments. The equivalent things are there in a translation of *Hamlet*, and may be a revelation to a new audience, as in the Paris production of 1826 which left hardly a dry eye in the house. Hugo and Delacroix and the other French intellectuals were responding to the gaiety and melancholy of Hamlet and the pathos of Ophelia in the same way that English audiences had done in the eighteenth century and presumably in Shakespeare's time. Poetry changes and yet remains the same. As Auden put it in his poem on Yeats, the words of the dead are modified in the guts of the living, and a poem could be said to be dead if it is not continually revived and revised by the reception of new readers.

T. S. Eliot on the other hand expressed the opposite truth: that the words of the dead are tongued with fire beyond the language of the living. In recognizing the paradox we should also recognize that there is no single problem about translating 'poetry': that the problem is both multiple and different in the case of every poet. A poem is in varying degree both unique and modifiable, both potential and complete. The peculiar density of a Horatian ode lends itself by its nature to different sorts of rendering, changes of emphasis, verbal paraphrase to suit the smell of another language; and the original poem gives hospitality to these new developments. Hence the quantity and diversity of Horace translations. But a Shakespeare song, a lyric by Heine, or by Pushkin, is quite a different matter. They have, as it were, total stability, announced in the most uncompromising way; they cannot adjust to the genius of another language.

A long poem is different again. Wordsworth's *Prelude* has no stability. It was constantly being modified by the poet himself.

Shelley's long poems too, like river or cloud formations, coil and reform in the same sort of extra-linguistic sublime, and could accommodate themselves to the parallel flow of another language. The same is true of Whitman, or of Wallace Stevens. Instability, and therefore translatability, is in fact a paramount feature of the longer poems of the Romantic period, to which Pushkin is a latecomer, and of poems that revived or continued its tradition. Such poems are in general both organic and incomplete; they come to a stop naturally, rather than being furnished with a beginning, middle, and end, and we shall see what unexpected and effective use Pushkin makes of this tendency.

He has often and conventionally been compared with Byron, and Byron was certainly an inspiration to him, but the linguistic instability of *Don Juan* shows how wholly different it is from *Evgeny Onegin* or any other poem of Pushkin's. Byron's form is in its own way as loose as Wordsworth's or Shelley's, as interchangeable and 'uninevitable', holding its spirit in its whole corporate being. It is typical of him to take on a stanza form so difficult in English, and make a virtue out of the very clumsiness that difficulty entails. Rhymes and sentences seem to revel in the very insecurity of their improvisation and in the difficulty of performing such a feat in English. Reckless and drunk with living they can reel with comparative facility into other languages and perform their act there. Inspired in fact by Byron (though he claimed it was by Pulci) de Musset started to write the same sort of poems in French, which, given the language's different style of vivacity, have much of the same kind of life as the original. Byron seduced Europe and its tongues as Tasso and Ariosto had done before, and like the romances of Sir Walter Scott his *Corsair*-type poems were even more popular than *Don Juan*, and more translatable. Pushkin profited from the translatability of the Romantics as Chaucer had done from his French and Italian models. But the commerce is only one way.

Two factors are involved. Truly international or cosmopolitan literature depends not so much on its style as on its climate of ideas, on the way it initiates and spreads intellectual and emotional fashion. Pushkin takes up fashions which then become lost in the depths of his genius, returned as it were to primary matter, as in the case of his adaptation from Goethe of a dramatic scene between Mephistopheles and Faust, or his own version of the Don Juan story, *The Stone Guest*. Drama is the most potentially international of art forms, as is demonstrated by Ibsen, Strindberg, and Chekhov,

Artaud and Beckett. One of Pushkin's 'little tragedies', *Mozart and Salieri*, is used by Peter Shaffer in his play *Amadeus*. Opera, most international form of all, also borrows Pushkin scenarios, most notably his story *The Queen of Spades*. But in these borrowings all is vulgarized: nothing that is truly Pushkinian is returned to general circulation. His own special inwardness remains unaffected, his real materials have not been naturalized or transformed as those of international literature can be, indeed should be.

The other factor is more disconcerting. Pushkin is probably the only great poet, at least in the European tradition, whose greatness is not only not revealed in translation but actually depreciated by it. It is not that he is 'untranslatable' in the sense that admirers and experts like Nabokov have claimed, for his plain words have their literal equivalents in other languages, but that when he is translated literally he does not seem much good. 'But he's flat, your poet', exclaimed Flaubert in genuine astonishment when his friend Mérimée tried to give some idea of Pushkin in plain French. And flat in a sense he can seem – it's an uncomfortable fact. *Evgeny Onegin* does indeed fizz like champagne, and some of the fizz – or at least the notion of it – does come over in a spirited and accomplished verse translation, like the one lately achieved by Sir Charles Johnston. It is much harder to render the flat, quiet side of Pushkin, which has such simple perfection, economy, and suggestiveness. *Tikho* – 'quiet' – is a word he uses often. But when most quiet and most masterly he is also, in terms of translation, most flat. The last line of the *Iliad* – 'and in this manner was held the funeral of Hector, tamer of horses' – strikes like so many other single lines in epic a powerful chord of majesty across the language barrier. And the same when Horace claims that he will be read 'as long as priest and silent virgin shall climb the Capitol' (an enormous understatement, as Fraenkel observes in his commentary). When Dante takes leave of his old schoolmaster in hell the words and the simile send an authentic shudder of poetic meaning down the spine, no matter how or in what language they are rendered.

Pushkin is not like this. His most authentic poetic electricity never jumps between languages. Maurice Baring said that one of his finest lines was a simple statement in the 'little tragedy', *The Covetous Knight*, 'And the sea, where ships were running'. This has no depth of meaning or expression, neither is it 'pure' poetry in the self-conscious sense. It is a plain statement. My own favourite is from another and in a formal sense unfinished 'little tragedy', the latest of them in time of composition, *Rusalka*. It is a typically Pushkinian narrative, half fairy-tale, half ancient and commonplace sad story, Heine's 'alte Geschichte'. A prince falls in love with a miller's daughter and when she is with child leaves her to marry an appropriate princess. In despair she drowns herself in the river Dnieper, to become metamorphosed into the 'cold powerful rusalka' of legend. The poem breaks off as she prepares to take vengeance on her lover, who since his marriage has continued repeatedly to return and linger at the scene of his lost love. His huntsman tells the princess that 'he has remained / Alone in the forest on the Dnieper's bank'. In Russian the decasyllabic line is indescribably haunting. The black verse of the drama has a calm precise realism and intensity unequalled even in Pushkin's other 'little tragedies'.

Reviewing some years ago my study of the Russian poet's art (*Pushkin: A Comparative Commentary*) Christopher Ricks quite justifiably commented that it was no good to tell us that the line about the forest on the Dnieper's bank was so wonderful when in English it seemed either prosaic or, still worse, feebly poetical. This is indeed the centre of the problem. Like Flaubert, Ricks from his own standpoint was quite right. It is no use shaking one's head knowledgeably and regretting that one cannot savour the original. Dostoevsky used to talk a lot about Pushkin's 'secret', which is irritating but not more irritating than the claims made by those who read Pushkin (and he is easy to read, even with the most elementary knowledge of Russian – all his metres are immediately familiar) to those who don't. But the worst aspect of this failure in communication is that the reader's impatience with its flat, mildly poetical air in translation will hinder him from looking in on the poem itself and on its particular dimension of meaning, its power to move, to impress, and to compel his attention. Feeling how limp is the texture of the poetry in English, he will assume that the story it tells is equally limp, equally banal.

No one could call *Evgeny Onegin* banal, even in translation. But here the problems are very different. Pushkin's verse novel was composed over a period of eight years or more; it is dense with wit, comment, and observation, but it is also leisurely, exploratory, partaking both of the nature of a prose novel (*Tristram Shandy* was one of Pushkin's models) and of a brilliant experiment in a graceful and complex stanza form. Pushkin succeeds in doing two apparently incompatible things: delighting the reader with the brio and virtuosity of his verse patterns, and at the same time directing the reader's attention through them – as if they were a clear window – into the world of his novel, its events and characters. The many translators into English who have attempted to reproduce the verse pattern have all succeeded at least in doing that, as a zealous trainer succeeds in teaching a dog to dance on its hind legs; the reader applauds, not at the poem itself, but at the spectacle of our native language being somehow distorted into performing such a curiosity. Fitting into English the complex and delicate rhyming form which Pushkin, in an inspired feat of adaptation, had picked up from La Fontaine, calls for a prodigy of visible effort with recalcitrant rhymes and consonants that not only embarrasses the reader but distracts him from what the novel itself reveals.

For Pushkin is here the opposite of Byron. He perceived that this stanzaic rhythm made a perfect mate for the Russian language, a natural verbal melody not possible in French or English. With it he can glide into rhymes and rhythms like an expert skater on to ice. The stanza works like the steps of a dance which the reader, embraced as it were by the poet, is beguiled into treading without feeling the difficulty of what seems so easy. The unfortunate translator has to pretend to do the same, while his efforts inadvertently draw attention to every step. No wonder Nabokov poured scorn on the ill-fated wretch, and himself composed the definitive translation, scrupulously accurate, in irregular lines, unrhymed, and substituting for Pushkin's play of wit and camaraderie his own particular brand of verbal eccentricity. The result is Pushkin fantasized, into a sort of airy baroque not at all unsuited to the genius of his own verbal charm.

Nabokov has been attacked on the ground that his verbal capers are wholly unlike Pushkin's, but I believe this objection irrelevant: what matters is that they afford precisely the equivalent of the easy play of verbal intimacy with which Pushkin engages us while artfully making us attend his story. Nabokov does not distract us, as the rhymed translators do, from looking in on Pushkin. Pushkin is both telling us a story and – as the formalist critic Shklovsky pointed out – having a game with that story. Nabokov manages to give the 'game' element its authentic air of negligence and charming ease while the plain reality of the tale itself emerges simply. Certainly one of Pushkin's 'secrets' is the way he combines a sense of form, of the right form for every work he undertook, with a very precise awareness of the need for 'freedom', the quality for which he

admired Byron and Shakespeare and the best of the new romantic
writers. 'A free novel', as he describes *Evgeny Onegin*, is of course a
contradiction in terms, but he manages to harmonize the contradiction by drawing attention to it. His four characters, Onegin and
Tatiana, Lensky and Olga, are puppets moving in a formal dance
(Tatiana loves Onegin and nothing comes of that: then he falls in
love with her and nothing comes of that either) who serve as a
foreground for the author's running commentary on life, society, his
tastes, his friends. But these figures are also real flesh and blood
people whom their creator becomes more and more interested in and
attached to – indeed he emphasizes and expresses surprise at his own
attachment. Lensky's death in a duel with Onegin, and Onegin's
final rejection in Moscow by a married Tatiana, are as moving and
true as anything in the novels of Tolstoy and Turgenev.

A rendering into English, particularly English verse, is not up to
this play of alteration. Even Nabokov and Johnston, the two most
accomplished translators in their different styles, find it necessary to
point out in notes when Pushkin is parodying a conventional style in
describing the sad death of the romantic poet Lensky –

> The bloom has withered on the bough;
> The altar flame's extinguished now . . .
> (Johnston)

and when he himself takes over, so to speak, and provides a haunting
image for the young poet's sudden extinction. A house is empty, its
windows whitened with chalk, the mistress departed. The wholly
natural transition in Pushkin's art from a parodic style, which can in
itself be as moving as Mozart, to a personal one, defeats both
translators, because it cannot be drawn attention to literally or by
means of any equivalent in 'poetic' English.

And this is the real cause of the impoverishment of Pushkin that
takes place when the sense of his poetry is rendered in another
language. It is the same whether he is put into literal prose or into a
version of his own metre. A translator might feel that plain honest
prose *must* be the answer, but it is no more of one than is a metrical
rendering. Nabokov no doubt perceived this, and it is probably the
reason for his own exotic practices. The problem is even greater,
though less obvious, in the case of *The Bronze Horseman*,
Pushkin's poetic masterpiece and a poem that sums up and
exemplifies, as *Evgeny Onegin* does not, the development of his
poetic genius. The only part of it published in Pushkin's lifetime was

the prologue celebrating St Petersburg. The tale that follows is both tense and terse, compounded equally of dynamic brio and plain quiet pathos. Here again the problem is to convey somehow the changes and modulations of a style.

Walter Arndt had some success at this in his *Pushkin Threefold*, which hit on the solution of presenting both a literal and a poetical version of the poems chosen. At the end of the prologue on St Petersburg the poet recalls an event about which he is now to tell us. *Pechalen budet moi rasskaz*: 'Sad will be my tale'. That takes us again to the heart of the problem. As another translator has observed, 'The night is tender' is not the same phrase as 'Tender is the night'. English poetry can play with word order as part of its poetic licence but in inflected Russian there is no natural word order to diverge from poetically. The laconic force of the Russian tetrameter becomes limp if its word order is faithfully rendered. 'Quoth the Baron: "Sad will be my tale"' is the sort of line over which our eye might pass languidly in any standard romantic narration, Scott's *Marmion* for instance. Arndt renders it 'Sorrowful will be my tale' in his literal version. Here is his poetic one:

> There was a time – our memories keep
> Its horrors ever fresh and near us . . .
> Of this a tale now suffer me
> To tell before you, gentle hearers.
> A grievous story it will be.

In spite of the 'hearers /near us' rhyme, the awkwardness of 'before you', and the padded line 'Of this a tale . . .' this version does at least manage to carry a true echo of the original in the punch and placing of that last line. The success is shown by the way in which the best plain prose version goes, that of John Fennell in the Penguin Poets series.

There was a dread time – the memory of it is still fresh . . . I will begin my narrative of it for you, my friends. My tale will be sad.

That shows how misleading literalism can be, even when rendering Pushkin at his simplest and quietest. The accurate prose makes a mere anticlimax out of the poem's calm intensity.

The latest translator, D. M. Thomas, has succeeded in part by taking a different course. As Nabokov combined the literal and the poetic by using accuracy with his own verbal fantasy, Thomas has used a subtler means of trying for the *tikho* and the tense in the same moment. Instead of the Russian tetrameter he has used blank verse.

> There was a dreadful time – the memory of it
> Is still fresh . . . I will begin my narrative
> Of it for you, my friends. My tale will be sad.

Just the same? The only change is the substitution for the poetic word 'dread' the more commonplace 'dreadful', which exactly corresponds to the Russian adjective. But by putting the lines into blank verse Thomas has changed the whole tone of them, suggesting something of Pushkin's quietly coiled potential – his *pruzhina* – 'spring', as the Russian critics put it. For blank verse is as natural to English as rhyming tetrameter to Russian, and as capable of the same variations in mood, pace, style. Indeed because of our Elizabethan dramatic tradition it is more capable of them than prose. It can render the glow and glitter of Pushkin's prologue as well as the calm bleached tones of his ending. Above all it does not distract us from looking in on the story itself. Thomas's feat is not so much to produce a translation as to restore the simple spell of Pushkinian narrative, so that we seem to be looking straight through to the story of the great Petersburg flood, and its sad consequences for one minor citizen, in the same way that the other character in the story – Tsar Peter himself – resolved in building the town to cut a window through which he could look out on Europe.

The tension of Pushkin's swift masterpiece comes from the contrast between 'Peter's creation', the cold beautiful city with its hundred-year history of national progress and autocratic power, and the private dreams and hopes of a young clerk who only wants to marry his sweetheart, settle down and 'go hand in hand with her to the grave', to be buried by their grandchildren. The Neva flood which drowns her drives him mad, and in his night wanderings he finds himself standing before the monumental equestrian statue of Peter. Arndt's free version here for a moment admirably renders his vision.

> And high above those rails, as if
> Of altitude and darkness blended,
> There rose in bronze, one arm extended,
> The Idol on its granite cliff . . .

Overcome with a sudden violent emotion the clerk shakes his fist at it and hisses 'Wonder-worker, just you wait!' Then in terror he thinks he sees the bronze head turn slowly towards him, and all night he flees about the city pursued by the clangour of brazen hooves.

The poem ends with the clerk found dead on an island offshore, where a little house, presumably that of his beloved, has been washed up. The heartless phantom city, in which the bustle of life itself can seem but a dream, has destroyed him. This is Pushkin at his quietest, and neither literalism nor rhymed artifice can give us a sense of his tone. Here is Arndt:

> A little island
> Lies off the coast. There now and then
> A stray belated fisherman
> Will beach his net at dusk and, silent,
> Cook his poor supper by the shore,
> Or, on his sunday recreation
> A boating clerk might rest his oar
> By that bleak isle. There no green thing
> Will grow; and there the inundation
> Had washed up in its frolicking
> A frail old cottage. It lay stranded
> Above the tide like weathered brush,
> Until last spring a barge was landed
> To haul it off. It was all crushed
> And bare. Against the threshold carried
> There lay asprawl my luckless knave,
> And here in charity they buried
> The chill corpse in a pauper's grave.

Unfair to pick on details: the point is the illustration of how our attention is necessarily fastened on the translator's performance, rather than being compelled by the tale. At what should be the last moving moment we cannot help noticing the need for a 'luckless knave' to rhyme with that grave. In Thomas's version we can forget everything except what the poetry is actually saying:

> A small island can be seen offshore. Sometimes
> A fisherman out late will moor there with
> His net and cook his meagre supper. Or
> Some civil servant, boating on a Sunday,
> Will pay a visit to the barren island.
> No grass grows, not a blade. The flood, in sport,
> Had driven a ramshackle little house there.
> Above the water it had taken root
> Like a black bush. Last spring a wooden barge
> Carried away the wreckage. By the threshold
> They found my madman, and on that very spot
> For the love of God they buried his cold corpse.

In *The Bronze Horseman* power confronts impotence, the subject his sovereign. The latter's small human concerns are of no moment to the archetypal ruler, even though his despotism is intended to be benevolent and to carry the people forward to their greater good. The populace suffers the penalty when grandiose schemes go awry, whether the founding of collective farms or of a capital built on a swamp. The censorship of Nicholas I presumably saw the point when they declined to let the uncut poem be published. They objected principally to the *Kumir* – the Tsar-idol – who in one form or another is still with us. Pushkin is now a national institution, safely in the past, and the Soviet state need not perceive any connection. But then as now the individual is always powerless. After his one wild outburst Pushkin's young clerk removes his cap and averts his eyes whenever he comes near the statue. The poem has no moral, or if it has it is not one for Russia only: it comes alive for us not in the poem's imaginative scope and absolute artistic mastery, unavailable as they are in translation, but in the moving sadness of the tale itself. Thomas was accused of plagiarism because his best-selling novel *The White Hotel* borrowed from the Russian author Kuznetsov its account of the massacre of the Jews in Kiev by the Germans at Babi Yar in 1941. The same accusation has been made about his Pushkin translations on the grounds that he often follows almost word for word, as my quotation showed, the prose translation of John Fennell. But there is nothing fraudulent about this similarity. The plagiarist hides behind the material he has borrowed, but Thomas scrupulously acknowledges both debts. It is honesty in a translator to follow his predecessor where the latter has achieved words and phrases both easy and exact: it would be mere conceit to change them for the sake of leaving his own mark. Thomas has translated *Rusalka* and *The Stone Guest*, as well as the more famous *Bronze Horseman*, and in these cases his own blank verse produces more than an echo of Pushkin's. It also is spare and quiet, avoiding any immediately striking effects and concentrating on a similar overall transparency of meaning.

Both in poetry and prose Pushkin's most characteristic trait is his art of implication; he never draws attention to his meanings or makes statements about them. Because of this he saw the possibilities in that characteristically romantic form, the dramatic fragment, which he picked up from the now forgotten English poet B. W. Proctor, whose pseudonym was Barry Cornwall. Pushkin was arranging for a translation from Cornwall to appear in his magazine *Sovremennik* (*The Contemporary*) only an hour before he drove out in the snow, 27 January 1837, to the duel in which he was mortally wounded. (An odd literary cross-connection here: in old age Barry Cornwall's widow became a great friend of young Thomas Hardy.)

Cornwall's dramatic scenes are a curiosity now and hardly worth reading, but they reveal an occasional glimpse of what gave the hint to Pushkin. This might be described as a melodramatic, even as we might say a 'corny' situation, which none the less contains a genuinely imaginative query, something true and penetrating that gives food for thought. Pushkin liked sentimental and melodramatic themes in which there lurked a certain meaningful and often compassionate irony. He used them in his deadpan prose stories, the 'Tales of Belkin', in 'The Queen of Spades', and in the most piquant way of all in *Rusalka* and in the combined verse and prose tale *Egyptian Nights*. Its two personages, a Russian aristocrat and amateur of letters, and a poor Italian improviser with a genius for producing verses on any subject as a public performance, are two sides of Pushkin's own self.

Though both *Rusalka* and *Egyptian Nights* are formally incomplete there seems no likelihood that Pushkin intended to complete them. They break off at the moment of impending melodrama and leave its denouement to our imagination. From a tall vase a young Petersburg miss in long gloves has drawn a theme for the improviser – 'Cleopatra and her lovers'. The improviser looks embarrassed and confused. Humbly and uncertainly he asks what was intended – 'because the great queen had many'. General laughter and the young ladies blush. But at the moment when the artist seems most ill at ease and at a disadvantage, most the butt of a philistine society, 'suddenly he felt the approach of the god'. Dazzling verse, Pushkin's own incomparable tetrameters, stream from his lips. It is the queen's whim to offer herself for a night to all comers, but the price is death. Three very different candidates accept. At the most youthful and personable the queen glances with a certain tenderness of regret . . .

To follow such a situation through into a story would be merely banal. What we look in on in the sketch is something much more subtle and comprehensive: the vulnerability of genius; its lodgment in the most unexpected people; its robust vulgarity ('Perhaps I am elegant and genteel in my writings', Pushkin once wrote to a female admirer, 'but my heart is completely vulgar') and its sensitivity in the same moment. Its immediate impact upon an audience both demonstrates and is inspired by their secret fears and hopes, aspirations and cruelties. An artist need not enact these in order to reveal them, any more than he need follow out the cycle of fate and revenge in the story of the prince and the rusalka. The prince there remains for ever enchanted by remorse and longing in the forest on the Dnieper's banks.

In *The Stone Guest* Don Juan himself cries out ironically that 'the denouement approaches'. Like his predecessors in the legend he is carried off to hell, but he goes with Donna Anna, who in Pushkin's version is not the commander's daughter but his widow. What is implied for Juan, and spoken only between the lines of the increasingly tranquil and measured dramatic exposition, is the approach of his destiny not in the conventionally retributive vengeance of the commander but in the person of Donna Anna herself. This Juan has loved girls, not coldly in order to add to his list but adding their warm sense of life to his own. Now he meets one seductive in her very coldness and passivity, as Pushkin had been charmed by his own beautiful wife Natalia. There is an element of autobiography in *Rusalka* too, for before his marriage Pushkin had a peasant mistress on his estate who bore him a child. Turgenev and Tolstoy were to do the same. The contrasting female figures in *The Stone Guest* are done with an extraordinary tenderness and Shakespearean ease. And, how brilliantly Pushkin brings out, in *Rusalka*, the difference between the two women – the miller's daughter and the young princess who unwittingly supplants her – revealing their nature with vivid economy.

Pushkin is the only writer of his time who has this strength and sureness of touch when writing in one of the standard romantic forms – lyrical, fictional, or dramatic. Apart from its obvious popularity with a public accustomed to Scott and Byron, the dramatic tale appealed to Pushkin because he could contrast its high colour with his own cool pellucid style, its obvious effects with his own more latent and subtle ones. If we can read between the blank English lines of a translation this is where his meanings gradually appear, as if made visible through some chemical process. Even in his own tongue they do not come all that easily into view. In them, however appears the true universality of Pushkin, a quality that depends on the reader's own growing perception of how his art works. It is supremely true of him that he strikes less at first, as used to be said of Raphael, to impress all the more later on, as we become familiar, like the Russians themselves, with the world of his writings.

A Petrograd apocalypse: *The Poet and the Revolution. Aleksandr Blok's 'The Twelve'* by Sergei Hackel

How do poets respond, if they respond at all, to violent social convulsions and great public events? What is the relation of a poetic masterpiece to such an external catalyst? Since the Romantic movement the successful process has seemed to be one of internalization: the poet adds the event to the annals of his own imagination, and thence by synthesis and transformation gives it back to the world in a form that appears totally public, authoritative and articulate, having the universality of myth.

Paradoxically the shock of outer events concentrates the poet's awareness of his own inner resources. And the service he may render is to do the same for the reader, sharpening his sense of his own individuality in the face of crisis, of tremendous external pressures. As Shelley said, the poet can indeed be an 'unacknowledged legislator' of the world, in that he leads the world to retain – against itself – the knowledge of human separateness, the shapes and significances of the self for the self. This of course is not what the acknowledged legislators – the Peters and Lenins and Stalins – require of him; but, as Auden observed, such ogres 'cannot master speech', and their poetic henchmen cannot do it for them. Poetry, true poetry, may celebrate the will of a Robespierre or the deeds of a tyrant: it will never exemplify the conformity that such power desires to impose. Hence any poem that 'celebrates revolution', say, without the poet taking it into his sense of himself and sharply and subtly defining his own attitude towards it, is, at best, nugatory. Solidarity cannot make a poem: only the individual can, by defining himself in relation to it.

These are commonplaces generally accepted in the culture of an open society, but if their implications are pursued to a conclusion, in relation to a poetic masterpiece from a very different kind of society, they lead to considerations of the greatest interest for criticism. Sergei Hackel's title, *The Poet and the Revolution*, suggests a summation which his book does not attempt – rightly: it consists instead of a study of the most minute particulars, and leaves the reader to draw his own inferences. It examines one poem only, Aleksandr Blok's *The Twelve*, which is one of the most striking of all instances of a poetic masterpiece written in immediate response to great events by a poet who not only lived in himself to an unusual degree but who extended further in the poem his own esoteric and arcane mythology. He and his circle were necessarily involved – totally involved – in the trauma of revolutionary Petrograd; but artistic sense can only be made of that involvement in relation to the history of himself and his ideas.

And this is what Dr Hackel effectively demonstrates. His knowledge of Blok studies is exhaustive, and although much of what he says will have complete significance only for the Russianist, his exposition is so clear and so compelling that any thoughtful student of poetry will at once become absorbed. Dr Hackel's is that tradition of Russian scholarship which is infinitely meticulous but never dry: indeed his enthusiasm for the niceties of the subject makes him almost lyrical.

The poem itself, *The Twelve*, is 335 lines long, and was written down by Blok in a state of intense excitement during January 1918. On the fifth of the month the Constituent Assembly had met for the first and only time, and had been immediately and forcibly dissolved by the Bolsheviks. Detesting all such bodies as Western, devious, bourgeois-democratic, Blok was delighted. The fury of the re- volutionary storm which inspired him had no place for such a cumbrous and compromising institution. *The Twelve* contains two ironic references to the forlorn – 'All Power to the Constituent Assembly' – placard stretched from houses across the street and swinging in the icy gale. Below it in the street is heard the slang chat of St Petersburg whores announcing that they have held their own assembly and agreed to charge ten for a short time and twenty-five a night, with no undercutting. Like elementals of the Revolution ('Bolshevism – the elements', Blok noted more than once in his diary), snow-showers whirl demonically through the poem, as through Pushkin's *Besi*; equally shrill and demonic are the snatches imitated from factory songs – *chatushki* – and the contrast between priggish slogans from juvenile *Pravda* and the brutish comments of the Red Guardsmen.

All these voices give the poem the stunning impact which it still keeps today. But it is also most carefully constructed in accordance with the symbolic patterns of Blok's imagination and the kinds of iconic tableaux that had perennially obsessed him; and it is with the ramifying implications of these that Dr Hackel is chiefly concerned. Like Yeats, Blok was not in any real sense an intellectual, nor did he have the kinds of omnivorous, intuitive intelligence that inform a great primary poetry like that of Pushkin or Shakespeare. He required the stimulus of ideas and mystic theories that could be turned into poetic metaphor; he needed the religiosity of the magus – Bely, Soloviev, Ivanov, Merezhkovsky – as Yeats needed the notions of Pound or the Rosicrucians. The theoretical side of all this has been well expounded by James West in his book *Russian Symbolism*, but the particular interest of Dr Hackel's detailed study is to show how Blok and others adapted Russian symbolist doctrine to a policy of action, religious and sexual, political and apocalyptic. Whatever might be the case in practice, in theory they certainly did not feel that human activity existed to end up in art and poetry; not unlike the Futurists in Italy, they exalted the prospects of blood, fire and rapine, which in the pre-war Russian capital were certainly more readily imaginable than elsewhere.

The air of the arcanum was thus tempered with spontaneity and by that curious kind of shameless honesty, often found in Dostoevsky's heroes, which even the most inflated St Petersburg shaman could unexpectedly reveal. In this critical month, while he was writing *The Twelve* and often in the society of Ivanov-Razumnik, Blok noted that he felt especially well, 'at once comfortable and disturbed' (*uiutno i trevozhno vmeste*), a singularly frank diagnosis of the intellectual's enjoyment of a crisis which will be meat and drink to his nature. The representatives of Russian culture, even the brilliant Baltic intelligentsia incubating ideas in that overwhelmingly unreal capital, had always been paralysed, conscious of their separation both from the Russian people and from the machinery of imperial government. To welcome disaster with open arms gave them – at last – a kind of authority. And for Blok this acceptance was not simply that of the connoisseur. 'Beautiful in the splendour of his power is the oriental king Asarhaddon, and beautiful is the ocean of a people's wrath beating to pieces a tottering throne. But hateful – aesthetically displeasing that is – are half-measures.' So the poet Bryusov had commented in 1905. Blok's tone is more humble, if not much less irresponsible. He followed Carlyle, one of his heroes, in a literary glorification of Sansculottism, but he admitted his lack of knowledge and judgement. 'I have nothing to be proud of, I understand nothing.' The hero of Pushkin's *The Captain's Daughter* had the pious hope that he would never see another Russian revolt, 'senseless and merciless'; and quoting this, Blok emphasized that even the Pugachevschina had been 'a quest for the real', to be exalted over any accidental and undramatic reality brought about by the historical process. 'Musical' and elemental forces were at work – 'and shall we have the right to say that the flame is entirely destructive if it destroys only *us*, the intelligensia?'

Considering that the destruction and diaspora of her intelligentsia was a blow from which Russia has never recovered and perhaps never will, one can hardly, with hindsight, agree. That class, so easily extinguished, had taken many generations to produce. It was of course far too valuable and various to be generalized under a common premonition of doom, but Anna Akhmatova's *Poem without a Hero*, in which Blok appears, gives a remarkable poetic retrospection of its apocalypse. Symbolism accepted this with facility, shrugging off actual human suffering with what Yeats was airily to refer to as 'gaiety transfiguring all that dread'. Mandelstam and Akhmatova, whom history has made greater poets than Blok or Yeats, knew better: not so much because their Acmeist ideal was more sensitive than those of symbolism – though it was – but because they came to understand as poets what apocalypse really meant.

And yet *The Twelve* is a great poem; although how, one might ask, could a great poem emerge out of all this nonsense, this wilful desire for an external holocaust to match the inner need for self-destruction? The repeated chant of Yeats in 'Easter 1916' – 'A terrible beauty is born' – seems close to the kind of animation and impulse which runs riot in *The Twelve*. But just as Yeats could also command a tough, rational, reflective tone, the tone of Marvell many generations before in his Cromwell Ode, so the very inwardness of symbolism enabled Blok to achieve comparable kinds of balance and discernment, to impose his own patterns on the 'revolutionary music', even as he seemed most ecstatically and slavishly to yield to its powerful rhythms.

At least it may be so. Yeats takes the image of the stone which a fanatic heart becomes – 'the stone's in the midst of all' – but one does not quite see him first writing down 'the Irish cause – a stone' as Blok wrote 'Bolshevism – the elements'. Yeats was humanly divided: division in Blok seems more purely formalistic. Dr Hackel does not seek to make this point, but he implies it in the course of his careful examination of the multiple motifs that make up the poem's structure. There is, first of all, the tradition in popular legend of Pugachev and Stenka Razin, who in the interests of class solidarity threw his princess into the Volga. This is the closest we come to simple feeling in the poem (and the scale of its background is of course far larger than anything in Yeats), for Blok personally detested stupid officer types twirling their moustaches, and identified with the Red Guards who, like those rebels of old, have come to 'lay their wild heads down' in a revolt against the Tsar and his officials, a revolt of the people (Dr Hackel has even discovered the engaging fact that a Pugachev and a Razin are in the records as serving at this time on the Bolshevik military committee of Petrograd). Blok echoes his predecessors here – Pushkin above all – in the familial manner that is peculiarly strong in Russian literature.

Then there is the appeal to traditional orthodox faith, for the poem ends with a vision of Christ with a red flag, marching unseen by them at the head of the guardsmen. Christ can always be claimed, and with justice, by any revolutionary body; and we are just as familiar today with the modish use of him on behalf of the underprivileged and against any form of Church or state 'establishment' or conventional belief. But there is a further refinement here, for after many hesitations and alterations Blok finally spelt the name of the Christ who is invoked in the last line – 'Ahead – Jesus Christ' (*Vperedi – Isus Khristos*) – in the manner no longer sanctioned by the Orthodox Church but used by the Old Believers, a traditionalist sect persecuted in Russia for two hundred years or more, whose tenets and psychology had fascinated many authors, particularly Dostoevsky. The orthodox spelling of Jesus in Russian is trisyllabic – Iisus, not Isus.

But who is this Christ anyway? Mirsky rather grimly observes that whoever he is, he is not the Christ of the Gospels and the Church, and goes on to hint that his identity can be found in the peculiar personal mythology of Blok's earlier poetry. Most Russian critics have agreed, pointing out that the figure wreathed with white roses, drifting silently before the brutal and licentious soldiery, bears a striking resemblance to Blok's famous image of the *Neznakomka*, the unknown lady misty with furs and perfume, who appears in previous poems amid the sordid and drunken disorder of a low restaurant, where even the moon has an imbecile gape and the pretentious faces have a loathsome fatuity. This lady was a later (and incidentally a highly popular) version of the more subjective being whom Blok had invoked in his earliest poems, 'Verses about the Beautiful Lady' (*Stikhi o Prekrasnoi Dame*), poems which Blok was later to assert came as near as he had ever been to the real 'truth' of his vision.

But, in a very typical volte-face, Blok had written a few years later, in 1906, a short play called *Balaganchik* (The Puppet Show) in which Pierrot and Harlequin find that the mystic bride Columbine is nothing but a cardboard doll, who collapses into stupid immobility on the snow of a St Petersburg street. This brilliantly despairing and Strindbergian little piece is also in the background of the mystic figure at the end of *The Twelve* which suggests that Blok was taking over the guardsmen and leading them by the nose, as it were, after a cardboard phantom which they are not even aware of, but which the poet knows to be a sham; and also that in so doing Blok has 'taken over' the Revolution in the name of the symbolist intelligentsia, and shown that its confused ideal and wild elemental music are nothing but the images which he and his fellows have already yearned after and been utterly disenchanted by. 'Whatever flames upon the night / Man's own resinous heart has fed', as Yeats put it. The Christ who marches with majestic head at the poem's end is also 'the eternal feminine' (Blok knew his Goethe) which inspires man's endeavour, and yet is shown as it burns out to be a will-o'-the-wisp as well as a timeless image.

The poem, seen in this way, is already deep into irony, voluntary or involuntary (and Dr Hackel reminds us that Blok was always intensely curious to hear how others interpreted his poem). Every compressed poetic masterpiece must and should reveal such ambiguities. 'Christ only can be loved and hated simultaneously', noted Blok, and Dr Hackel's chief purpose is to emphasize his ambiguous but essential relation to Christian observance and belief. He also notices how closely Blok's Christ figure is related to contemporary figures in Remizov's 'Lay of the Downfall of the Russian Land', Rozanov's *Apokalypsis*, and Ivanov-Razumnik's 'Two Russias' (*Dve Rossii*). But more striking than this is his conjecture that while Rozanov's description of Christ, in a comparable circumstance, has the simple intention of discrediting his image, the silence and indistinctness of Blok's Christ gives him the suggestiveness of a whole host of figures, positive and negative, drawn from Russia and the scriptures as well as from Blok's own mythology. 'Unfortunately, Christ', was Blok's own concluding comment, after a host of queries and speculations, mostly hostile; and his figure has indeed something of the impenetrability of an icon. Dr Hackel is surely right in suggesting that its relation in the poem to Katka, the cheerful tart who has gone off with Vanka the villain (Judas, or

John?) and who is shot by the Twelve in the course of their prowl, becomes in the end almost like that in an Assumption or Dormition: the Christ figure is seen together with the prostrate body in the snow, who is all unconscious victims, and even Russia herself.

Within weeks of writing *The Twelve* Blok was plunged in the deepest gloom, from which he never recovered. He died three years later without having written another poem, though he made occasional efforts to continue work begun earlier. 'All sounds have stopped', he said. 'There are no more sounds.' What else could he have expected? The elemental fury of revolution and liberation were over: the stifling aftermath of repression and regimentation had begun. But the very simplicity of this disillusionment shows the poet's essential honesty, the honesty that made Gumilev remark that with other poets you read their works: with Blok you read the man himself. And this of course is the very opposite of Yeats, the indomitably protean survivor, who discards his personality and gets a new one in order to remain a poet. Overwhelmed with committee work, Blok now noted that 'there is something inexpressibly disgusting in the air', presumably all that bustle of reconstruction, already and sinisterly censorious, over which he spiritlessly presided as president of the Poets' Union.

The lightning flash of *The Twelve*, its lack of any deeply matured and considered background, make the story in it seem curiously stilted, more of a puppet show (*Balaganchik* again) than an enduring drama. As Wordsworth said about Goethe's poetry, it does not seem inevitable enough. But this of course was not how Blok's genius worked; and was in fact why he was unable to finish the long retrospective poem 'Retaliation' (*Vozmezdie*), still only a fragment when he died. As a poetic *coup de foudre*, *The Twelve* remains intensely present to us, and Dr Hackel has shown – for the first time in a book written for the English-speaking public – how arresting is the workmanship behind its explosive and enigmatic power; but nevertheless it is not the sort of poem which continues to grow in the mind. During his lifetime the Soviet authorities continued zealously to put out new editions, and when Blok queried this on the ground that the poem 'had a somewhat, dated note' a commissar told him that this was 'correct', but that a decision had been taken to publish the best works of Russian literature, 'even though they only have a historical significance'.

Blok's reaction is not recorded, but the commissar may have had a point. The same could not be said of *The Waste Land*, Akhmatova's *Poem without a Hero*, or Pushkin's *Bronze Horseman*, three poems that in their various ways transcend the situation out of which they were written and to which they remain closely linked. All are 'sleepwalking' poems, as Blok's was; poems, that is, which seemed to arrive out of the air, without their authors' conscious volition, and which are seen to have the quality of classic summation, the apprehension of a time and place focused in the experience of the individual. All three, however different, are supremely *impassive* poems, and it is this kind of authority above all which *The Twelve* must be said to lack. Whatever their esoteric meanings in the techniques of the poet's history, Blok's dramatis personae seem confined to their role as puppets, while the denizens of the other poems – Pushkin's Evgeny supremely – transcend pattern and purpose. Blok himself is a character in *Poem Without a Hero*, a haunting figure like all the others in that poem, whose most terrible and most casual personification – the 'noseless slut' of the epilogue, symbolizing, perhaps, all the callous horrors of the regime – is more suggestive in her one-line role than Blok's Christ in his.

It must be admitted though that *The Twelve* is virtually impossible to render into any sort of English (though there is an outstanding German version) whereas *Poem Without a Hero* survives a literal and simple translation (and there is now a really masterly rendering of it by the English poet D. M. Thomas). Dr Hackel gives us in an appendix *The Twelve* in the pre-revolutionary orthography that Blok himself insisted on, but though the rendering he provides on the opposite pages is extremely helpful it is uncomfortable to read. The feebleness of any possible English colloquial and rhythmic equivalents must be blamed for this, and not Dr Hackel, who has composed a commentary of outstanding scholarship and general interest.

He quotes in conclusion Blok's remark: 'Even in despair the world is beautiful, and there is no contradiction in this.' For Blok the world could not have been beautiful without the validity of that despair which died in the vacuum of Soviet complacency: Soviet-style man is no more entitled to it than to the elemental thrill of anarchy to which *The Twelve* has given its music. In his last lecture, on Pushkin, Blok made clear that he understood what would happen. Like Pushkin himself, like any Russian poet, he was habituated to the principle of censorship, but he now urged the bureaucrats 'to beware of a worse name than Pushkin's "rabble"', if they sought to condition poetry socially, 'threatening its mysterious freedom and preventing it from carrying out its mysterious function'.

The secrets of Gogol: *The Creation of Nikolai Gogol* by Donald Fanger

With his usual tendency to exaggeration Dostoevsky said – or is reported to have said – that all the Russian novelists came out from under Gogol's 'Overcoat'. A generous tribute, though with a faint hint of patronage about it, and in any case not really true. What is true is that Gogol himself owed everything to Pushkin – themes, treatments, characters, the idea of being a writer, the way of being a writer. It is also true that all Russian writers who followed Pushkin owed him a tutelary idea of form: the piece of writing that is not quite like any other category, a 'free novel', in Pushkin's phrase; not quite a story or a comedy or satire, polemic or exploration or apologia, but partaking of all of them, and appearing – for reasons connected with the singularity of its form – uncompleted, if not incomplete. That appearance is illusory, though it is an illusion which is part of the unique satisfactoriness of the work of art, whether it is *Evgeny Onegin, Dead Souls, Notes from Underground*, even *War and Peace*.

Another unique feature of the great renaissance of Russian writing in the early nineteenth century is what, for want of a better term, might be called its Shakespearean quality. It went against the grain of the age in Europe, however much it was copying European models, and against the grain of Romanticism as it was developing in France, Germany and England. There the writer was the man, the voice and personality: the age of the author as hero, and of the *Dichter*, was under way: in England it was to end in Westminster Abbey and three-volume biographies. The writer came to stand for his country and its genius, as Goethe had done, or for the spirit of the age itself, like Byron. But the first great Russians were not a bit like this. They had no posture, no pretension, not even that of a 'man speaking to men'. They wanted to find out the authentic masterpiece, but they did not know how to be themselves, with that absolute authenticity which Europe was learning to recognize in its authors.

This not knowing how to be an authentic self was especially true of Gogol, and it worried him as it never worried Pushkin: it virtually worried him into the grave. Pushkin's indifference to the writer as self was serene and harmonious; but this was not possible for the genius who was his disciple and follower. Although Gogol's native talents were of quite a different kind they had the same divine *absence* behind them, an absence that Gogol became more and more obsessed with filling up. (It is significant that he used the phrase 'an abyss of space' about the effects of Pushkin's greatest poetry.)

This then is the paradox of Gogol, which neither he nor his critics later on could make any definitive sense of. He has attracted explicators into his vacuous oddities as if into a black hole; thinkers and theorists have taken him as their text while professing to expound him; later writers, of whom Andrei Bely was the most subtle, have ingested his work into their own and interpreted his inspired negations as positive techniques. Dostoevsky, typically, stated that both he and Pushkin had a 'secret' which it was the task of later Russian writers to discover and profit by. More recent studies by F. C. Driessen and Simon Karlinsky ('The Sexual Labyrinth of Nikolai Gogol') have sought to explain him, and the motifs of his stories, in terms of repressed homosexuality. As this aspect of sex had no official existence in the Russia of Gogol's time, and has if possible even less of one in the Russia of today, it might seem an appropriate key to a writer the nature of whose existence and point as a writer was always of such anguish to him. It is certainly true: the case is pretty well proven; but in the world of Gogol it is not much use proving things.

Though Nabokov's little paperback will probably remain for the English-speaking reader, bedevilled as he has been by bad and incomplete translations, the most instantly illuminating thing on Gogol, Donald Fanger's *The Creation of Nikolai Gogol* is the most comprehensive, balanced and scholarly critical study that has yet appeared outside Russia. Fanger is an equable and good-natured expert, who gives all other experts and technicians in the field their due, and has the knack of producing just the right quotation from one or another of them to help make his point.

Gogol is Shakespearean in the sense that he can be interpreted in almost any way, and what is latent or negative in him can be made to appear profound and positive. It is for example, a slight shock for the reader of Bely or Nabokov to turn to the Gogolian text and find it much less *fin de siècle* and fascinating or less Nabokovian, than it there appears. Indeed part of Gogol's trouble, which came to bother him exceedingly, is that he excited everyone madly without their quite knowing why; and they expected the greatest things of him without knowing – nor did he – what form these would take. Both he and his audience expected him to be prophet and lawgiver, roles which by temperament and talent he was totally unsuited to fulfil. A sympathetic contemporary, Count Sollogub, put it as follows:

Gogol suffered long from his impotence before the demands of the literate Russian public, which had chosen him as its idol . . . He broke down under the weight of his calling, which had, in his eyes, taken on enormous dimensions. He died from an internal struggle, while Pushkin died from an external one. Pushkin could not withstand his enemies: Gogol could not withstand his admirers.

His admirers expected a sort of Russian Schiller, and they got something more like a Ukrainian Groucho Marx. Though it is certainly relevant, the effect of Gogol's Ukrainian provenance can be exaggerated: its chief consequence was to make him determined to become a specifically *Russian* author. Much more important is his passion when young for all things fashionably German – 'the high, the lofty, the beautiful' – passions which Pushkin gently satirized in young Lensky, the friend of Onegin, who falls asleep the night before the fatal duel reading a poem by Schiller. On arrival in St Petersburg the youthful Gogol spent far more than he could afford on a complete set of Schiller, whom he was mad about, and wrote to his mother that he was striving to think beautiful thoughts every day.

The crucible of St Petersburg, the background of the early hallucinated stories like 'The Nose' and 'Nevsky Prospect', transformed him. The most important thing was his introduction to Pushkin. Gogol needed a principle on which to work, and it seems likely that Pushkin supplied him with one, either by precept or example, as he was later to supply him with ideas for stories, including that of *Dead Souls*. There must have been something about the young man which charmed and won over discerning elders. Perhaps it was the intuition of an unhoused talent, a Russian 'soul' and potential that might be going anywhere. The academic Pletnyov, who introduced him to Pushkin, was 'touched and delighted' by Gogol's multiple enthusiasms. Pletnyov wrote to Pushkin, 'he was at first inclined to go into the civil service, but a passion for pedagogy led him to my camp: he has gone into teaching as well. I am impatient to bring him round for your blessing.' As a result of this kind of thing Gogol was actually given a post as professor of Universal History at St Petersburg University. The job was far from a sinecure; Gogol knew nothing and extemporized desperately, grasping at information from any quarter and compiling voluminous notes on the folklore of little Russia, geography teaching, classical agriculture, the Middle Ages, sculpture, painting and music. His position was as dazzling but precarious as that of his own Khlestakov in *The Government Inspector*, as he asserted his right to speak and to print 'all sorts of things about all sorts of things'.

In the meantime he had perpetrated a lyrical effusion in verse and prose of the most ludicrous kind, which he called *Hanz Kuechelgarten* and took the precaution of publishing under the pseudonym 'G. Alov'. The piece met with such general derision that Gogol bought up and burnt all the copies he could find and then fled to Germany for a six-week vacation. And yet in a sense *Hanz Kuechelgarten* contains the embryo of all that Gogol was later to achieve and is a more essentially Gogolian work than the stories called *Evenings on a Farm at Dikanka*, which established his reputation a little later, and for which he used his store of concocted Ukrainian folklore. The attempts of his earlier work to be German – the lofty lyric outpourings, the passion for Greece – are already beginning to be transmogrified into a kind of Russian hilarity and dishevelment, that majestic dishevelment that runs riot in *Dead Souls*.

Gogol's originality was enormous, but it lay unknown to him beneath a mass of banal plans and ideas, of the kind attempted by bright young men who will never amount to anything. His method appears to emerge precisely out of the fatuousness of such attempts. He was the first man of the nineteenth century to bring the 'ideal' into the area of the hopelessly contingent; and the ideal did not vanish in the process but was in some way apotheosized in the incorrigibility of the *ne to*, the not quite, the nothing exactly. In the world of Gogol's style his 'energetic imputation', as Fanger calls it, is left hanging in the air. Idealists like Küchelbecker (his name bears a Gogolian resemblance to that of the hero of the adolescent romance), a charming and naive young Russian critic of German origin, could be said to have helped form the climate in which the process took place, and even contributed to what seems Gogol's originality.

All Küchelbecker's friends were fond of him and found him

absurd (Pushkin was particularly attached and may have thought of
him when inventing Lensky) but he was a shrewd thinker who,
wrote in his diary, when in Siberian exile after the Decembrist
conspiracy, 'In the foolish and stupid, when carried to the highest
degree, there is a sort of loftiness . . . pure joy.'

If Gogol had formulated that and acted on it the results would not
be what they are: the originality of his process is intimate with its
obfuscation and contradictoriness. His method was far from being
that artfully closed circuit of the absurd that it had been in Sterne
and was to be in Beckett. On the contrary, the pleasures and rewards
of Gogol's art depend on the freedom of its always being apparently
provisional, hurrying on to something else – he knows not what – as
if transported by the notorious troika, and strewing incongruous
possessions behind him on the way: a nose, an overcoat, a tacky old
travelling-carriage, a tie-pin in the shape of a pistol. His way of
writing never settles down into being itself. If it did it would cease to
have the showman's magic of 'now you see me, now you don't'. Nor
would Gogol have virtually committed suicide by starvation when
he found that the writing which was his whole life had no other place
to go, no new world of living souls to reveal and rejoice in. His
theme, as Fanger justly says, is 'mere existence', but the point about
mere existence is its volatility – it is made of dreams and always
trying to get somewhere else.

'Not a single line was written without my imagining him before
me', wrote Gogol after Pushkin's death. 'What he would say, what
he would laugh at, what would elicit his eternal and indestructible
approval – that was all that concerned me and roused my powers.'
Pushkin's prose experiments related especially to form: the right
way to do a historical novel, a novel of society, short story,
melodrama and miscellany. If things did not go well he broke off and
tried something else. The number of these unfinished experiments
indicates that he found prose a constricting medium, less free than
the verse in which his novel *Evgeny Onegin* had been so much at
home. As Fanger observes, 'where Pushkin's pursuit of this problem
– an artistically serious Russian [prose] fiction – was mediated by
existing literature, Gogol's turned out to be unmediated and
radical'. Both writers were influenced by the situation of literature in
Russia at the time, the sense of great possibilities but also of
frustration; for the potential audience, though growing, was still
very small, and the financial arrangements were chaotic. In so far as
what Balzac called 'la littérature marchande' existed it consisted of

novels imitated from the West, though with a Russian setting, and Fanger is particularly good on the logistics of the writer's world with which both Pushkin and Gogol had to deal.

But it is arguable that neither writer in fact solved the problem of what the new Russian novel would be like: that was left to the great second and third generations, to Tolstoy and Dostoevsky. Gogol clung, it would seem, to the example of Pushkin's poetry rather than his prose. His more or less straight historical novel, *Taras Bulba*, is the feeblest of his mature performances, though it received a warm welcome from readers who were totally puzzled about *Dead Souls* and how to take it. Gogol composed his own frontispiece for *Dead Souls*, which Fanger reproduces. Conspicuous in very large print in the centre is the word 'Poema', which – rather than poem – means some long epic or lofty narration, heroic or mock-heroic. Though some of the critics jibbed, the point on the whole was taken that this was not a novel as such, even though the censor had insisted on adding as the main title, 'Chichikov's Adventures'. What is significant is the way Gogol was clinging to the example of the Pushkinian verse narrative, and particularly to that aspect of such a narrative which Pushkin in *Evgeny Onegin* had called 'pied' – i.e., partaking of every sort of tone, grave and gay, sad and witty, low and lofty and so forth. For Pushkin, always preoccupied with form, this was the only part of 'Romanticism' that mattered, and for him it was not a modern phenomenon but a perennial one, something that could be found in great writers like Shakespeare, Cervantes and Molière.

It seems banal today because it has become the standard modern novel formula – 'a novel funny, relentless and obscene, savage, poignant and touching', etc. – though Sterne was already exploiting a not so different formula in the eighteenth century. But though Pushkin and Gogol were well aware of what materials they were working with, there remains something gloriously discrepant and incongruous between the way they put the idea before themselves and their readers, and what actually happened in their works as a result. Pushkin's 'free' verse novel turned out not to be so free after all: all of a sudden he saw that its structure was completed, even though it seemed merely to be resting at an impasse. In Gogol's case the incongruity is much more helpless, more owlish as it were. A rambling article by him appearing as 'Petersburg Notes for 1836', in the journal founded by Pushkin, *The Contemporary*, affirmed that 'what surrounds us daily, what is inseparable from us, what is ordinary, only a deep, great, extraordinary talent can notice'. Who can doubt it? Jane Austen would have agreed; so would Pushkin, with his ability to show us in peerless poetry how a young girl's heart is broken in the corner of the vegetable garden (something, incidentally, that Byron could not possibly have done). Gogol is trying to formulate what he could not have afforded fully to understand, but which gave him something to hold on to.

Still more banal, even in 1836, are his further comments on the aesthetic seriousness and social value of comedy, of laughter and tears, and on the desirability for the artist, and particularly the playwright, 'of reading a lively lesson at once to a whole crowd where . . . a familiar vice that has been trying to hide is exposed and, with the secret voice of universal sympathy a familiar, timidly revealed, lofty feeling comes to the fore'. The real clue – or *clou* as Henry James would say – lies not in what is actually said here but in that characteristic juxtaposition of loftiness and lowness, grandeur and timidity. Nabokov was surely right in stressing how much Gogol was obsessed with *poshlost* – self-satisfied vulgarity – but it is even more important that the *poshlost* officially under attack in his satiric comedy is in Gogol's art the only way to the sublime. And again, this is something Gogol could not say, or even perhaps think, for the only true way to use vulgarity in art is unconsciously to worship it.

No doubt Gogol suffered from being condemned by his art to disingenuousness. Sincerity with him is always a matter of invoking the idea of the sincere; and as Fanger observes, his attempts 'to speak frankly in his letters are all attempts to speak *about* frankness'. At that pregnant moment in the history of Russian letters there was bound to be tremendous theoretical interest in Russian art and what it meant to be a Russian writer, but in Gogol's case there is a quite extraordinary hiatus between creation itself and the ways in which creativity can be programmed and justified. Where Pushkin, in his good-natured way, had gone calmly on with the business of trying out different literary forms, Gogol sought feverishly in his middle period to produce things that would triumphantly exemplify his ideas – state comedies, historical novels, and most of all the 'positive' second part of *Dead Souls*. But success as an artist always turned out to be in terms of *ne to* . . .

That useful formulation was first made by Alex de Jonge in a seminal essay in the Faber Studies, *Ten Russian Writers*, handsomely acknowledged by Fanger. The thing that does not really happen, the fact that fails quite to reach progression and articulation – such matters are both disquieting and, as we come to know Gogol,

satisfyingly addictive. De Jonge neatly makes the point by remind-
ing us of Chekhov's gun, which, if it is mentioned in a narrative as
hanging on the wall, must sooner or later go off. In Gogol's world
the gun never does go off. Hence the sharp division in his critics
between those who thrust great truths upon him, at Schelling did on
Shakespeare and Heidegger on Hölderlin, and those who stress that
there is nothing to him but performance. His stories are a paradise
for formalist and structuralist commentators: indeed, the critical
premises of Shklovsky and Bakhtin could be said to be largely based
on Gogolian precedents. And he perfectly fits Barthes's definition
of irony as 'the question posed to language by language', and of
'baroque irony' (as opposed to 'poor Voltairean irony, narcissistic
produce of a language too self-confident') as what 'expands the
language rather than narrowing it'.

Writers like Joyce and Dickens use language in ways that offer
parallels here, but essential differences remain. For one thing their
use of incongruity is much more precise. Joycean platitude and
cliché are contrived and meticulous, a sort of Platonic essence of
cliché, and Mrs Gamp would never have said anything so disturb-
ingly simple as the Welfare Commissioner in *The Government
Inspector* who reports that his patients are 'recovering like flies'. The
language of Gogol and his characters has none of the self-confidence
Barthes speaks of, and with which Dickens endows Mrs Gamp. That
is something literary language can hardly bear to lose, or hardly
knows how to lose, but Gogol's language could be said to give the
feeling that it has never acquired it. Meaning and syntax are
sometimes paralysed in their most basic capacity. 'How happy I am',
Khlestakov declares on being presented to the mayor's wife, 'that I
have pleasure of a kind in seeing you'. What he thinks he means and
what she thinks she hears merge in a kind of shapeless suggestion of
the things heard and said in polite intercourse. When flirting with
her daughter he tells here that her eyes 'are better than important
matters'; and when he turns his attention to the wife again – 'With a
flame in my breast I ask for your hand' – the gratified lady can only
reply that she is 'in a certain sense . . . married'. Conversational
platitude has spread its nerveless powers over and above reality. As
Fanger says, 'the speakers have been deprived of the capacity to
recognize nonsense at any level, their own or others'. But so
apparently has language itself.

There is a sense in which Gogol's art as performance should
appeal particularly to modern fashions for the 'happening', whose
effect is not durably engraved, as with art, but dissipated like the

contingent moments of life. Certainly to read Gogol is to experience a wonderfully uneasy immediacy, as if the experience had never happened before, had been improvised and run up for one at a moment's notice. Fanger puts the finger on this impression when he says that such an artist 'does not evoke vitality, he *confers* it'. Nothing, so to speak, was there until he conjured it up for us, just for the time it takes to read. Logically, therefore, nothing in it can refer to what other sorts of art evoke: the experiences of life and our response to them. This goes some way to explaining why Gogol was so much 'misunderstood', and was driven mad by the tendencies of his own talent. The story of 'The Two Ivans', in Mirgorod, has a famous concluding sentence – *Skuchno na etom svete, gospoda* – 'It is dreary in this world, gentlemen' – often taken as a comment on life and Russia of a summatory kind, a sort of verdict, however unexpectedly and incongruously produced. But, as Fanger observes, its aesthetic function is merely to signal the withdrawal of vitality, the unique vitality generated in the telling of the tale but absent from 'this world'.

In the same way it might be said that the famous 'Overcoat' needs the structure it has for the same reason. Nothing is happening, nothing that could be called life or consciousness. Then life begins to stir, in the form of a vision of a new overcoat, reaches a feverish pitch of excitement and intensity when the overcoat is obtained, and vanishes again with the theft of the overcoat, the death of its owner, and the final manifestation of what is taken to be his ghost. The overcoat, or rather the hero-with-overcoat, is the source of vitality summoned up by the author, and as his tale ends it can only be withdrawn. The coat is in a sense his art in tangible form, and when art is finished with them owner and coat vanish back into limbo.

Having suggested which, I experience a sharp revulsion and a desire to separate the story from this kind of criticism, which seeks – as always in Gogol's case – either to interpret a parable or to explain the working of a performance. Certainly the hero's coming to life is also the coming to life of the tale. But life itself in Gogol is, of course, an ambiguous affair. It might seem a matter of pure Pavlovian conditioning which recoils upon the reader himself, as Charles Bernheimer claimed in his essay 'Cloaking the Self: the literary space of Gogol's "Overcoat"':

We laugh at the unresponsive, mechanically repetitive quality of Akaky's existence, at his self-absorbed blindness and mute hesitancy, exulting thereby in our own flexibility and freedom. But the joke is really on us. We feel superior to Akaky in our adaptability to this world, but he has found a mode of being that eschews all such degrading compromises . . . by being undefined as an individual.

Borrowing from the 'You are laughing at yourselves' of *The Inspector General*, this criticism suggests that the story conceals a sort of moral trap. In its world none of us are individuals, and Akaky is destroyed by his attempt to become one through possession of the overcoat. Are most human beings only really at home in the humble little hell of the *ne to*? Does the overcoat spell hubris, a fatal temptation, even the Fall? Certainly some Russian critics have seen it as the occasion of the kindling of the human soul to love – 'albeit of a very special kind' – while others suggest that the 'unfallen' Akaky's name echoes that of a specially meek saint in the Orthodox calendar. Certainly when he gets his overcoat Akaky sheds much of his meekness, feels sexual interests stirring, drinks champagne . . . Is this a moral point being made, or merely what another critic calls 'a travesty of hagiography'?

In face of such hermeneutic dilemmas it is no wonder that the most authoritative Russian critics have settled for a description of the performance, as Eykhenbaum gives it us in 'How Gogol's "Overcoat" is Made'. In the making of 'The Overcoat', everything positive, every hope, wish or assertion is paralysed by oddities or 'filler words' – 'somehow', 'even', 'sort of', 'all the same', 'it seems', etc. When Akaky visits the tailor to see if his ancient garment can somehow be patched again, he finds the door open, 'because the lady of the house, preparing some fish or other, had filled the kitchen with so much smoke that you couldn't see even the cockroaches'. The 'even' and the 'some or other' are essential here to feel and sense, as is the fact that the lady of the house doesn't even see Akaky, as if he had no existence.

All the same, none of this is really relevant to the story, any more than comparable ingenuities of interpretation or technical perception are to Pushkin's poem, *The Bronze Horseman*, the preceding tale with a poor clerk in it. Pushkin, incidentally, probably supplied the idea of 'The Overcoat' with a true story of a clerk who lost a much-coveted gun the first time he took it to the marshes, but was able to get another one after a generous whip-round at the office. Gogol adapted this: the clerks do have a whip-round for Akaky but there have been so many contributions to other causes that very little is raised. This change, though, which would be significant *as* a change between, for instance, a Shakespearean source and the resulting play, has little if any relevance to the genesis of Gogol's tale. It seems both inevitable and unimportant. The disquieting thing to the Gogol critic, which makes him as it were run mad in methodology, is: what is relevant? Anything and nothing, the simplest response and the most ingenious hypothesis. Perhaps, as Karlinsky implies, an author who is uncertain about his own sex is likely to make his reader uncertain about everything else. Both Karlinsky and Fanger discuss the question of *identity*, which indeed with many authors is the simplest way of establishing the question of relevance. In C. P. Snow, for instance, personal identity comes from serving on a committee; in Dickens it is often a matter of deception, of hypocrisy – the Dickens character can be imagined as saying, in various grotesque ways, 'none of them know what I am really like', and this is effective because the reader at once recognizes how closely it represents his own experience of secret identity in the world. It does not matter that there is no way of being 'really like' yourself: Dickens's characters seem in their sly or anxious way to be confident that there is.

But Gogol's grotesques are quite a different matter. For them the notion of pretence, of acting a part, has no meaning, Khlestakov does not *pretend* to be a Government Inspector; it just turns out that he is taken for one. Even parodic comment in the characters' mouths, as when Poprishchin says 'Maybe I myself don't know who I am', does nothing to clarify matters. It is an ironic echo, in one sense, of Gogol's invisible sexual feelings. Absence of identity also seems to render impossible the function of satire and caricature, where function depends on the existence of a norm, the aberration from which we recognize and respond to. 'The Gogolian being refuses any autonomous conscious apprehension of reality . . . fails even to suspect its possibility.' With that kind of pronouncement the critic – in this case one of the most respected of the Russian experts – gives us his sense of satisfaction of knowing at least where *he* is.

Gogol leads one on to make all sorts of such suggestions. It is not Professor Fanger's fault: he is not sold on any one critical method, he is a humane and subtle scholar, who himself perceives just what the difficulties of talking about Gogol are. But is there not some more ordinary compromise to be made between the relevance of the formalistic approach and the fact that Gogol cannot help striking most readers as a great realist? I feel the connection must and should be made, for only by making it do we rescue Gogol from the world of Borges, Nabokov, Beckett – writers who compound in their various

ways with the formalist premise about literary art and make their
constructions inside its boundaries. (Only *Lolita*, the most Gogolian
of Nabokov's works, breaks triumphantly out of those boundaries.)

Of course, what used to be called realism can be dissected and
explained in formalist terms with no difficulty and no problem.
Realism knows what it is setting out to do, which Gogol's art does
not; but nor does his art seem conscious, as the art of Borges or
Nabokov is, with its own dedication to performance. The modern
novelist's route to creation is seldom hard to make out, but Gogol
confers his vitality on the real without studying it, or knowing what
he means by it. For one thing it is strictly true, as academician
Vengerov pointed out in 1913, that 'Gogol Absolutely Did Not
Know Real Russian Life', that those wonderful and vivid descrip-
tions of provincial towns, inns, and people, are based on the
scantiest and most fleeting acquaintance. But realism, in its turn, has
no trouble in answering that one: let us refer the academician to
Henry James's observation that a good novelist could catch a
glimpse, of, say, a French Protestant family at dinner as a door
closed, and produce on that basis a novel about such people which
carried total imaginative authority and conviction. No, the problem
is a still simpler one; it is of trusting our ordinary immediate
responses to Gogol instead of approaching him under the aegis of
formalist interpretation. For here the contrast is all too genuine.
Bocharov, for instance, sees the structure of 'The Overcoat' as
determined by the fact that its hero, Akaky 'has no relation to life in
the first person'. Unable to tell or even conceive of his own story he
has no personal existence within the word-play of its narration.

So it may appear to a structuralist, but as in any other masterpiece
of realism the common reader is impelled by identification and
sympathy to invest Akaky with absolute existence, existence the
consciousness of which has been not only focused but created for the
reader by the art of the story. We follow the story of the overcoat
with bated breath, and the coat itself, with its wadding and its calico
lining, but of such good quality calico that it might almost have been
silk, etc., etc., has the absolute reality that only objects in very great
art possess. We can feel it and stroke it, wear and be warmed by it,
and in so doing we experience the sensations and being, the hopes
and fears, of Akaky himself.

I shall never forget the sickening sensation of dread as it became
apparent, while I read, that Akaky was not going to be allowed to
keep his overcoat. If we were in Dickens there would be some way in

which he might have done, but not here: and I would maintain that the pathos of the story, its power to move and to actually make one wretched, without being in the slightest degree sentimental, is in the way Akaky is first brought close to us – as close as can be – and then taken a great distance away. This is not a sensation that formalism would wish to express or to analyse, but it certainly occurs in life, of whose dreariness it is, indeed, a marked aspect. We have it here with all the intensification that art can provide, and there is a natural irony in the fact that in being compelled to take Akaky's overcoat away from him the story is not only doing its own thing, as the formalists would have it, but is also being all too faithful to a common human experience.

Because, to be pacific, we are talking of assets only, as Chekhov used to say, when we have different opinions about how to take works of art, and in particular works so masterly and yet so equivocal as Gogol's. In a Shakespearean medium there is always apt to be what Fanger calls 'a hermeneutic challenge'. Such art has a scale and perspective of meaning quite different from that of the great novelist like Tolstoy and Dostoevsky, more fundamentally idiosyncratic and peculiar, mysterious even. Yet we should not exaggerate this; what is true of 'The Overcoat' or *Dead Souls* is also true of *Evgeny Onegin*, the clearest, most open and Mozartian of verbal inventions: and the death of Lensky, the love of Tatyana, are as moving as the story of Akaky and in the same simple way. Pushkin and Gogol share, we might say – and we have the same impression where Shakespeare is concerned – a totally *artistic* attitude to a human story of wide appeal: they are not involved emotionally in that story, as Dickens or Dostoevsky would be, as even Flaubert so signally was. But the artist's lack of involvement does not mean that the reader must be uninvolved, and must ask not what effect it has on him but only how it is done.

Our first response to 'The Overcoat', and I do not believe mine is unusual, in fact involves us most deeply in the true originality of Gogol. Annensky described it as his 'ecstatic live for existence – not for life, but precisely for existence'. The ecstasy is for what the great Germans had loftily labelled as *Das Gemeine* – the mere meanness of things. Gogol's ecstatic vision of them – in *Dead Souls* he describes his blissful communion, when young, with all the tedium of a provincial street scene – brings Romanticism right down to earth. And whatever the formalists suppose, such elemental Romanticism must also be at the heart of 'The Overcoat'. To Akaky 'there appeared a bright visitor in the form of an overcoat', so that he too could have said with Holderlin: 'Einmal/Lebt ich wie Götter, und mehr bedarfs nicht.'

Gogol and the critic Belinsky are the two great German Romantics of Russia. The heroic and disastrous Belinsky, though himself rejecting and despising art with a 'social purpose', none the less had an influence that eventually helped to lead Russian literature into the Soviet gas chamber. And in a memorable letter he denounced Gogol's failure to embody in his art the spirit of consciousness and progress. Gogol's influence, transforming for us into ecstasy the totally commonplace, is by contrast a seraphic one. But it did not save him, either from Belinsky or from himself. The Romantic travesty, which is not really a travesty, reminds us that Gogol himself had his own peculiar version of the fate common to so many of the Romantics: to die after the vision had departed. The tragedy of their lives – the gaining and losing of the overcoat as it were – is an inherent aspect of their art, and without it art would indeed be what the formalists say it is.

So simple but essential a secret could not be communicated. That is why Dostoevsky did not, in any true sense, come out from under Gogol's overcoat. His version of an Akaky type of existence, in *Poor Folk* and in the Marmeladov scenes of *Crime and Punishment*, is pointed and intellectualized in a way that for all its detail makes it seem a flat diagram beside the unmeaningful perspective of Gogol. Still more revealing is the transformation of the marvellous Manilov, one of the land-owners of *Dead Souls*, into Svidrigailov in *Crime and Punishment*, the handsome open-faced creepy character who is 'nothing in particular'. You cannot turn the *ne to* into an idea, as Dostoevsky seems to have intended. Both characters are memorable, and comic, but there is a certain staginess about Svidrigailov that confines the drama of his being to rumour and report; whereas Manilov resides whole and entire in the essential vacancy of *poshlost*, he and his wife embraced 'for about the time it would take to smoke a small cigar'.

The greatness of Akhmatova: *Requiem* and *Poem Without a Hero* translated by D. M. Thomas

No woman in English poetry has written like Blake, or like Eliot. Nor, for that matter, could either Blake or Eliot have written with the conscience and the fury of a sibyl, the status of a society beauty, the experiences of a divorced wife, terrorized widow and persecuted mother. No other woman poet has had the opportunities given to Anna Akhmatova, and it may be that such opportunities – the kind not vouchsafed to Emily Brontë, or to Sylvia Plath – are what a great female artist requires and can make best use of. Akhmatova was a very unselfconscious poet in many ways, she had qualities of elemental force, utterance haunted and Delphic; yet these went together with elegance and sophistication, even a certain kind of mirror-gazing and a cunning which is *chétif*, or, as the Russians say, *zloi*. She is not in the least like Blake or Eliot, and yet those are the English poets – different as they are – who offer some sort of parallel with her finest work. The incongruity in coupling such names shows how exceptional is her own poetic being.

Her individuality was not likely to recommend her to the men at the top – nor did it. At the time of her expulsion from the Writers' Union, Zhdanov called her 'a nun and a whore'. Sound archetypes for a great poet, observes D. M. Thomas, in the introduction to his translation of her two greatest poems, *Requiem* and *Poem Without a Hero* (his is the first complete version of the latter in English).

But though it is nice to think the party hack uttered praise without knowing it, such a description is in fact wholly incongruous with the kinds of contrast in Akhmatova's personality. Strangely enough she has as a poet more in common with what are – in a degraded form – Soviet ideals; restraint, correctness, propriety. Her poetry is dignified in the grandest sense without pretending to dignity, an equivalent in art of what she called the severe and shapely spirit of Russian orthodoxy.

Blok, or Yeats, would have been delighted to see themselves as archetypes of nun or harlot, libertine or sage – it would be a part of the methodical build-up of their poetic selves. She was herself in a more absolute sense. Though full of admiration, her attitude to Blok was as to some sort of unstable demon or actor in a seductive but dangerously wicked farce. The majesty of her own being seems to declare: 'One doesn't behave like that'; and she says the same thing in the same tone to state tyranny, to the horrors of the *Yezhovschina*, to all the destructive convictions of inhuman conceit. She knows – none better – that offence comes, but woe unto them by whom it cometh, whether it be the perverse and deliberate invocation of madness and violence, or the policy of cruelty and persecution in the name of some abstract good. A curious feature of *Poem Without a Hero*, which irritated some of her friends and well-wishers as it did the priests of the new regime, is the resurrection and expiation of old St Petersburg sins as if they were one with the new torments of Leningrad.

The central part of the poem's 'triptych' bears the epigraph 'My Future is in my Past', a version of the device of Mary Queen of Scots: 'In my Beginning is my End.' Thomas's notes point out that she refers to Eliot as the source for this, and only discovered that it was Mary's motto just before her death. Probably she knew of the *Four Quartets*, and their provenance in besieged London. Certainly the passage in 'Little Gidding' that begins 'In the uncertain hour before the morning' gives a more direct impression of the tone and movement of her poem than any translation can do.

One does not believe like that; one does not do such things. If one is tempted, if one is compromised or guilty, one is haunted by the dead and devoured by conscience. To meet throughout life, as in a mirror, one's image or double – an idea which constantly recurs in her poetry – is not for her a way in which the artist escapes himself or by which he profits: such an identification may be with a great fellow-spirit in suffering, as was Akhmatova's with Mandelstam, but it was more often like a warning, an admonition of sin and shortcoming. The role of conscience in her poetry reminds us how unfamiliar such a possession is to most poets, whose natural tendency in the Nietzschean and modern era is to say that 'such as I cast out remorse'. She was deeply religious, and religion – as Dr Johnson noted – does not come over in poetry, but conscience, its precursor and attendant, can and does.

It figures largely, and strangely, in *Poem Without a Hero*, whose title itself suggests the collapse of a Nietzschean world in which men of action, or the hero as poet and seer, could play a part. Its denizens, including Blok, including the poet herself, are in one sense poor creatures, not the heroic figures into whom an intense vision of the past transmutes so many. For this is a poem about remorse, and about a past 'in which the future is rotting'.

Thus although it is arbitrary to attach a single life and its interior shaping, as Akhmatova does, to the ordeal of Russia in the revolution, to the years of terror and invasion, the theme of remorse – for one and for all – unites these things as they could not have been united in any artificial poem in which such events were directly lamented or celebrated. She refused to be 'melted to a state hymn'; hers is not a 'public' poem as is, for example, Margarita Aliger's moving *Spring in Leningrad*.

Poem Without a Hero was more than twenty years in the writing, and appeared to the poet, during that time, as a recurrent and inescapable malady. On its smaller scale *The Waste Land* had the same characteristic of a visitation, painful to suffer, more painful to evade. And another phenomenon is significantly true of both poems: they derive their status from the reality of the *fait accompli*. Though critics may seek to demonstrate after the event their underlying 'unity' and so forth, such poems only now seem so inevitable and so public because they made a total success of being so private and so arbitrary.

As might be expected of Akhmatova, however, *Poem Without a Hero* is extremely literal, as concerned with place and event as a Hardy poem, and closely connected to the poet's life in pre-war St Petersburg. A child of the professional middle classes – her father was a naval architect – she grew up in the capital at a time when its artistic life was at its most febrile and brilliant, the height of the 'Silver Age', not only in poetry but in painting, ballet, music; and her poem makes full choreographic use of these forms. She married the poet Gumilev, and together with Mandelstam they began the Acmeist movement, which best defines itself negatively as a reaction against Blok and the Symbolist poets, a kind of classicism which their admiration for Dante links with the nascent notions of Hulme and Eliot. Her poetry at this time has an unstylized purity, sometimes simplistic, absorbed in what might be called the moral nature of things, and assuming its own kind of confidence from them.

But Akhmatova was also assiduously of the fashionable artistic coterie. Like other poets she recited her poems at the Stray Dog, a cabaret decorated by the leading stage designer Sudeikin, whose wife Olga Glebova-Sudeikina performed there in productions such as Belayev's *Blundering Psyche*, and danced in the Fauns ballet half naked and wearing horns, a 'goat-legged nymph' as Akhmatova calls her. Blok was a revered member of the group, as was Mikhail Kuzmin, a poet and homosexual whom Akhmatova deeply distrusted, and who makes appearances, though briefly, as the evil genius in her poem.

He was probably in love with Vsevolod Knyazev, a young dragoon officer and apprentice poet, the Petruchka of the poem and its 'senseless sacrifice', who was himself romantically devoted to the fascinating Sudeikina. When he discovered that Blok – handsome, famous, and a great womanizer – was his successful rival for her affections, he shot himself on the landing of her flat, after seeing her return home in the small hours with Blok, as related at the end of the poem's first section. By that time estranged from her husband, Akhmatova was sharing the flat with Sudeikina, and she herself went round to the young officer's quarters to look for compromising evidence, as the poem suggests: she leaves the place 'on tip-toe'. She refers to herself as Sudeikina's 'ancient conscience', and is obsessed with her as a double or mirror-image of herself, an empty-headed, amiable but amoral beauty. A photograph in the French *édition bilingue* of the poem shows the two statuesquely handsome women together, with clasped hands.

After the war and the terror and starvation of the revolutionary years Sudeikina fled to Paris; Akhmatova stayed in what had become Leningrad. The poems of this period are grim, spare and laconic, but it was not till the mid-1930s, when the Yezhov terror began and Mandelstam was arrested, that the full horror of what was in store became apparent. Her son Lev Gumilev was arrested, solely because of his father's name; sent from Siberia to fight in the war, he was then rearrested and not finally released till after Stalin's death. At the time of his first arrest Akhmatova joined every day for months the queue waiting outside the prison for news of relatives, and from this experience came the poem *Requiem*, written between 1935 and 1940, or rather committed during that time to memory and to the memories of friends – it was not published until 1963, and then outside Russia and without the author's consent.

The theme of *Poem Without a Hero* came to her, she tells us, on a night in December 1940. Much was written before the German invasion and the siege. She was later evacuated with other artists, including Shostakovich, to Tashkent, where the poem was completed. There is a certain irony in this Soviet solicitude for intellectuals, which probably saved her life: but it is consistent with persecution. They were an asset of the state, and the state, since Pushkin's time, had set a high value on the power of poetry. Her popular status grew in the war years and became an embarrassment to the authorities, who withdrew permission for her collected poems to be published and subjected her to increasing degrees of persecution, including constant escort by the secret police. After Stalin's death came a degree of rehabilitation, a visit to the West, a great and growing reverence on the part of all intellectuals and lovers of Russian verse, for whom she was its voice and conscience.

The action of *Poem Without a Hero* opens on New Year's Eve 1940, the moment when its conception took place. The scene is a house on the Fontanka canal, a white room full of mirrors, in which 'instead of the expected guest, the author is visited by shadows from the year 1913, disguised as mummers':

> From childhood I have feared mummers.
>   It always seemed to me that someone,
>   A kind of extra shade
> 'Without face or name', has slipped in
>   Among them . . .

The phantoms play roles from the old St Petersburg world, notably Don Juan, from Mozart and Byron, Pushkin's Stone Guest, one of Blok's most famous poems 'The Steps of the Commander', and from Molière's version, which was staged in 1910 by 'Dapertutto' – Vsevolod Meyerhold. The multiple references are typical of the poem's method but – as in *The Waste Land* again – the clarity and trenchancy of the verse makes its immediate impact without any need of notation.

These roles were associated with Sudeikina, and Blok is there 'in the motley stripes of a milepost', an image that recalls through Pushkin's poem about devils in a snowstorm the blizzard of *The Twelve*, the literal correlative being the verst-marks of a Russian high road, striped black and white. Then a parenthetic passage refers to the actual 'expected guest':

> Guest. from the future, will he really come
> Taking the left turn across the bridge?

That was the way to Akhmatova's apartment near the Fontanka; and though he is not named, the 'guest from the future' is Isaiah

Berlin, who visited there shortly after the war and talked all night, giving her encouragement at a time when the state, which during the war had maintained her as if she had been some potentially valuable asset or machine, had apparently decided to phase her out and consign her to silence.

An intermezzo gives snatches of talk and laughter from the past – in the next scene a voice is reading in Sudeikina's bedroom. Knyazev haunts the movement, his cry 'I am ready for death' coinciding with Mandelstam's words to Akhmatova at the time of his arrest:

> Is this the guest from behind the mirror,
> The shape that flitted past the pane?
> Is the new moon playing a joke, or
> – Between the cupboard and the stove – is
> Somebody standing again?

His shape now that of the selfhanged Kirillov standing 'in a terribly strange manner' in *The Possessed*. But for all its macabre images (the capital is called Dostoyevskian) the poem here is full of a vital gaiety and conveys the same animated celebration that Pushkin did in his 'sad tale', *The Bronze Horseman* a line from whose prologue – 'I love you, Peter's creation' – is the heading of Akhmatova's epilogue.

Part 2 is headed *Reshka*, i.e., 'tails', the obverse of the coin, with a further significance of defeat and, in its variant, of prison bars. An editor complains about the poem and its obscurities; the author disowns interpretation and the idea of state or public recognition. Her intimacies will remain her own, and her poem's, and the muse informs her that the poem has no traditional romantic ancestry, no kinship with the heroes of the nineteenth-century pantheon. The third and last part begins with a brief prose evocation of Leningrad under siege, breaking off into poetry, spoken by the author's voice, 7,000 kilometres away. At no point does the poem become 'public', even when the poet remembers her friends.

> who stayed to perish
> In an iceblink of waters, a glitter of spires

and not even when in flight she sees below the road to Siberia, along which her son and so many others have been driven. The end is a vision of Russia herself, 'knowing the hour of vengeance', walking eastward before the poet, with clenched hands and dry eyes. 'Vengeance' refers to the German invaders, but the image of suffering Russia has a wider significance. This is confirmed, it seems to me, by the more singly and conventionally 'wartime' conclusion written and then taken out (the poem was never 'finished', but intention seems clear here) in which 'young Russia' is seen emerging from Ural and Altai, and advancing, like a mirror reflection, to the faithful defence of Moscow.

Such an account cannot by itself carry conviction of the poem's authority and grandeur; like most such masterpieces it is about as non-international as could be, and it is saturated, besides, in the communal references of generations of Russian art. *Requiem* is much more simple, generically moving; a number of reasonably adequate versions have already appeared, and D. M. Thomas's, to my mind the best so far, has much less to persuade us of than in the case of *Poem Without a Hero*. Persuasion is the point. Auden, characteristically honest, said that he could not feel Mandelstam was a great poet, 'because the translations I have seen don't convince me of it'. Thomas's version of *Poem Without a Hero* is not of course itself a great poem: but it makes us feel the original is one, and that is a remarkable achievement. For the translation is itself a good poem; in writing poetry as a translation, rather than translating poetry, Thomas shows that it need not be, as Nabokov said, 'a parrot's screech, a monkey's chatter'.

Yet his is far from a Lowell-type 'imitation'. He quite occludes his own personality and style; he has profound reverence and affection for the original; and like the politician (except that the translator deals in the art of the impossible) he knows he is compelled to endless compromises in which the absolute of poetry will dissolve. Lowell, greatly egocentric and as honest as Auden, made no bones about his intention to create a different kind of absolute – 'as if it were written now and in America'. Thomas's 'Akhmatvan' poetry, cannot be Akhmatova, but it does not seek to create an English equivalent. Although by intention not always accurate – sometimes it departs quite far from her actual words – it never takes over or transforms her sense and tone, as Lowell does in his translation of *Requiem*. That poem opens with a statement of biblical simplicity, a literal claim; Akhmatova was proud of her refusal to emigrate and her power to bear witness in the time of terror:

> No, not under the vault of a foreign
>   sky, not under the shelter of foreign wings
> I was with my people then, there
>   where my people, unhappily were.

Lowell's version:

> I wasn't under a new sky,
> its birds were old familiar birds.
> They still spoke Russian. Misery
> spoke familiar Russian words.

This takes us right out of Russia, as far as William Carlos Williams's comment about 'plain American which even cats and dogs can understand'. Playing it cool in this way produces an idiom that calls for quite different expectations in the reader. Thomas, like his original, is gravely poetic:

> No, not under a foreign heavenly-cope, and
> Not canopied by foreign wings –
> I was with my people in those hours,
> There where, unhappily, my people
>   were.

That at least gets in the sculptured commas, though it cannot manage the deliberate emphasis of the inflected forms (*byla, byl, narodom, narod*). Thomas remarks that he is not happy with his 'heavenly-cope', 'which is literally and metrically close to the Russian but sounds stranger in English'. English verse since the eighteenth century can rarely sound both simple and wholly 'poetical'. A compact tradition and the flexibility of the language perpetuates this possibility in Russian, as it does the classical metres for which Brodsky complains that few translators with pretensions of their own even try to find a near equivalent. 'Sky's vault' – *nebosvodom* – is pure Pushkinian poetic diction, and native, through him, in Akhmatova: a paradox of dependence and independence for which again there is no English parallel. (In *Poet Without a Hero* she even follows Pushkin in indicating the omission of a stanza, or part of one, in order to formalize ironically the effect of cuts by the censor.)

Robin Kemball's version tries bravely to 'render the sense, the spirit and the music . . . while strictly retaining the *form*':

> No, not far beneath some foreign sky then,
> Not with foreign wings to shelter me, –
> I was with my people then, close by them,
> Where my luckless people chanced to be.

Metrically this is excellent, but 'close by them' weakens the sense just where it should be strong, suggesting that the poet was around but not of them, as the next line incongruously implies that Russians just happened to be in Russia. This unfair but of course the whole thing is unfair, for great poetry only comes into being by making the fullest use of the properties of one particular language. As Thomas points out, the 'same' metre tends to emerge not the same, partly because the old circumlocutions make it sound odd, and also because even iambs and spondees sound different in a different linguistic context. This is crucial in *Poem Without a Hero*, which has a remarkable metrical form; it should be monotonous and over-emphatic, and in a faithful English reproduction would certainly be so. With great delicacy Thomas has echoed its liturgical power and subdued it, though still recognizable, to a calm but forceful English rhythm, that has the flexibility of the original and something of its haunted utterance.

Quantity is as unreliable in analysing Russian metre as it is for English – accent and syntax diversifies and overrides it – but in her masterpiece the Akhmatovan line consists roughly of two anapaests and an amphibrach, or two with an iamb, a combination probably never used before in the modern era and certainly not on this methodicial scale. Reproduced, a section from the 'lyrical digression' which evokes the phantom of the real twentieth century approaching pre-war St Petersburg comes out something like this:

> Since up every street there was drumming,
>> Since past every porch it was coming
>>> The shape feeling its way in gloom,
>> Gusts tore the placards off the palings,
>>> Smoke spun its dance over the railings
>>> And the lilac flowers smelled of the tomb,

Increasing tension, as in the account of the suicide, adds a third rhyming line to the pattern:

> And measureless in his distressing
>> Whose time to live quickly is lessing,
>>> Who only for death asks God's blessing
>>> And who will be ever forgot;
> He strays by her window benighted
>> As the street-lamp indifferently lighted
>>> His form with its lividest tone.
> He attends. And most slender of maskers
>> To have trodden the boards
>>> 'from Damascus'
>> She comes back at last . . . not alone!

That is reasonably accurate, as a reproduction of sense and metre, but it can only remind an English reader of Edgar Allan Poe, or even 'The Dong with the Luminous Nose'. It shows how right Thomas is that 'the "same" metre tends to emerge *not* the same: translated in the *Midsummer Night's Dream* sense'. Russian can sustain this astonishing movement, for 800 lines or so, with hypnotic variation and unremitting intensity. And though the poem's strong and straightforward theme – retribution and expiation – resounds in the rhythm like the hoofbeats of Peter's steed in *The Bronze Horseman*, one never feels that the movement is taking over and determining the sense, as one does with Swinburne, or in *Locksley Hall*, or even in such an apparently cerebral poem as 'Le Cimetière Marin'. Eliot, in his brilliant use of a comparably hypnotic metre in 'Little Gidding', is careful not to go on too long.

In English, moreover, as can be seen from several lines of my version, such a metre can often be 'scanned', crudely, in two ways, which here does nothing to enhance its authority (a subtle rather than crude example is the last line of *Paradise Regained* – 'Home to his mother's house private returned' – where the iambic deliberation has the ghost of an anapaestic outrider mounted on it).

Thomas's parallel metre, however necessarily muted, is both durable and eloquent. Compare his version of the tricky three rhyming lines and a fourth, in the suicide episode:

> His agitation cannot be sounded
> Whose whole life is running
> aground and
> Whose only prayer's for a
> boundless
> Forgetting and forgotten
> sleep.

That gets the despair of the original, and its half-rhymes reproduce the fluid and less positive rhyming of Russian. Of course his sedulous skill cannot convey Akhmatova's simple atavism, plunging excitement and drooping pathos – in fact the very qualities, bizarrely enough, that Lear *did* get into 'The Dong with the Luminous Nose'. And the 'difficulties' of the poem seem more formidable in English, more saturated and obscure, because the reader is not carried on by the brio of the narrative. Sudeikina, for instance, had been taking part in a show at the Stray Dog called *The Road from Damascus*, which is the point of the reference to her return – a return *into* sin, the opposite of Paul's – but the beat of the Russian makes this evident subliminally, without the need for pausing and pondering. Not that the poem is anything but arcane. Akhmatova calls it a Chinese box 'with a triple base', and its numerological patterning is as complex as its references to real people, events, works of art. But it is essentially a voice poem, in that tradition which Pushkin stylized in the figure of the 'Improvisatore' in *Egyptian Nights*, who denies any idea of how complex verse comes to him suddenly, rhymed and in regular feet, so that it can be instantly declaimed. Like so many Russian masterpieces the poem has the form of an open secret, at once spontaneous and enigmatic. 'I frequently hear of certain absurd interpretations of *Poem Without a Hero*', writes Akhmatova in her foreword. 'And I have been advised to make it clearer. This I decline to do. It contains no third, seventh, or twenty-ninth thoughts. I shall neither explain nor change anything. What is written is written.'

And she ends with a dedication to 'its first audience', the fellow-citizens who died in Leningrad during the siege, which reveals the deep source of her simplicity and her greatness, both in this poem and in *Requiem*. 'Their voices I hear, and I remember them, when I read my poem aloud, and for me this secret chorus has become a permanent justification of the work.'

Two pieces on translating Mandelstam

Of the Indo-Germanic languages, English is probably the most recalcitrant in matters of rhyme and rhythm, Russian the most obliging. This does not mean that it is any easier to write poetry in Russian than in English, but it does mean there can be very little poetic communication between the two, and even this little constantly diminishes. English poetry is compelled by the stubbornness of the language continually to renounce the too obviously poetic: but in seeking to be more precise, more dense and more allusive, Russian poetry has never had to give up the straightforward traditional intoxications of sound and rhyme. To put it another way, the lack of inflection in English and the inflexibility of word-order makes its 'poetic' area at any given moment very narrow and hence potentially claustrophobic, requiring constant modification. In Russian, the area of the poetic goes on being exceedingly inclusive and wide.

Russian poetry is still written to be heard and declaimed. Osip Mandelstam's recitations were famous and he composed in the mouth, carrying poems there for weeks or months together. 'I alone in Russia work from the voice', he wrote in his last days, 'while all round the bitch-pack writes.' A preoccupation with paper was, for him, Soviet-style – the Soviet writer being, 'not a creator of verbal pyramids out of the depths of his own spirit, but one of Pharaoh's modest slave-drivers overseeing the slow but sure construction of actual pyramids'. This growth of meaning in the mouth, as it were, adds to the insuperable translation problem. Mandelstam's matter is 'modern' – allusive, richly and obscurely idiosyncratic, full of compression and dislocation – but the *shum*, the sound and rhythm of his lines, has no motive within the scope of his genius to be other than sonorously and soothingly traditional. The effect is a little as if it had been quite possible for Eliot to have composed *The Waste Land* in the metrical cadence of Gray's 'Elegy', or Pound to have done Cantos in the stanza-form of the 'Ode to a Nightingale' or *Locksley Hall*.

That being so, the reader without some Russian cannot form much of an estimate of Mandelstam, though since he became a hot property that has not stopped the poetic PR men from trying: his widow's memoir *Hope against Hope* has not done any service to the poetry by enabling them to substitute for its reality the usual PR big words like 'compassion'. (*'Hope against Hope*, a book almost as fine in its sardonic compassionate way as Osip's own poetry' – A. Alvarez. Not knowing, as he says, any of the language, how can he know? What are his grounds of judgement? The take-over of the Christian name suggests some special and intimate hot line to the poet's *manes.*)

Fortunately Professor Clarence Brown and the poet W. S. Merwin do not see matters in this light. Clarence Brown's critical biography of Mandelstam is a model of its kind – scholarly, scrupulous, witty at times, unpretendingly informal and sensible. His discussion of some of the most difficult and rewarding poems in *Tristia*, the collection produced by Mandelstam during the Revolution and its aftermath is outstandingly lucid and helpful, pursuing, as it does, the threads of friendship and literature, history and idea, that Mandelstam wove into his poems. Imagism was in the air: T. S. Eliot was doing much the same at the time in *The Waste Land*, but Mandelstam's configuration of intimacy with other poets from Pushkin to Akhmatova (a famous line of whose he echoes verbatim in the poem 'Tristia') is much denser, and also more homely and direct. In spite of the grave splendour and elaboration of his poems, which often move into shape like great buildings, arches and domes – with the hidden symmetry of Hagia Sophia, or as obviously as the Kazan Cathedral in Petersburg, both poetic subjects of his – one often apprehends something more like Thomas Hardy in them than Yeats or Eliot: not remarkable, perhaps, since Hardy was an architect who also, as Donald Davie has pointed out, brought to verse-making something of the precision and passion of the Victorian engineer. Hardy-like, too, is the extreme informality of approach that Mandelstam often has in his later poems, written during the increasing darkness, deprivation and persecution of the thirties: both poets retain the chant of a liturgy while saying things that are piercingly commonplace, as in the poem of Mandelstam which begins,

We shall sit for a while together in the kitchen,
The white paraffin smells sweet,

and relates the small jobs they must first do,

So that we can leave for the station
Where no one would ever find us.

But the limp little light lines in English are each in Russian a heavy
sound-carved couplet, carrying the tone of a farewell religious rite
that is muttered and impersonal, its newness as if familiar with
constant repetition.

Clarence Brown is enlightening about the Acmeist movement, in
which Mandelstam and his contemporaries Gumilev and Akhmatova came together in Petersburg before the First World War: at
the same time, he is surely right in not taking it very seriously. T. E.
Hulme and the Imagists and Pound were saying some of the same
things, but Mandelstam's poetic practice is not a bit like theirs, and
he regarded Acmeism as an atmosphere to be rendered rather than a
programme to define and follow out. Gumilev said it was harder to
be an Acmeist than a Symbolist, as it was more difficult to build a
cathedral than a tower: this suggests Mandelstam's verbal architecture as it does Yeats's symbolism, but in fact it was a private joke –
Symbolist HQ in Petersburg, the apartment of Vyacheslav Ivanov,
was nicknamed 'the tower' – and really means no more than that
poets and novelists are always having to decide to be more
condensed and 'real' than their predecessors, and to 'make it new'.

The term itself was invented satirically by Andrei Bely to descibe
those who considered themselves the apex, the chosen few – prime
souls – and Gumilev (who was to die before a Bolshevik firing-squad
in 1922) accepted the imputation with humorous defiance. His wife
Akhmatova was then certainly sometimes too much of a 'soul' in her
poetry, about which Mandelstam himself wrote sharp criticisms in
the early Soviet epoch: and in the statement of Gorodetsky we can
see how that adroit hack poet was to be able to convert the arcane
disciplines of Acmeism into a celebration of the new regime. 'It is
first of all a battle for *this* world, its sounds, its colour, its forms . . .
for our planet Earth. For the Acmeist the rose has again become
beautiful for itself alone, and not for its supposed likeness to
mystical love or anything else.'

Mandelstam says something which is apparently similar but
really very different: 'To be – that is the artist's greatest pride. He

desires no other paradise than existence, and when he hears talk of reality he only smiles bitterly.' Socialist reality was not going to appreciate that, nor Mandelstam's insistence on what Cranmer's rubric so well calls the 'true and lively word', the logos which 'does not signify a thing: it freely accepts as its dwelling-place, so to speak, this or that objective significance. The word wanders in the vicinity of its thing like a soul round its discarded and not forgotten body.'

David McDuff's volume of translations, English and Russian interleaved, is accurate and impersonal, satisfying Mandelstam's canons of restraint, a fine job throughout and containing an admirable version of the marvellous poem '1 January 1924'. He provides an effective introduction to the poems, and along with Clarence Brown's study his book would make a good beginning for the serious student with a little Russian.

In his foreword to W. S. Merwin's versions (the book has a charming cover reproduction of the Fabritius goldfinch – Mandelstam's *shchegol* – which occurs in several poems) Clarence Brown makes the just point that Mandelstam himself, translating Petrarch, turned him into Mandelstam. 'Lowell does not translate into English but into Lowell; Nabokov can be said to translate into literal English only by those who will accept his definition of literal English: in reality it is Nabokov. Merwin has translated Mandelstam into Merwin.' But I doubt if this is quite fair to Merwin. If he sometimes inevitably makes Mandelstam read like modern American poetry, there are some versions – notably 'The Twilight of Freedom' (a powerfully equivocal poem about the age, the *vek*, that opened in 1918), 'Tristia' itself, and, above all, 'We shall meet again in Petersburg', where the whole poem seems to swim over into its new setting.

The reason for the final arrest and sentence of Mandelstam, though not for the malign if desultory persecution to which he was always subjected, was his poem on Stalin which begins:

> Our lives no longer feel ground under them;
> At ten paces you can't hear our words.

It is entirely characteristic that one or two later poems which were written to rehabilitate himself and which adopt spasmodically a tone of humility, almost of recantation are actually better, more subtle and more rich as poems, than this fiercely scornful commentary on 'the Kremlin mountaineer'. The fact of himself, a Jew with his roots in the Russian language and in the Western classical tradition, is criticism enough of the regime that could not accept him. Blok remarked on the gloomy roll-call of history's tyrants and executioners, and opposed to it 'a bright name' – Pushkin's. Like Ovid and Pushkin, Mandelstam reveals the nature of tyranny simply by being himself and by writing the kind of poems that he did. In one of his poems Pushkin has a fine description of Ovid in exile, half-crazed but offending no one, captivating the tribe with his 'gift of poetry and voice like the sound of water'. That could also be Osip Mandelstam before his final disappearance where no comparisons or words follow.

He had no poetic forerunners. In all of world poetry I know of no other such case. We know the sources of Pushkin and Blok, but who will tell us where that new divine harmony, Mandelstam's poetry, came from.

What Anna Akhmatova said of her fellow-poet might apparently also be said of Mallarmé, and of the Imagists, of that sudden surprise turn in poetry around 1910 that in Pound's words 'made it new'. But, as in the ideology of politics or of painting at the time, that was a deliberately revolutionary programme, its dislocation extending into line and syntax. 'Acmeism', with which these two greatest Russian poets of the century are associated, is not a bit like that. Indeed Mandelstam's widow declared that 'unlike *innovators*, such as Mayakovsky and Pasternak, he composed verses in *tradition*, which is far more difficult to imitate'.

His 'divine harmony' is certainly like nothing else, for though it can only be heard in Russian its shape and weight seem to embody a whole European sense of forms, particularly architectural forms, the space of domes and temples, the stretched curve of sails and ships.

Just before his arrest and death in a camp in the far east Mandelstam, perhaps a little tongue-in-cheek, defined Acmeism as 'a homesickness for world culture'. Homer and Dante constantly manifest themselves in his poetry, not only as images of legend and learning but in the cadence and weight of their words. With what is probably a conscious irony he associated this weight of tradition, whose tensions he wanted his poetry so exactly and evenly to carry, with what is in a sense the equally historical Mongolian and Petrine weight of the Soviet regime:

> I too one day will create
> Beauty from cruel weight.

His sense of Europe makes his poetry not less but more difficult to bring back to it, so to speak; and James Greene has done a fine job. He feels that in order to live a translation of Mandelstam must also be a new poem, exploiting the genius of English as fully and as subtly as the poet has used that of the Russian language. In this metamorphosis resides the whole problem, but Greene has solved it as effectively as D. M. Thomas succeeded in his version of Akhmatova's *Poem Without a Hero*. Donald Davie, whose bold paraphrase of Mandelstam's 'Octets' appeared in *Agenda*, observed that 'current British idioms preserve the arc of the poem's form only by filling in, by not having the content of the poem pressing up against the curve of its form with equal pressure at every point'. Greene's versions have an impassive fullness and roundness which is rare: when accurate – perhaps especially when accurate – verse translation can often make words seem meagre in their too great anxiety to be right.

It is instructive to compare how he does the first stanza of a famous early poem, written in 1909, with the way Clarence Brown translated it in the admirable critical biography to which all Mandelstam's admirers are indebted. Its fourth line contains an unusual use of an impersonal verb – the birch twigs *nezametno vechereli* – 'unnoticeably eveninged':

> On the pale blue enamel
> conceivable in April
> the birches raised their branches
> and vespered imperceptibly

Clarence Brown's is an elegant and accurate solution of the difficulty, but unfortunately its very elegance conceals the pellucid simplicity of the original, Greene has:

> April-blue enamel:
> Inconspicuous
> And pale,
> A birch-tree hammocks in the evening sky.

This produces a different but equally unusual verb usage, making a new picture to twin the Russian one.

His versions of 'Hagia Sophia', 'Sleeplessness' and 'Tristia' are remarkable poems in their own right, as are his lines for Psyche descending into the underworld:

> She breathes on the mirror
> and is slow to hand over

> The lozenge of copper to the
> master of the ferry.

He is alive to the poet's omen-haunted humour, which helped to destroy him when he wrote poems about Stalin. An early poem, the one best known in Russia, inimitably describes his sense of his own body – *Takim edinim i takim moim*. Greene's 'So much at one with me, so much my own' recreates the rhythm perfectly, though it must be admitted that Brown's 'so one and so my own' is closer to the nub of the sense. A critic once objected to the tone of this poem, and Mandelstam wrote a little quatrain in reply:

> Don't be glum,
> Sit on the tram;
> So desolate,
> So wholly No. 8.

Much later he imagined in a poem the future of his name:

> What street is this?
> 'This is Mandelstam Street.'

The joke is complex, because 'Almond-Tree Avenue' – his name in German – might occur in all the world's suburbia, but he imagines some Russian or slum 'sewer' called after him. Not so; though he has been 'rehabilitated', not even the meanest street throughout the USSR is named in his honour.

A poet's tragedy: Marina Tsvetaeva

Marina Tsvetaeva is the most Russian of poets in the same sense in which Hardy could be called the most English of poets, or Whitman the most American. Paradoxically Russia's greatest poet, Pushkin, is not, in the obvious sense very Russian. Of course a Russian poetry-lover would rightly say that this is a meaningless observation, but it does none the less remain true that Shakespeare and Pushkin are not placed by their nationality. Other poets are, and Tsvetaeva is one. It alters the case not at all – in fact it confirms it – that her family origins were also part Polish, part German: the most intensively English persons often come from Ireland, and American expatriates have been known to be more French than the French.

The Russianness of Tsvetaeva's poetry and prose – singularly direct and forceful as they are – consists in an obvious authenticity of the emotions. Everything is felt instantly and strongly; everything is *strashny* and *vesely* – terrible and joyful – and yet about this directness there is nothing historic, sloppy, or self-indulgent. It can however be contemptuous. Isaiah Berlin has remarked on the 'emotional superiority' implicit in the Russian outlook:

a sense of the west as enviably self-restrained, clever, efficient, and successful, but also as being cramped, cold, mean, calculating, and fenced in, without capacity for large views or generous emotion, for feeling which must, at times, rise too high and overflow its banks . . . and consequently condemned never to know a rich flowering life.

The flowering of life is immensely strong, immensely spontaneous in Tsvetaeva's poetry, but that goes with an equally extraordinary precision and technical skill, an originality which was discerned by some of her poetic contemporaries but both in émigré circles and the Soviet establishment not fully recognized until the present decade.

But she has always been a poet's poet. Her first privately printed poetry, *Evening Album*, came out in 1910 when she was eighteen, and the young Pasternak was at once struck by the poems of her second collection, *Versty I*, written after Russia had been two years at war. He probably did not read them until the chaotic civil war years, when Tsvetaeva was producing her series of poems about the White Guard in Southern Russia, *Lebednii Stan*, *The Demesne of the Swans*, which now appears for the first time in an excellent bilingual edition with a scholarly apparatus and notes.

What impressed Pasternak, one supposes, was the absence of preciousness, of *littérature* in the sense in which it had obtained a stranglehold on symbolist and post-symbolist poetry. For Yeats, life existed to end up in a poem, and why not? But art must always try to crawl under the net of its own artifice. Probably it takes a poet, at the outset, to see how another poet has done it. Yeats made his style stark and brutal, saluting the arrival of the Savage God. Aleksandr Blok used meter and style in *The Twelve* to take the poem into the streets among brutal, illiterate revolutionaries. But no one is deceived. Their poems remain as upstage as ever, which is not to say they are not marvellous and magical. 'Gaiety transfiguring all that dread', writes Yeats, and a contemporary friend of Blok observed that terrors and splendours for him were what could be made terrible and splendid *in poetry*.

Tsvetaeva's poems are not like that. Even her very great and elder contemporary Akhmatova can write of 'joy and terror at the heart' without making the reader feel that these are anything but the emotions that the poet is working on. Brodsky compares her to Auden: a surprising judgement but one sees why. Both had very strong moral convictions – a rare thing among poets – which ultimately control their poetry, rather than the poetry creating by itself an image and likeness of the poet. Principle in both of them anticipates poetry. Tsvetaeva's passions, hatred of injustice, anarchy, and corruption, profound admiration for duty, honour, loyalty, and trust, are as it were the standard strong feelings, but they seem to belong to her as a person not as a poet, even when she is writing poetry. Nothing could be less modish than her feelings or her poems, which may explain why they have never quite fallen in with, or been discovered by, followers of poetic fashion, like the recent ones for confessions, suicides, the violence of nature, 'The Savage God'. Tsvetaeva's suicide cannot be seen as Sylvia Plath's could, as an aspect or requirement of her art.

It was simply the end of the road, a long and agonizing one. Like most Russian writers of the time Tsvetaeva had a sheltered and happy childhood. Her father was professor of art history at the University of Moscow, and her mother, who came from both German and aristocratic Polish stock, was a lover of art and a talented pianist, a former pupil of Rubinstein. She was educated at boarding schools in Switzerland and Germany as well as Moscow and later studied French poetry in Paris and attended lectures at the Sorbonne. Precocious, her verses had already attracted attention from Russian poets such as Gumilev (Akhamatova's husband), the symbolist Bryusov, and Max Voloshin, who ran a kind of permanent house party for young writers at his home in Koktebel on the Crimean coast. It was there at the age of eighteen that Tsvetaeva met Sergei Efron, who was a year younger than she and also hoping to become a writer. She made her decision in a typically firm and forthright manner. 'I resolve that no matter what I will never part with him, and I [will] marry him.'

Efron could be a character out of Conrad's *Under Western Eyes*: he would fascinate any great novelist. He was also the right choice for Tsvetaeva, at least in so far as she conformed to the description given by Nadezhda Mandelstam in *Hope Abandoned*.

She was absolutely natural and fantastically self-willed . . . cropped hair, loose-limbed gait – like a boy's – and speech remarkably like her verse. Her willfulness was not just a matter of temperament but a way of life. She could never have reined herself in, as Akhmatova did. Reading her verse and letters now I realize that what she always needed was to experience every emotion to the very utmost, seeking ecstasy not only in love, but also in abandonment, loneliness, and disaster.

Of course nobody, least of all a genius, quite conforms to that sort of stereotype. But the wish to shock, the bobbed hair, the cigarettes, the adolescent affairs – these are certainly the hallmarks of the period and were being tried out by strong-minded young women everywhere, by Katherine Mansfield in New Zealand and London, by the heroines of Lawrence's *The Rainbow* and *Women in Love*. Incorrigibly novelistic as we are we could see Tsvetaeva as incubated in such emancipated fictional fashion as those of Artsybashev's *Sanin*, or Bely's, or Remizov's, Lawrence's too if we transpose to an un-Russian key – but then entering and growing up into the real thing, into a work of Dostoevsky or Conrad.

The most touching photograph in the remarkable collection that Ardis have put together for their *Pictorial Biography* of Tsvetaeva (edited by Ellender Proffer and translated by J. Marin King) shows

her with Efron in the spring of 1911. With his childish good looks
and party clothes, her soft hair and pince-nez and sturdily chubby
features, they look like Hansel and Gretel, young lovers in a fairy
tale. Four lustrous eyes gaze at the camera with stern concentration
and melting candour. The features could be those of young
revolutionaries from the eighties of the previous century, but the
look is wholly different, both gentler and more determinedly
egotistical.

Their first child, christened Ariadna, was born a year later, and a
second daughter in 1917. In the meantime Mandelstam had fallen in
love with Tsvetaeva and pursued her from Petersburg to Alexandrov
before giving up. Both commemorated the abortive affair in poetry,
Tsvetaeva in the lyrical diary of *Versty I*. After the Bolshevik coup
Efron got away to the south and joined the White army: she was
caught in Moscow during the famine with the two children, and the
younger died of malnutrition in the orphanage where she had been
compelled to leave her. From 1917 to 1922 she never saw her
husband or knew if he still lived. She wrote in her diary: 'If God
performs a miracle and leaves you among the living, I shall serve you
like a dog.'

When she heard from him they agreed to emigrate together, and
met in Prague, moving to Paris after a few years. Although
Tsvetaeva had written a passionate and beautiful poem cycle
celebrating the cause of the White army she was not accepted or
thought well of among the émigré sects. Though her sentiments
were orthodox, even xenophobic, they sensed that her art was in its
own way revolutionary. Good poetry has in any case its own ways of
refusing to identify wholly with 'us', as against 'them', and perhaps
nobody was ever so conscious of 'us' and 'them' as a Russian at that
time. Number 36 of the Swan poem cycle gives us Tsvetaeva's own
kind of poetic individualism, which her adored Pushkin would have
appreciated. A 'winged soul' is indifferent to class warfare, to the
arrogance of the haves, and to the envy of the have-nots. 'I have two
foes in the world, twins inextricably interrelated – the hunger of the
hungry and the glut of the glutted!' And though that sentiment
would have got past the authorities in the Soviet Union, the
technique, like Mayakovsky's was too avant-garde for the growing
conservatism of the new Red orthodoxy.

She herself put her dilemma pungently. 'In the emigration they
began (enthusiastically!) publishing me, then, on reflection, they
withdrew me from circulation, sensing it was not in-our-line but
from-over-there. The content seemed to be "ours", but the voice –

'*theirs*!. . . For those on the Right it is Left in form. For those on the Left it is Right in content.' When Mayakovsky came to Paris she attended one of his readings at the Café Voltaire. When journalists asked her afterwards what the recital made her think of the present Russia, she replied, 'That strength is over there'. She meant, which was true, that the best Russian poets were still in Russia, and it was their strength which was lacking among the poets of the emigration. But the comment was held to be pro-Soviet, and her work, on which her family depended for its small income, was boycotted from all the émigré magazines.

The same spirit of division obtained in the family itself. Efron, to whom she remained wholly loyal, had himself acquired Soviet views; their daughter and the son born to them in Czechoslovakia, now growing up, followed their father's example and wished like him to go back to Russia. They were desperately poor; at one time Tsvetaeva wrote that their only income was the four or five francs a day their daughter earned by making bonnets. This Dickensian touch was no doubt strictly accurate, though it is clear from the many photographs in the *Pictorial Biography* that things were not always so bad and that help of some kind was usually forthcoming. None the less it seems that simple poverty was one factor in her family's wish to leave for the worker's paradise that Soviet propaganda depicted, despite the many disillusioned letters they had from friends who tried it.

There were other factors too. Efron, who was partly Jewish (his family were connected with the famous Efron-Brockhaus encyclopedia), had never been a convinced 'Orthodox', and his experiences on the supply lines of the White army had not been such as to promote chivalric faith. It is touching that Tsvetaeva herself gloried in her husband's mixed ancestry and wrote a poem about his handsomeness, his face 'narrow as a sword' and eyes 'beautifully without purpose': 'In his face tragically intermingle two ancient bloods.'

> In him I am faithful to chivalry,
> To all of you who lived and died
> without fear!
> In times of fate such men
> Write verses – and go to the block!

Efron, one imagines, was not always disposed to follow this model and the liberation of Russian Jews in the early idealist days of the revolution may itself have had an appeal for him. 'If only you knew', his wife wrote to a friend, 'how ardent, magnanimous, profound a young man he is.' Though they were a loving couple Efron's answer to this was to cultivate on the side his own style of individuality and dedication. One feels in him the odd presence of a wary, unspontaneous, perhaps bewildered man, weakened by illness and privation – he was a consumptive of long standing – and wanting to exhibit his own talents as a story-writer. That may have something to do with his becoming involved in the most sinister of stories. Without telling his wife, he had joined in 1932 an organization known as 'The Union for the Return to the Fatherland'. He became a full-time official of what increasingly became a Soviet front organization – the name significantly changed to 'Union of Friends of the Soviet Fatherland' – and was secretly recruited by the European department of the OGPU.

In September 1937 the Swiss police discovered a bullet-riddled corpse in a country road near Lausanne. It proved to be that of a defected OGPU agent who had been murdered by his former comrades on orders from above. Investigation clearly pointed to Efron as having helped to organize not only this killing but that in France of Trotsky's son Andrei Sedov. Efron had to disappear, and he did so via Republican Spain, ending up in the Soviet Union. Not long afterwards he was arrested in the purges and summarily shot, presumably because he knew too much. His daughter Ariadna, who had earlier returned to Russia and become a devoted supporter of the regime, was sent into the Gulag and re-emerged in the fifties – a crumpled photo in the *Pictorial Biography* shows a haggard woman with huge staring eyes. The eloquence of the photographs in this book is positively creepy. The last ones of Efron himself, in Paris and the Crimea, present a tragic yet strangely tranquil face, barely recognizable as that of the rather passive little dandy whom Tsvetaeva had carried off.

She refused to believe he was implicated in the murders, and when she heard he was in Russia prepared at once to join him there. It was her duty. Recalling the promise she made to herself at the time of their first separation she wrote on the same page of her diary '*Voi i poidu – kak sobaka*' – 'And here am I, about to go – like a dog (21 years later).' This recalls the archetypes of the strong loyal Russian woman and the weak indeterminate man she loves – Pushkin's Onegin, Turgenev's Rudin, Chekhov's Ivanov. But life is worse than fiction: the strength of that 'fantastically self-willed' girl, whose loyalty was a kind of superb egotism, was nearly at an end. She was not persecuted in the Soviet Union. The authorities who had destroyed her husband and daughter, converts to the cause, seemed uninterested in one who had been always conspicuously against them. But to fellow writers she was bad news; they kept well away, and she and her son, now aged fifteen, were reduced again to extreme poverty and isolation.

She had been devoted to him as a little boy. Napoleon had always been one of her heroes, and physically her son resembled the great man to an extraordinary degree.

Mur lives torn between my humanism and the virtual fanaticism of his father. He is very serious. His mind is acute, but sober: *Roman*. He loves the magical too, but as a guest. All hope rests on that forehead. He loves me like his very own possession. And already – little by little – he is beginning to value me.

But that relation seems to have vanished by the time they were back in Russia. Another writer recalled later her bewilderment and loneliness – 'she and her son, in my observation, had no common language'. Natural enough, at that age, but in the circumstances tormenting and heart-breaking. She felt that her position and reputation would ruin his life. When war came they were evacuated to Elabuga in the Tartar republic, and there, at the lowest ebb, she decided to carry out what she had long contemplated. 'For about a year I have been looking around for a hook . . . I think I am already posthumously afraid of myself. I do not want to die, I want *not to be*. Bitter wormwood.'

When the house was empty she climbed on a chair by the front door, put a rope over a beam and hanged herself. The note she left disappeared into Soviet police archives. Her son joined the army a year later and was killed, aged nineteen. In a strangely touching last postcard from the front he writes he is 'absolutely confident that my star will bring me through this war unharmed and that success will certainly come to me'. He has seen dead people for the first time in his life, for 'up till now I have refused to look at the dead, even my mother'.

Poets in Russia mourned Tsvetaeva, and felt guilty about her. Pasternak, who had visited her in France and been rather less than forthcoming in advice and assistance, wrote in his autobiography that 'the common tragedy of her family exceeded my worst fears' and unhesitatingly answered 'I am' when his friend Gladkov asked the rhetorical question, who was to blame? All of us, Pasternak added; but this is the natural display of guilt in a naturally warmhearted society where terror ruled, and where a fellow author would normally have been helped and cherished far more than in any comparable situation in the West. Pasternak described her as 'more Russian than any of us . . . in the rhythms that inhabited her soul, in her tremendous, uniquely powerful language'.

Those rhythms are indeed individual and highly effective, in prose as well as in poetry. Russian critics are perhaps apt to make too much of a mystery of the phonetic or acoustic side of Russian poetry, and the originality of new metrical or sound effects produced by Tsvetaeva or Mayakovsky. Russian poetry is deeply melodious and (as her translator Robin Kemball points out) even at its most modern retains much of the traditional harmony of metre, alliteration, and onomatopoeia. Kemball cites another expert, Simon Karlinsky, who remarks of Tsvetaeva's mature style that 'words are not used to connote or to imply or to suggest: they are selected equally on the basis of their shape, sound, and meaning, each of these qualities being equally necessary for the total impression'.

Well, yes; but the same could be said of almost any good poet in any language: the process is instinctive as well as individual, each poet producing his own kind of linguistic character by his own sense of words. The nature of Russian is apt to make the process more dramatic and emphatic, suited to a long tradition of recital. One feature of Tsvetaeva's style, on which Karlinsky writes very interestingly, is *bezglagolnost* – verblessness – a dislike of the verb compensated by a brilliant and characteristic use of inflection, especially dative and instrumental case endings, a tactic beyond the scope of any translator. As Kemball says, her syntax sets more problems than her prosody.

With this in mind he has favoured metrical translations, unfashionable today, but in this case probably justified because they give some conception of the vigorous and vivid style of *The Demesne of the Swans*.

> Your temple, so stern and so stately,
> You quit for the scream of the square . . .
> – O, Liberty! – Beautiful Lady
> Marquis, Russian princes, found fair
>
> So far we've some fearful choir practice –
> Communion has yet to take place!
> – O, Liberty! – harlot, seductress,
> In some giddy-brained soldier's embrace!

The trouble is that though the metre is the 'same' as in the Russian you cannot really divorce metre from everything else in the poetry. In English it is bound to be non-poetry except for the metre and the rhyme, and thus the metre and the rhyme become non-poetry too: what jiggles in English does not appear to do so in its natural Russian.

> Iz strogago, stroinago khrama
> Ty vyshla na vizg ploshchadei . . .
> – Svoboda! – Prekrasnaya Dama –

The strength of the original, its discipline yet immediacy of response, expresses itself naturally in that forceful alliteration. Like much of this diary of poems, history is a kind of instant feeling: Philippe Egalité of the French Revolution and the aristocratic Decembrists of the Russian bid for liberty in 1825 are brought together with the drunken soldiers and their girls whom the poet had before her eyes in the squares of Petersburg, that town of severe harmonious lines which Pushkin in *The Bronze Horseman* had celebrated with the same alliterating adjectives:

> Liubliu tebya, Petra tvorenie,
> Liubliu tvoi strogii, stroinii vid . . .
>
> [I love you, Peter's creation, I love
> your severe harmonious look . . .]

When she made a fair copy of these poems before leaving for Russia in 1939, Tsvetaeva noted that her friend the poet Balmont, to whom she read the poem during the revolution, said, 'I don't like the way you treat the harlot. Some harlots, well –' and he turned up his eyes. She replies, 'What a *great pity* I can't say in answer to that "Some soldiers – well." ' The rhythm of 'To the cadets who fell in Nizhni' comes over very well, and is moving even in translation, a real tribute to Kemball's version:

> Swords held high –
> And the bugles sadly sighing –
> Bid good-bye
> To the dead.
> Cap with sprig of green-leaf lying
> At their head.

Another poem, glorifying and identifying with the White officers, was read by the author to thunderous applause at a recital in Red Moscow. Not really paradoxical: the poem does not mention the Whites specifically, and the idea of the officer, and officer qualities, was already just as popular – after the first giddy bout of egalitarianism – on the revolutionary side.

Ardis publishers are to be congratulated on the three excellent books under review, all lovingly produced and annotated. Marin King's edition of the prose and Kemball's of the Swan cycle are both supplied with a discerning and admirably complete *apparatus criticus*. This is the more desirable because Tsvetaeva, like many other Russian poets, is extremely allusive, and takes for granted the reader's familiarity with Russian history and poetry. Her prose does much the same thing, and is in its way as idiosyncratic as her poetry. Her description of Voloshin, in her portraits of contemporary writers, is memorable, and so is her account of her childhood in Germany in 'The Tower of Ivy'. (The title, as she tells us, came from her misreading of the name of Rilke's patroness, the Fürstin von Thurn und Taxis. *Thur* she connected with French *tour*, and she knew the botanical name *taxus*, yew, which she thought meant ivy.)

Her most interesting prose pieces, though, are her reflections on Pushkin, to which like Bryusov she gave the title 'My Pushkin', and still more so her essay on Pushkin's two versions of the famous eighteenth-century Cossack rebel, Pugachev, one in his history of the rebellion and the other in his historical novel, *The Captain's Daughter*. The aesthetic implications of this are profound, and never more so than today, when art prides itself on getting things just as they were, and devoting its artifice to an appearance of factual realism.

Tsvetaeva, an idealist, will have none of this. For her the sober factual account of Pugachev in the history lacks the love with which Pushkin the poet created the portrait in his novel, a love which he made the hero feel for the villain, despite his villainy. For her, as for Pushkin – she quotes his poem 'The Hero' – the idea of a hero is more important than any diminishing facts about him.

A truth, by the fact that it is low, is *not* truth any more, an an elevating lie, by the fact that it elevates us – is *not* a lie any more. There are no low truths and high lies, there are only low lies and high truths . . . there are happy cases, when destiny is perfected. What poet writing about Jeanne d'Arc does not adjust the record of the facts?

Hagiography has seen to it that she herself has become one of those 'happy cases when destiny is perfected'. In these three books we have both the legend of Tsvetaeva and her history. No doubt the legend has the greater appeal but the history is true too. And in its way as impressive.

The novelist as pedagogue: *Lectures on Russian Literature* by Vladimir Nabokov

People will sometimes say: 'I was lucky at such and such an age. I had a teacher of genius.' And it turns out that what this genius could do was – in a *coup de foudre* – to open the eyes of the young person to the transcendental realities of literature. There was such an eccentrically lovable pedant – a Mr Chips or a Mr Pnin – in Professor Nabokov. In his teaching he was a genius of a distinctly old-fashioned sort.

This might seem to make it all the odder that as theorist and practitioner of the novel he should still have such a reputation among the modernists. When today it enters the field of education modernism does not seek to open our eyes to the old-fashioned sublimities of literature. It seeks instead to inculcate a method by which literature may be judged, parcelled, and synthesized by rule of thumb, or rather by mastery of jargon. Nabokov's own novels may be 'taught' in just this fashion, the instructor displaying the ways in which their verbal techniques stage a carnival of language, the verbal signifiers rejoicing in and playing out their elaborate games and patterns.

In practice Nabokov had entered on his career as a modern novelist by the back door, and by way of the wholly unclassifiable world of the Russian classics. His debt to Russian formalism is clear and evident; but that formalism, as expounded by such brilliant critics as Shklovsky and Eykhenbaum, was itself a reaction against the earlier emotional and nationalistic attitudes taken by the Russian populists and their public about Russian literature.

The formalists took an admirably astringent line with such admirers: for instance those followers of Dostoevsky's famous lecture on Pushkin who wept over Tatiana, the heroine of *Evgeny Onegin*, as the incarnation of warm and outgoing Russian womanhood. Is Pushkin weeping with us over his bittersweet tale of

Tatiana and Onegin, demanded Shklovsky, or is he really having a game not only with the characters themselves but with the notion of a bittersweet tale about them? Nabokov perceived the importance of the distinction, or rather the fact that in drawing it the critic is not in fact compelling us to decide. The formalist critic is not telling us to choose between shedding tears over the characters of fiction and treating them as figures in a game. One must be conscious of the respective propriety, in their contexts, of both responses.

Nabokovian formalism is in this sense a long way from both structuralism and its deconstructive progeny. Nabokov's view of literature is by no means that of 'a world of words to the end of it'. On the contrary. He told his students that in the course of giving them some instruction in the development of Russian literature, 'I may, if I am lucky, tap the deep pathos that pertains to all authentic art.' Nabokov had immense tenderness for the divine status in art of the object, the thing; and like Virgil he saw that the mortal things that touch the heart touch it all the more in a masterpiece of fiction, when they cease to be evanescent and ephemeral and become immortal. The fact is the sweetest dream that fiction knows.

And particularly Russian fiction. These lectures on the Russian masters are in a less completed state than Nabokov's previous volume of *Lectures on Literature* – many are made up of notes and contextual points for class delivery, and they have been given just the proper degree of coherence by the expert editing of Fredson Bowers, who incorporates as an appendix some photostats of Nabokov's notes and lecture worksheets. Nabokov of course made up his own class notes on Gogol into a brilliant short book, and a sizable chunk of this is included. His comments on the style of *Dead Souls* and the plot of 'The Overcoat' are the most illuminating written in English on those great works. The overcoat and its owner, thing and person, are virtually synonymous and interchangeable, melded together in a dream of possession and identity. As one reads Gogol one's eyes may become gogolized, Nabokov observes, and bits of his world may appear in unexpected places. 'I have visited many countries and something like Akaki Akakyevich's overcoat has been the passionate dream of this or that chance acquaintance who never had heard about Gogol.'

It is the same with that young man who appears and disappears for good in a single paragraph at the beginning of *Dead Souls*, and whose significance Nabokov was the first critic to notice. His significance consists in the absolute lack of it, plus the fact that he wears a Tula-made bronze tiepin in the shape of a pistol; and it is this object which establishes and authenticates his total contingency. Although Nabokov does not himself make the connection, the reader may place side by side in some happy compartment of his mind the vast sturgeon, a 'wondrous produce of nature', which Sobakevich (literally 'dogman', the uncouth but effective *barin*) consumes in its entirety in *Dead Souls*, with that other sturgeon in Chekhov's 'The Lady with the Little Dog', to which we are never actually introduced, but which the hero's restaurant acquaintance judges to have been slightly 'off'. Like the tiepin both fish do their part, and the importance of the part is defined only by how memorable they are.

Nabokov's discussion of Chekhov's 'The Lady with the Little Dog' is one of the high spots of this volume, on a par with his wonderful analysis of Kafka's *The Metamorphosis* in *Lectures on Literature*. A comparison of the two treatments tells us a lot about his basic methods and how effective they can be. With both stories he has it both ways, and in subtly different ways. Of both he implies, and in the case of 'The Lady with the Little Dog' states openly, that 'there is no special moral to be drawn and no special message to be received'. Naturally not. No true work of art appears conscious of its moral and its meaning: nor for the client is it ever in fact without them. Nabokov knows that quite well, and like the artist himself he shows us what the moral is without stating it.

Both stories are on a different level of art from what he calls the 'special delivery' stories of Gorki and Thomas Mann. (Note that odd juxtaposition of names and the airy way in which Nabokov proffers it without further explanation.) The 'special delivery' story, whether by Gorki or Maupassant, and – yes – possibly in most cases by Thomas Mann as well, depends on a determination of tone, which leaves the reader in no doubt how his responses are being directed. No great story tries to impress its 'realism' upon us, as Gorki and Maupassant did in their different ways, and as any run-of-the-mill story-teller up to a quarter century or so ago would have done. And conversely no great story tries to impress us with its 'non-reality' as many new tales would do today, making capital out of the deliberate artifice of its fabrication, as Robbe-Grillet and Calvino and many others make a habit of doing.

Under Nabokov's examination Kafka's story reveals that only the hero-victim who becomes an insect is human. The rest of the family and the lodgers in their house demonstrate an insect-like inhumanity in their relations with the victim and their attitude toward him. A yawn or a laugh, physical acts of the species poor Gregor Samsa no longer belongs to, become less characteristic of the human race than are the feeble wavings of his many-jointed legs. In the last sentence of the story his sister 'flexes her young body' in the spring warmth on the tramcar. The nightmare is over, the insect son and brother is dead and disposed of, and her action cruelly contrasts with her beetle brother's pathetic movements. Within a family, even a national family, every cruel contrast can take place. Nabokov might well have been thinking of that most marvellous of Russian stories, Pushkin's poem *The Bronze Horseman*, where the hoofbeats of the brazen tsar's steed ring out behind the panic-stricken clerk who has dared to shake his puny human fist at the great statue, the father of his people.

Gregor Samsa and Pushkin's clerk, like Gogol's more famous clerk Akaky Akakyevich, are little men whose humanity takes the most unavailing and therefore pathetic form. But power and impotence take unexpected forms too. Any of Nabokov's fortunate pupils would have perceived from his discourse the fact that the story's art evangelizes the author's self-pity, his hidden conviction that neuroses give their victim a greater awareness of life, and thus the moral and aesthetic status of a seer, a status denied to the healthy persons around him. Two further observations of Nabokov shed light on the way allegory works in a narrative, as he has already shown the most effective technical way a moral works. With the meticulous attention to the factual which is the secret of his pedagogic process, and presumably too of his skill as a lepidopterist, he points out (a) that Kafka fails to establish just what sort of beetle Gregor has become, but that (b) he has wing-cases and therefore must have wings and be capable of flight. Freedom of speculation, as with a discussion of Shakespeare; and no further comment is needed to make the critical point. A narrative masterpiece both defines and abandons us to the unpredictabilities of its moral and symbolic life.

In the case of 'The Lady with the Little Dog' the initial approach is similar. The inwardness of this story, its 'moral', is that the secret life is what is really precious to a person; that he may never discover one, but if he does make the discovery – through falling in love for example – the visible part of his life, and other people's lives, will seem intolerably dull, meaningless, and humdrum. This moral, we might note, is both dubious and romantic, conceited and woolly minded: exactly the moral we might expect to be drawn by a man who has fallen in love.

That directness, and that dubiousness, are precisely what the story is able to make into its total success. Gurov, the hero in love, perceives what the story also perceives, but the story perceives it with a difference.

Judging others by himself, he did not believe what he saw, and always fancied that every man led his real, most interesting life under cover of secrecy as under cover of night. The personal life of every individual is based on secrecy and perhaps it is partly for that reason that civilized man is so nervously anxious that personal privacy should be respected.

The irony in that last sentence should be pondered on today, when so many have decided that personal privacy is not so important after all, and least of all to art. The story leaves not only the secrecy of the love affair intact, but also the dignity of its participants. Chekhov's comment on his hero is also one that places his story inside the social and cultural frame of an age. Nabokov celebrates the timeless triumph in it of 'beauty plus pity'; but though that phrase is illuminating of the Nabokovian aesthetic, about which a general misunderstanding was often wilfully encouraged outside the class-room by the author himself, it ignores the historical dimension of the tale.

For the really significant fact is surely that Chekhov is able both to endorse and exploit the idea of the truly private life. In the heyday of privacy, novels and stories could have a special kind of authenticity: the power both to assume secrecy and to violate it. The success of Chekhov's technique here is to leave the open and the secret side by side, and immobile. Gurov's wife and colleagues never discover his secret, nor does the husband of the lady with the little dog. The peculiar success of the story follows logically from this stasis. Nothing can happen and yet everything has happened, because the world of the love affair can be shown in contrast with the outer world of triviality.

The decisive moment occurs when Gurov himself feels the urge to bring the two together. After dining with a colleague he suddenly blurts out about what a wonderful woman he met at Yalta. But the departing friend fails to respond because he has been reflecting on something Gurov said earlier: was their sturgeon at dinner 'off' or not? The everyday world and the secret world meet only in the dumb substantiality of things – the ambiguous sturgeon, the slice of watermelon which Gurov slowly masticates after he and the lady have first made love.

The peculiar insistence of such things must never be exploited. Nabokov lays a finger here on Turgenev's weakness for what he refers to in a schoolmaster's phrase as 'purple patches'. 'When Turgenev sits down to discuss a landscape, you notice that he is concerned with the trouser-crease of his phrase; he crosses his legs with an eye upon the color of his socks.' Chekhov's lack of concern conveys 'an impression of artistic beauty far surpassing that of writers who thought they knew what rich beautiful prose was'. Nabokov is wholly fair to Turgenev, indeed enthusiastic about him, but he shows his pupils unerringly why Turgenev is not in the same class as Tolstoy on the one hand or Chekhov on the other. 'When you read Turgenev, you know you are reading Turgenev. When you read Tolstoy you read just because you cannot stop.' Nabokov the aesthete is quite clear why the obviously aesthetic writer is inferior to the two who seem to care nothing about the matter.

And he gives Tolstoy the same loving treatment he gave Pushkin in his great commentary on *Evgeny Onegin*; not so exhaustively, for these are only lecture notes, but with the same recognition that this is the only way we can give such a master his due. But first an important generalization. Tolstoy is the first great writer to think of obvious things, like describing childbirth:

The whole history of literary fiction as an evolutionary process may be said to be a gradual probing of deeper and deeper layers of life. It is quite impossible to imagine either Homer in the ninth century BC or Cervantes in the seventeenth century of our era – it is quite impossible to imagine them describing in such wonderful detail childbirth. The question is not whether certain events and emotions are or are not suitable ethically or aesthetically.

In these lecture notes Nabokov's style is lacking in its usual elegance, but the point is an important one. Tolstoy does not 'go deeper' in any ordinary sense: he concentrates on what has previously been taken for granted. And the reader too must concentrate, for example on the way that fact, pattern, and symbol meet and merge·in *Anna Karenina*. He must see what Tolstoy is describing as clearly as the artist himself has done. 'To comprehend certain important aspects of Anna's night journey [the train journey from Moscow to Petersburg just after she has met Vronsky] the reader should clearly visualize the following arrangement.' There follows a meticulous description of the facilities, still fairly primitive, obtaining in a first-class carriage on an overnight railway journey between the two

Russian capitals. (There is even a sketch of them reproduced in the notes.) In the same spirit Nabokov traces the patterns of symbolism, such as the little peasant muttering and beating iron, which lead us to Anna's death, and the way in which time in the novel is adjusted to the pace of different families and of the three interlocking pairs – the Oblonskys, Anna–Vronsky, Kitty–Levin. 'The mated move faster than the mateless.' The three pairs are 'time-teams' ('a good Nabokovian term . . .; use it with acknowledgements').

Where names are concerned the fastidious can extend to the pernickety. Nabokov never refers to Levin but to Lyovin, pointing out, not unjustly, that the 'Leveen' sound uttered to themselves by most readers becomes entangled with a Jewish surname having a different root as well as different associations. Moreover, just as Tolstoy perfunctorily fictionalized the ancient Russian surname of Obolensky into Oblonsky, so he gave his hero another leonine version of his own name, Lev, pronounced 'Lyov'. These pedantries of Nabokov's are highly salutary, and far removed from the critical jargon which has displaced them in the modern lecture room; and yet it must be admitted that the mania for accuracy can lead him at these times into an outlandishness less excusable than the high-spirited neologisms which in his version of *Evgeny Onegin* paralleled in some sense the wonderful fizz of the original. Why insist on calling Chekhov's story 'In the Ravine' 'In the Gully'? No doubt because the translation is Constance Garnett's, and Nabokov delights to twit that well-intentioned and hard-working if unreliable lady. 'Gully' in English is associated with drainpipes rather than with those abrupt crevasses that seam the flat steppes of southern Russia and have no geographical and thus no lexicographical equivalent in English. 'Gulch' would be more graphic but also more distracting verbally. 'Ravine' does at least suggest the symbolic overtone of primitive debasement in the Russian title.

And why must he call Gogol's overcoat 'The Carrick'? It cannot be denied there was such a term in English, though specialized and unfamiliar even in its own day, for a many-caped coachman-style cloak, with sleeves made almost supererogatory by the voluminous breadth of the shoulders. Poor Akaky schemes for, saves for, and finally obtains such a garment, before a mugger takes it off him. But the story is entitled *Shinel*, a Russianized version of French *chenille*, a furry sort of cloth, and this is the *normal* word for overcoat. The 'Carrick' draws attention to the cut of the coat itself – fair enough in view of Nabokov's passion for accuracy and justice to the semi-divine status of the thing in fiction – but it suggests this is going to be the significant point of the tale. Such a title points the story's plainness and pathos quite the wrong way. Yet Nabokov's discussion of it is one of his best things, the centrepiece of the triptych, as it were, of which the wings are formed by *The Metamorphosis* and 'The Lady with the Little Dog'.

What comes out so strongly in each case is the absolute compatibility of the story's 'touchingness' – the way it finds the heart and brings water to the eyes – with an extreme elaboration of artifice, a heaping up of aesthetic Nabokovian detail. And in cataloguing the latter with such joy Nabokov also shows us the subtle grounds on which we feel the former response. All the great Russians excel in combining simple feeling with a sense of the infinite contingency entailed on human existence. Dickens, by contrast, is apt to suspend the complexity of his art when he wants us to cry; and Aldous Huxley long ago pointed out that if we compare the death of Little Nell with that of the child Ilusha at the end of *The Brothers Karamazov* we are struck by the multitudinous vitality of the detail with which Dostoevsky surrounds the touching event.

But Dostoevsky is one author about whom Nabokov can be of no use to us. He is too good at authors he loves to be of help when he doesn't love. He tells us that Dostoevsky's early story 'The Double' is his masterpiece, because it is virtually an imitation of Gogol. Dostoevsky

is not a great writer in the sense Tolstoy, Pushkin, and Chekhov are . . . Not because the world he creates is unreal – all the world of writers are unreal – but because it is created too hastily without any sense of that harmony and economy which the most irrational masterpiece is bound to comply with.

That is not criticism, but it performs the negative function of showing that if we find Dostoevsky no good it is no good trying to invent reasons why not. It is not just a question of temperamental incompatibility either: plenty of readers who find his ideas and personality repugnant are nonetheless entranced by the marvellous dishevelment of his drama and comedy. Nabokov actually goes so far as to say that Dostoevsky 'has little humour in the description of his characters or their relations, or in the situations'. Considering that humour makes Dostoevsky's world as it makes Gogol's – and if Gogol's humour is like a bed-sitter, Dostoevsky's is a Gothic cathedral – that judgement is quite inexplicable. Yet it may be that

Nabokov was right in finding no humour in Dostoevsky *as a man*,
even though the strange genius of his books runs riot with it.
This brings us to a point of crucial importance in Nabokov's
attitude to Russian life and literature: his dislike and avoidance of its
profoundly dualistic nature. Aesthetic patterns, productive of
aesthetic bliss, never produce dualisms; and though acknowledging
that one cannot separate Tolstoy the preacher from Tolstoy the
artist Nabokov says he would like to

> kick the glorified soap box from under his sandalled feet and then lock him
> up in a stone house on a desert island with gallons of ink and reams of paper
> – far away from the things, ethical and pedagogical, that diverted his
> attention from observing the way the dark hair curled above Anna's white
> neck.

A superb bravura passage in *Gogol*, reprinted in the present
collection, makes play with the idea of *poshlust* (German *Kitsch*,
English – though too generalized to be accurate – vulgarity). The
passage has given the Russian term for sickly high-flown sentiments
and sweetly coloured daydreams a certain notoriety. In the West it is
usually, as Nabokov has observed, a wholly commercialized affair,
stereotyped for advertising, the *Reader's Digest*, the women's
magazines.

But in Russian literature and society *poshlust* can have quite a
different implication, and one that Nabokov ignores or seems
unaware of. It exhibits the duality between aspiration and reality,
what Brodsky calls 'the dialogue between the spheres and the
gutter'. Handled by a great artist such as Gogol or Chekhov it shows
a geniune pathos in the soil, divided between intimations of beauty
and the banality of living, as Gurov is in 'The Lady with the Little
Dog'. Chichikov in *Dead Souls* – for Nabokov the embodiment of
poshlust – converses with his fellow crooks in nonsensical and high-
minded platitudes while engaged in speculating in the mortgages of
defunct serfs; but Gogol has a vision of a redeemed Chichikov,
travelling toward some glorious goal just as Russia – the headlong
troika – will do.

Of course that glorious goal has turned out to be the gleaming
heights of socialism, and Nabokov had scarcely the need to waste his
contempt on the jargon of Soviet *poshlust*. In the lecture which
opens this collection, 'Russian Writers, Censors, and Readers', read
at the Cornell Festival of the Arts in 1958, he indicates the
institutionalization of *poshlust* in Soviet art. Although there is a

comparable formula in Western book clubs and prepackaged thrillers, 'there is no governmental law in Western countries to ban a story that does not comply with fond tradition'. And thus we have passages like this from *The Big Heart*, by Antonov, published serially in 1957.

> 'Why can't you love me as I love you?'
> 'I love my country', she said.
> 'So do I', he exclaimed.
> ' And there is something I love even more strongly', Olga continued, disengaging herself from the young man's embrace.
> 'And that is?' he queried.
> Olga let her limped blue eyes rest on him, and answered quickly: 'It is the Party.'

Readers of the monthly journal *Soviet Literature* will know that the formula has become a little more flexible since then, but not much.

What is worst about it is the disappearance of that saving dualism which animates the Russian literature of the nineteenth century, and in the end one's strongest criticism of Nabokov must be that he comes perilously close to equating what he calls the 'unctuousness' and 'sentimentality' of Dostoevsky with the same *poshlii* qualities in present-day Soviet literature. Sentiment and human interest are not bad things in themselves. We may agree that Gorki's 'Twenty-Six Men and A Girl' 'is all pink candy with just that amount of soot clinging to it to make it attractive', but Nabokov goes on to observe, as if it were an inexplicable and on the whole distasteful phenomenon, that however degraded the scenes Gorki presents he always retains a childlike faith in human nature and a boundless enthusiasm for its potential. That paradox is just what Nabokov as a critic and teacher would rather not take into account. But it has always been vital to Russian literature and remains so even today. Its greatest art has never been about art but about love and the soul and human progress – matters which Nabokov would prefer to ignore or to depreciate by taking for granted – but indispensable to his fellow countrymen.

Canetti and power

Henry James writes of a very grand lady that she had 'an air of keeping, at every moment, every advantage'. Paradoxically, the same would be true of the literary personality of Elias Canetti. Behind its approachable modesty, its avoidance of every publicity and image-making process, there is a loftiness, an assurance, a stance of absolute superiority. Indeed the modesty and the dignity make the same point: why make a fuss about your greatness?

Great writers usually do, nonetheless. 'Fame wants to find safety', as Canetti has put it. Thomas Mann was notorious for his self-importance and his suspicion of anyone whom he felt might be detecting signs of weakness in him; Thomas Hardy spent his last days writing venomously bad verses against fellow authors whom he felt had patronized him. Across the Atlantic the Hemingways and Mailers positively seethe with anxiety about their status and reputations. Such unease does not mean they are not great: it just shows the extreme vulnerability which usually goes with true creative powers.

Canetti's superiority is reverenced and proclaimed by his disciples, who feel something different from enthusiasm for an admired writer. He is sage and master of an art which only the initiated can fully perceive. The American firm which has begun to publish all his books – the novel, the essays, the play – simply print 'Canetti' in big black letters on top of the jacket, as it might be 'Socrates' or 'Confucius', and the full name and title in smaller print below. A critic writes of his memoir *The Tongue Set Free* that 'all readers – even those not yet exposed to the writings of Elias Canetti – will appreciate 'this self-portrait.' The idea of such an 'exposure' – a magic ordeal yet to come – is typical. Nor, in this case, does it seem absurd.

The Unknown God, dwelling in splendid intellectual isolation, is always a potent cult figure. Canetti chose a language and its literature, but his genius has no setting or home. He was born in 1905 in Ruschuk, Bulgaria, into a merchant clan of Sephardic Jews originally from Spain, and retaining from it a four-hundred-year-old cultural memory. Among themselves, they spoke the Spanish dialect called Ladino, and they had until recently been Turkish citizens. The Canetti and Arditti clans were acquainted for business purposes with some fifteen or seventeen languages, and the importance they attached to this kind of fluency was shown by the story handed down from Canetti's great-grandfather of the journeys on Danube river steamers, when earth merchants kept his heavy money-belt round his waist. Because he knew some Greek, the Canetti patriarch could understand the plotting of two passengers who thought it secure: they were plotting to rob him or another rich man.

Language became an art of magic and a key to power – one language in particular. Canetti's grandfather cursed his son for wanting to leave Ruschuk and set up with his brother-in-law in the cotton-exporting Sephardic community in Manchester. But the family did move, and not long afterwards Canetti père died of a heart attack at the breakfast table while reading the *Manchester Guardian*. The little Canettis had loved England, and with their father's help had joyfully learnt its language: relatives rolled about laughing when Elias recited a French story he had learnt at school with a strong British accent. The father, a gentle, civilized man, hoped that his eldest son would go to university in England and perhaps become a doctor or teacher. Had he lived, his son's destiny would have been very different.

English, then, was not to be – could it ever have been? – the magic language. Canetti's mother, who was intensely proud of her family's status – as an Arditti, she ranked above a Canetti – was devoted to Vienna where she had lived as a child: 'Vienna loves you', a later admirer was to remark. Elias became, at the age of nine, the head of the family, his mother's confidant and helpmate. He had heard with envy his parents talking the magic language, German, and now his mother set out to teach it to him, with a ruthless single-mindedness that made his days a nightmare and estranged him from his English governess and his two younger brothers. His portrait of his mother in the memoir is of the deepest interest. He adored her, but she was not, like Proust's, a worshipping and self-abnegating mother. Her eldest son, to whom she confided her fitful and spontaneous literary enthusiasms – she loved Strindberg and Baudelaire and her favourite character was Shakespeare's Coriolanus – was like a lover with several rivals. Jealousy was an early and lasting obsession. With her half-reluctant connivance he learned to dispose ruthlessly of his mother's admirers, and later came to feel that his childish and adolescent egotism had wilfully failed to realize her need for another husband or sexual relation. This was indeed an apprenticeship in power, its infliction and reception. 'I recognise the words that Genghiz Khan's mother spoke to him', noted Canetti, when he was working on *Crowds and Power* and reading *The Secret History of the Mongols*.

Years later, his mother told him what had really happened when his father died. Relatives supposed it had been the shock of the Balkan war, announced in the headlines, but in fact for a day and a sleepless night he had refused to speak to his wife, who had just returned from a spa cure in her beloved Austria. Radiantly communicative, she had told her husband of a doctor there who had wanted her to elope with him. Her husband could not believe that nothing else had occurred. Her pride was at stake. Mother and son shared the same pride, but the son came to understand its mysterious connections – as in the case of Kafka – with powerlessness and humility.

They were in Vienna when war came, the moment which both Canetti and Akhmatova write of as the real beginning of the twentieth century. No personal problem – the Canettis are now British citizens. They leave for Zürich, but not before the boy sees, and will always remember, a trainload of Jewish refugees from Galicia (what struck him was how motionless the freight cars were, and the faces of those looking out of them). Canetti loved his Swiss school and Zürich, where he now lives, but his mother was contemptuous of his love for a complacent and self-approving provincial society. She wants him to be educated in Vienna, and after the war they return there. He studies for a doctorate in chemistry, and at the age of twenty-five begins to write a novel. His secret and steadfast intention, to study and made a general theory of power, will now manifest itself.

The novel which emerges, *Auto da Fé*, has been seriously called the most remarkable of this century. A meaningless judgement, and yet what could be said is that it is the most remarkable attempt at an intellectual imagination of the true nature of the twentieth century, an apotheosis of the immensely weighty and serious Faust tradition of German letters. It could only have been written *in* German, and yet it could hardly have been written *by* a German, a man too physically at home in the *gemütlichkeit* of his native speech. Canetti's use of the language is enormously mental, magical and dynamic. During a thirty-year residence in England after his return in 1939, he often suffered what he called 'word attacks', a compulsive urge to make lists and patterns of German words as if they were counters in a spell to conjure, or to abjure, power. He also began to keep the extended diary of thoughts and aphorisms now published as *The Human Province*. Full of fascination but verging on the portentous as such compilations in an English translation unavoidably do, it contains such comments as 'So long as there are people in the world who have *no power whatsoever*, I cannot lose all hope', and 'I have never heard of a person attacking power without wanting it.' Portraits of the powerful in history rekindle his hatred of power, 'and warn me of my own power over people'.

Everything Canetti writes is obsessed with and transformed by this abstract passion, even his academic but strangely haunting play *The Numbered*, written in England after the war. His own creative dynamism comes from the love–hate relation with power, and from 'confronting' its special nightmare in our own century. *The Human Province* is a sort of Caesar's *Commentaries* on power geography. One of Canetti's strengths is that he never discriminates between the public and the private spheres of power, just as he never admits, even tacitly, a division between his own abstraction of it and the thing itself. A profound admirer of Hobbes, he wastes no time on the anatomy of modern power systems – Communism, Fascism – which absorb the individual into an ideal of overall social cohesion. He sees the crucial area both of power and of freedom in the private life, the area which Hobbesian authority exists to encourage and protect. Yet it is here also that the worst abuses take place, as is shown by the vision of a father and daughter relation in the chapter of *Auto da Fé* called 'The Kind Father'.

For Canetti, it is self-evident that *Auto da Fé* engrosses as a novel the most central significances of our time, and in his other writings he speaks of it as Goethe spoke of *Faust*. What about such a novel as *Ulysses*? That would be by comparison a piece of random jewellery, a plaything with the popular appeal of such a craft object. The same with *A la Recherche du Temps Perdu*, even with *The Magic Mountain*. They are essentially independent of their time, floating above it: they are *literature*. In art Canetti had, as he tells us, a contempt for 'salvation and joy', for anything that was 'relaxing'. Art should have the atmosphere of revolution, the excitement, as in

Goethe, of a potential, 'manifest in each of its moment'. A favourite text of Canetti is Stendhal's account of growing up in the French Revolution, *La Vie de Henri Brulard*. Dostoevsky, Büchner, Kafka also point the way to *Auto da Fé*. Writers who don't, even great ones like Tolstoy, are of minor interest; Canetti's essay on Tolstoy, one of his very few pieces lacking in compulsive interest, merely makes the point that Tolstoy at the end of his life became like the hero of *Auto da Fé*.

'Truly to confront the age' – great art does not often do that so self-consciously. Stendhal does it with lightness and élan; the painter Beckmann did it after the First World War with mythic violence and horror. Beckmann's painting is probably the closest parallel in art to Canetti's novel. Canetti does not mention him, but when writing his novel he surrounded himself with reproductions of Grünewald, who also inspired Beckmann. And apart from the intention, an art that confronts the age must not give way to it. It must be highly organized technically, to survive its own picture of disintegration.

The thought came to me that the world should not be depicted as in earlier novels, from one writer's standpoint as it were; the world had *crumbled*, and only if one had the courage to show it in its crumbled state could one possibly offer an authentic conception of it . . . When I ask myself today where I got the rigour of my work I come to heterogeneous influences . . . Stendhal it was who made me stick to clarity. I had just finished the eighth chapter, now titled 'Death', when Kafka's 'Metamorphosis' came into my hands. Nothing more fortunate could have happened to me at this point. There, in utmost perfection, I found the antipose to literary non-commitment which I hated so much; there was the rigour that I yearned for. There, something was achieved that I wanted to find for myself. I bowed to this purest of all models, knowing full well that it was unattainable, but it did give me strength.

Kafka seems to be not so much an influence on *Auto da Fé* as totally absorbed by it, almost as Shakespeare's sources were absorbed by Shakespeare, and it is revealing to find out that Canetti discovered him in the actual process of writing his novel. But the greatest formative influence in Vienna at that time was Karl Kraus, the extraordinary nature of whose achievement – partly because it was histrionic, acted out in his recitals – can probably never be adequately presented to an Anglo-Saxon readership. Indeed, it would probably not be too much to say that *Auto da Fé*, which has been effectively translated, and which contains beside the potent forces of Canetti's internationalism, even his 'Englishness', his

Shakespearean side, gives the best intuition that a non-Germanist can get of Kraus's peculiar genius.

It is, above all, a genius of commitment – to language and to emotion. That was the same with Kafka. How to combine, in art, a pure, fastidious rigour with the simplest feeling of rage and sorrow agains the dreadfulness of life, the domination of the powerful, the torture of beetle Gregor by his family, of Woyzeck by the captain, of Jews by Nazis, Russians by Communists, Oliver Twist by Bumble, of Smike by Squeers (*Nicholas Nickleby* was one of Canetti's early and passionate enthusiasms)? For such an artist, the inner world, the world of his invention, cannot and should not be any different from the world of human and historical reality. In his study of Kafka Canetti writes that his strength was increased by the horror with which he saw the 'mass events accompanying the outbreak of war'. The rigour, the totality of his art is a direct expression of the wholeness of that sense of horror, the 'bond between the external hell of the world and his inner hell'. 'He did not have for his private and interior processes that disregard which distinguishes insignificant writers from writers of imagination. A person who thinks that he is empowered to separate his inner world from the outer one has no inner world from which something might be separable.'

Canetti has written nothing more significant than that. Most people do, in fact, feel empowered to achieve a normal equilibrium by separating their own world from the outer one. What is more, most art exists to aid, comfort and satisfy that natural urge. Our inner world is supported and confirmed by it against the outer world – which is the reason thoughtful Nazi officials could read Goethe and Schiller, and listen to Mozart, while going about their business of persecution and domination. Many artists of real honesty will admit the fact, tacitly or openly. Jane Austen, possibly not a genius in whom Canetti takes much interest, writes in a letter about a bloody battle in the Napoleonic war: 'How dreadful that so many poor fellows should be killed, and what a mercy that one cares for none of them.' There speaks the voice of a certain kind of common sense, the kind that most of us have to live by.

Not Canetti's great masters, however. Shakespeare may not have wept over King Lear, may indeed have written the play in a passion of relish, but he *suffered*: the play is a correlative of his total capacity to suffer. That is perhaps self-evident and tautologous. In a climate of pseudo-scientific structuralism, a bloodlessly mechanistic approach to literature, Canetti's insistent emphases are decidedly salutary. In what sense, though, is Kafka for him the 'purest of all models'? That in which suffering is most absolute, most evident? But the message of great works of art is more ambiguous than that, and in a sense more comforting. As Auden wrote in Jane Austen vein: 'You can only tell them parables, from which each according to his immediate and peculiar needs may draw his own conclusions.' And as with the client's need, so with that of the artist himself. Kafka suffers all in himself, but by writing he accepts and takes possession of that suffering. By becoming a beetle, his hero paradoxically has found how to keep, 'at every moment, every advantage'. There is nothing 'pure' in the spectacle of Kafka's pleasure in discovering the perfect way of separating himself from his hated family: for the reader, it is too touching for that, too 'human, all too human'.

That vulnerability is not to be found in Canetti's novel, a work of pure schematic power and ferocity, in which every sentence crackles with violent intelligence, violent humour.

There was not *one* voice that he did not hear, he was possessed by every specific timbre of the war and rendered it compellingly. Whatever he satirically foreshortened was foreshortened effectively; whatever he exaggerated was exaggerated so precisely that it only first existed in this exaggeration and remained unforgettable . . . unsparingly, uncomfortingly, without embellishment, without reduction, and above all and most important, without habituation. Whatever was repeated . . . remained horrifying through every single repetition.

What Canetti wrote of Kraus's play *The Last Days of Mankind* is true of his own novel. As the First World War 'completely entered' Kraus's play, so a horrifying sense of the modern world completely enters his novel. But it is not in the slightest degree a self-consciously 'black' work, like Céline's; nor does it parade a ready-made metaphysic of gloom, like the novels of Graham Greene and Patrick White. It is not apocalyptic but dreadfully and intently domestic, like Dickens's world of Todgers.

It is divided into three parts: 'A Head without a World', 'Headless World' and 'The World in the Head'. Kien, the hero, a recluse and a distinguished Sinologist, with an enormous library, is the head; the library his inner world. His housekeeper Therese, the most memorable portrait in the book, is a world without any head. Everything in the novel can be distinctly 'heard', Therese and her speech particularly so. Having no contact with life, Kien has no speech, only an interior utterance. But he (and his creator) are painfully sensitive to what Canetti apropos of Kraus calls 'acoustic quotations': the sense that everything in the world – newspapers, people, and now radio and television – has a *voice*, its own sort of unique propaganda, which the artist must render unsparingly. He must 'let everybody speak', though most artists do not know how to listen: 'It is the hereditary vice of the intellectual that for him the world consists of intellectuals.' This no doubt is why the greatest acoustic artists, like Dickens and Shakespeare, are not in the German sense 'intellectuals' – they are naive rather than reflective. And it is perhaps the greatest achievement of Canetti to fuse in himself as artist the massive endowment and consciousness of a modern European thinker with an absolutely precise and humble sense of other people, their irreducible, untranslatable utterance of being.

Significant, then, that the speech reality of the novel is in its headless world, the world of Therese, the red-haired porter Benedikt Pfaff, the chess-playing dwarf Fischerle, his prostitute wife the Capitalist, and the other denizens of the café called The Stars of Heaven. Kien, a profound student of Confucius, becomes aware that Therese, whom he finds wearing white gloves to read a tattered book he has given her, *The Trousers of Herr von Bredow*, has a greater respect and feeling for books than he has. Amazed and humbled by this revelation, he decides to marry her. The sequence is one of the funniest in the novel and echoes the range of meaning in its German title *Die Blendung*, a noun which combines the literal with the metaphorical to signify blinding, dazzlement, delusion, deception. The married Kien is crumbled willy-nilly into the horrors of the headless world, beaten, driven out, and forced into the company of the denizens of The Stars of Heaven – particularly the dwarf Fisherle, who sets out to exploit him (there is a sort of grotesque reversal hereabouts of the adventures of Little Nell and her father).

Unhinged, Kien is convinced that he has removed his entire library into his head, whence it has to be laboriously unpacked when he lies down at night, and repacked again in the morning. 'Anything that appears in reality is seen in terms of the delusion as a whole.' This fantasy is remarkably like that set forth in a 'real' madman's book – *Denkwürdigkeiten*, by Schreber, a former president of the Senate of Dresden, whose paranoia was examined by Freud in an essay of 1911. Canetti suggests, rightly, that Freud has missed the point, and that Schreber's is really a very typically twentieth-century case of what he calls 'Power and Survival'. Schreber's delusion was that he was the one man left alive after some vast catastophe – the nuclear bomb, as it might now be. He was aware of other people around him in the asylum, but he explained their presence away by knowing that they were 'fleetingly sketched men', not real, manikins whom he can repack into his head as and when he needs, as Kien repacks the books, though for Kien books are the only reality, which is why in the headless world his survival depends on his continuing to hold them in his head. Kien, like Schreber, has entered, though by another route, what Canetti calls the extreme phase of power – the certainty of onlyness. Power is, ultimately, nothing but the refusal to believe that other people exist, and to act on that belief.

Kien is thus, by a grim paradox, reduced simultaneously to the state of ultimate survival power and of total degradation and powerlessness. As Gogol's Akaky can only apprehend the world through the reality of a new overcoat, so Kien survives by haunting the state pawnshop, 'releasing' by purchase all the books which headless people have brought to pawn, and repacking them in his own head. This is, among other things, a parable of the way in which we try to serve the world and come to terms with it, while retaining our own kinds of solipsism. The most important and terrifying statement of Kafka, says Canetti, is that fear and indifference made up his deepest feeling toward human beings. 'If one thinks about it with a little courage, our world has indeed become one in which fear and indifference predominate. Expressing his own reality without indulgence, Kafka was the first to present the image of *this* world.' The head without a world can only feel those emotions towards it, and it is the task of the artist like Kafka to bring the world into the head, to compel the two into coincidence. That is also what happens in the last section of *Auto da Fé*. Reunited with his library, Kien sets fire to it and perishes in the flames. The world has got into his head and he has voluntarily joined the crowd, the mass, the headless world, as Gregor in *The Metamorphosis* joins it by his humble death as an insect, something dry to be swept up off the carpet. Canetti records that his ending was suggested by the burning of the Justice Palace in Vienna by crowds protesting against the shooting of some workers, and against the acquittal of those responsible. He himself witnessed the scene and, like his puppet Kien, felt at last truly one with and a part of the crowd.

Schematic as it certainly is, the novel's extraordinary richness, the density of its wit and style, can only be travestied by such a brief sketch of its contents. It is not without faults, though these are more evident in the English version than in the German original. Even

though it was translated by the historian Veronica Wedgwood
'under the personal supervision of the author', English linguistic
forms and models cannot quite accommodate themselves to an
outburst of *Kunstprosa* that was in every sense intended for the
German language. There its fierce abstractness, its almost paralys-
ing intelligence, are wholly at home: even the tedium which it by no
means lacks seems, as it were, a wholly genuine and necessary
tedium, as essential and even dynamic part of its massive mental
specification. For the Anglo-Saxon reader accustomed to less
demanding works of fiction, even the endless multiplication of the
grotesque can be a little wearing, as if a computer had been
programmed to turn out an infinite series of scarifying intellectual
jokes, sometimes at its own expense. An example would be Kien's
comment to a student who brings a set of Schiller to pawn. 'Why
Schiller? You should read the original. You should read Immanuel
Kant.' In classic German literature there is nothing opaquely
'original': the prismatic radiance of intellect is reflected from one
work to another. Canetti's novel seems, in one sense, like the pinnacle
of every brilliant and transparent work in its language: in another
sense, as if it was already immanent in all of them. Exhilarating as it is,
and also so physically disturbing that some of the author's friends and
fellow writers hated it and couldn't bear to read it, it is at the same
time a purely intellectual and philosophic exercise. This tension
between a mental and physical plane is by no means unique in German
literature, and it continues today in massive fantasy novels probably
influenced by *Auto da Fé*, like those of Günther Grass.

It is also a tension unknown in naive art – art which slips without
a purpose into a particular perfection of its kind. *The Bronze
Horseman*, or *The Golden Bowl*, are just as much graphic studies of
power as *Auto da Fé*, but they are also halcyon structures of
consummated art, by their very natures tranquil and uninsistent.
The high-pressure blast of ruthless clarity in *Auto da Fé* seems to
blow away the whole world of art. This may be the reason some of
its greatest admirers, though they may also admire Proust or Musil,
tended in England to be intellectuals to whom it would never occur
to read and enjoy the standard English poets and novelists. Like
Voltaire or Nietzsche, Canetti seemed to them quite separate from
the mere banal arts of literature.

Nonetheless, it may be that the predicament of *Auto da Fé*'s
puppet hero, although he has none of the physical reality and
emotional pathos of Gogol's Akaky or Kafka's Gregor Samsa, has

for intellectuals not only a strong masochistic appeal, but conventional fiction's charge of fascination and suspense. Canetti has himself written, as any good novelist might do, that 'true writers encounter their characters only *after* they've created them': and yet his hero is obviously and by intention not a character in this sense. While the book was in progress, he was called simply B, or Bookman, and later Kant (the novel had the provisional title 'Kant catches fire'), finally becoming the combustible Kien (Pinewood) when the conflagration nears which ends the novel. Therese was based on Canetti's first impression of his Viennese landlady.

The finally completed novel was dispatched out of the blue to Thomas Mann, the author being confident that he would recognize it for the masterpeice it was. Mann replied apologetically that he found himself unable to read it. It remained in manuscript for a further four years and was published in 1935, achieving an immediate success. To Canetti's amusement, Thomas Mann wrote a warmly enthusiastic letter. But Canetti wrote no more novels: in that form there was no other subject for him. He had always been obsessed by the need to write his theoretical study of power and the mass, for which he had never ceased to read omnivorously. It was written mostly in England, and was finally published in Germany in 1960.

Crowds and Power could be said to ingest history, all stories about themselves and their behaviour which human beings have told, in the same way that *Auto da Fé* ingested the works of art that told in their different way the truths about power that Canetti was seeking. His favourite historian is Herodotus, a story-teller, with whom it hardly matters whether the story told is factually true or not, because it is always true to the psychology of the society it relates to. Conversely, he has little use for Aristotle the rationalist, who is more interested in the processes of knowledge than in those of suffering, of who does what to whom. As an analyst of the power process, Canetti is equally contemptuous of the empirical and factual historian and one of the men-of-destiny school, noting that both are on the side of power and have a vested interest in it, either because of their theories or from their very function as investigators.

Muhammad Tughlak has been defended by modern Indian historians. Power has never lacked eulogists, and historians, who are professionally obsessed with it, can explain anything, either by the *times* (disguising their adulation as scholarship), or by *necessity*, which, in their hands, can assume any and every shape.

He is instructive, as I have already indicated, on the psychology and powers of the survivor, and has two chapters on the paranoia of Schreber, which are far more illuminating than any of the 'explanations' of Freud. (We might note that Canetti is implacably hostile to Freud's view of literature as both a substitute for life and a way of achieving power in it. For him, great literature is the truest expression possible of the predicament of living and of its need to understand and renounce power.)

The survivor may be detested, as in the example of Muhammad Tughlak, who killed all those returning from an unsuccessful expedition, or he may be credited with almost magical powers, as in the case of Josephus, or Hitler. Josephus, probably the only historian to have actually been in this physical sense a survivor, drew lots with his soldiers in a cave after the fall of the fortress he was commanding. They were to kill each other on this basis, but Josephus cooked the deal in such a way that he and one other man were left alive. 'This is precisely what he brings the Romans: the enhanced sense of his own life, feeding on the deaths of those he had led.' This power he is able to sell, as it were, to Vespasian and his son Titus, in the form of a prophecy that they will become Emperors of Rome. Josephus's distinction as a survivor is so great that it quite outweighs his betrayal of his fellows and desertion of his country.

Surviving the crowd implies having been once a part of it. Hitler's survivor complex was based on the amazing deliverance from his enemies of Frederick the Great. When Roosevelt dies a few weeks before the end of the war, Hitler is convinced he is saved, as Frederick had been saved by the sudden death of his arch-enemy the Empress Elizabeth of Russia. This clutch of a precedent shows an almost pathetic stupidity – and the paranoiac's ignorance of and separation from the realities of the outside world. Yet Hitler had once been truly a part of that world, and of the German and European crowd at the beginning of the First World War.

He described how, at the outbreak of war, he fell on his knees and thanked God. It was his decisive experience, the one moment at which he himself honestly became part of a crowd. He never forgot it, and his whole subsequent career was devoted to the recreation of this moment, but *from outside*.

Hitler's response had been that of the crowd, which was given the same expression by men like Péguy and Rupert Brooke. His paranoia devotes itself to recreating that erstwhile solidarity, and his immediate instrument is the crowd: he perceives how to turn the old *closed* crowd of the German army, now forbidden under the Treaty of Versailles, into the *open* crowd of the National Socialist Party.

The orders, exercises and expectations essential to German psychology had to be procured again at all costs. 'Every closed crowd which is dissolved by force transforms itself into an open crowd to which it imparts all its characteristics.'

The many categories which Canetti makes – invisible crowds, double crowds, crowds as packs – claim to quasi-scientific status. So clearly and forcefully does he set them out that we seem to be recognizing something we have always known, as Molière's hero discovers that he has been speaking prose all his life. The human condition in history is seen as Montaigne might have seen it, in pictures and conversations: the mode of discourse is itself entirely open. This very openness can lead to a sense of repetitiveness: the reader may feel that he has got the point quite early on. But it is the strength of Canetti's mode of creative exposition that he is not out to prove anything and that his terminology does not imprison enquiry. *Masse* and *Macht* are more resonant and more menacing than their English equivalents – the word 'crowd' suggests flower-shows and football matches rather than the forces inherent in a human mass – and the material of Canetti's book is mythic and historical rather than contemporary, though it can also be curiously prophetic, as is indicated by cant modernisms like 'student power' and 'gay power'.

The nemesis of such an undertaking, steadfastly through so long a period of intellectual growth, must be that its director becomes himself charged in its emotional field. To study the operation of power is in some sense to love it; and Canetti's scorn for historians who enjoy the spectacle of power involuntarily and aesthetically cannot dissociate him entirely from their predicament. As a character of Saul Bellow's observes, the deepest ambiguity in intellectuals is that they despise the civilization which makes their lives possible, and prefer to contemplate one, or to create one mentally, in which this would cease to be so. But Canetti never commits that particular *trahison*. His calm, which is never ironic, can be directed against himself (he repeatedly queries the possibility of self-knowledge and praises Kafka for having come as near to it as a writer can). Some of the best things in *Crowds and Power* are detached essays or meditations, like that on immortality, the last infirmity of power, and the way a walk among the silent crowd in a cemetery feeds the sensation of it ('We draw from them the strength to become, and to remain for ever, *more* than they are'). Stendhal is again a favourite here, the least pretentious aspirant to immortality: such a writer 'will still be here when everyone else who lived at the same time is no longer here'. To live for ever in this way is Canetti's own expressed ambition.

His aura of extreme exclusiveness seldom irritates; even when, in his most brilliant essay, he does not so much explain Kafka as absorb him, the process seems biologically natural and benign – Kafka was the thinnest of men and Canetti is corpulent. *The Other Trial*, first published in Germany in 1969, analyses Kafka's correspondence with Felice Bauer, to whom he was twice engaged. Canetti sees these letters as decisive in Kafka's writing life: by writing to her, he discovered both how to love her and how himself to be a writer. Two nights after his first letter he writes 'The Judgement', the first tale which liberates his characteristic genius, in a single ten-hour sitting, by night, and a day or two later, 'The Stoker'. He produces six chapters of *Amerika*, and after an interval his finest short story of all, *The Metamorphosis*. It is a *mensis mirabilis* comparable to Pushkin's Boldino autumn, the most fertile writing period in Kafka's career.

He can feel she expects something of him, and he in turn expects of her an equal precision in recording her days and her feelings. 'He succeeds in imposing upon her his own obsession', his own way of being in love, which he would later transfer to her friend Grete Bloch. Felice has given him what she could, but he cannot give her marriage in return. He confronts her family and the two girls in Berlin, at what he called the 'Tribunal', with the war already impending, and a little later he begins *The Trial*, with its culminating scene of the two executioners leaning over Josef K like the two girls, their cheeks touching.

Canetti uses the word 'obduracy' to describe the way Kafka protected 'the tremendous world he felt to be in his head' – a new world in which the human situation appears in art in a new way. Canetti rejects any idea that Kafka is exploring the nature of God or the Divine Law: it is power itself, in its ultimately and impersonally human shape, which executes Josef K and oppresses the hero of *The Castle*. The implication of Canetti's short book, which reads like one of Kafka's own compelling stories, is that the truest and most significant modern literature can be seen as a withdrawal from power, even from literature's own magnificent pageant of mastery as it appears in the great creations of naming, recording and enjoying, in the worlds of Homer, Shakespeare, Milton or Dante. Kafka must find mastery in minuteness, in disappearance.

Kafka's sovereign perspective on psychoanalysis ought to have helped critics to detach from its constricting domain his own person at least. His struggle with his father was essentially never anything but a struggle against superior power as such . . . Since he fears power in any form, since the real aim of his life is to withdraw from it, in whatever form it may appear, he detects it, identifies it, names it, and creates figures of it in every instance where others would accept it as being nothing out of the ordinary . . . *Macht* and *mächtig* are his unavoided, unavoidable words.

Marriage is out of the question. The place of smallness in it is usurped by children, whom Kafka envied and disapproved of because they are not actually small beings who want to dwindle and disappear, as he wants to, but 'false smallnesses' who want to grow bigger. Himself an expert on Chinese literature, where the idea of smallness – in insects or animals – is subtly explored and imagined, Canetti claims that Kafka 'belongs in its annals', and quotes for this the authority of Arthur Waley, for whom Kafka was the one Western prose author to be read with passionate attention.

Canetti's feeling for the Orient is perceptible in *The Voices of Marrakesh*, a unique travel book, and, together with *Kafka's Other Trial*, the most formally satisfying of his works. A sentence referring to Kafka's letters gives the clue to the way he enters into and conveys to us the baffling and yet familiar quality of strangers met in such a scene: 'They are so enigmatic and familiar to me that it seems they have been mental possessions of mine from the moment when I first began to accommodate human beings entirely in my mind, in order to arrive, time and again, at a fresh understanding of them.' That sort of accommodation is the key to Canetti's creative vision, with its peculiar blend of intense abstraction and equally stunning physical reality, constantly creating images of power where others would see 'nothing out of the ordinary'.

Though he is a scholar and a man of the mind, Canetti's sense of human societies and his gift – as in the Marrakesh book – for familiarizing out-of-the-way places have something in common with the art of another and earlier Nobel Prize-winner, Rudyard Kipling. But the timely comparison and contrast is with a more recent winner, the Polish poet Czeslaw Milosz. Both authors have written in a wide range of forms and both are exiles – Milosz in America – though in Canetti's case exile is itself a mode made for genius, for his country is the entire European tradition. Milosz's wonderful record of a Polish-Lithuanian childhood, *The Issa Valley*, should be enjoyed together with Canetti's *Geschichte* of his own early years in Bulgaria and England, Switzerland and Vienna. Both are subtle analysts and historians of national fixations and complexities. There are, it is true, poems by Milosz – one of the great poets of our time – which move the reader more directly than anything by Canetti, who is by adoption a German *Dichter* but not

in the naive and direct sense a poet. He enchants and enlightens but
does not make the tears flow. But what a pair! The fact that two such
remarkable writers should have won it in recent years almost makes
one believe in the prize as an 'award' to literature.

Czeslaw Milosz

1. Emperor of the Earth: Modes of Eccentric Vision

Being Polish is of course no joke, but Polish intellectuals tend to possess a detachment and a kind of sardonic equilibrium unpretended to by, say, their Irish equivalents. There is nothing peripheral about Poland; indeed there is something almost painfully central in her position as mediator between two cultures and powers of which she is also the historical victim. To put it schematically: a French intellectual dances with an idea in a graceful minuet whose steps are self-determined by his language; a Russian is crushed by an idea and lies under it passively, like a man under a stone. Reaching out to France, Polish intelligence none the less remains clear-eyed about *la grande nation*, and can recognize the power of the Russian genius without succumbing to its *idées fixes*.

This is pre-eminently the case with the Polish critic and philosopher Czeslaw Milosz. His essays belong to a genre now alas nearly extinct, in which the man of letters combines with the thinker, critic of literature and ideology, and political commentator, each mingling with the other without any reliance on a metaphysical stance or persona. Milosz teaches in California, but in their different ways other Polish writers like Kolakowski and Morawski – the latter still from Warsaw – continue something of the same tradition.

Although Milosz's subject-matter in *Emperor of the Earth* is as modern as the latest hijack, he himself has the freedom and detachment that goes with a certain kind of old-fashioned literary good manners – Polish manners perhaps, the kind we are aware of in the prose of Conrad. A key essay in this collection is on the Russian-Jewish philosopher Lev Shestov, born in Kiev and thus in a historical sense as much Pole as Russian, and the most elegant incisive Russian stylist of this century. Shestov, as Milosz says, 'is probably the most readable philosophic essayist', developing arguments which 'especially in their original Russian, captivate the reader with their scornful vigour'. In a sense his philosophy is that of Conrad in *Lord*

Jim – the lifetime's jump in the dark and what follows – and without knowing Kierkegaard he explored lines of thought that reached many of the same conclusions. He was revered by Camus and by Simone Weil.

Milosz begins his essay with the mention of a young woman, a Romanian refugee in Paris, who lived a frugal and solitary life, like Razumov in *Under Western Eyes*, trying to support herself by writing, and then contracted cancer of the breast from which she died. When Milosz visited her she had just discovered Shestov, whom she urged him to read. Shestov did not console her so much as give her company in 'the purity of despair':

Shestov . . . lacked the polite indoctrination one received at Western European universities; he simply did not care whether what he was saying about Plato or Spinoza was against the rules of the game – that is, indecent. It was precisely because of this freedom that his thought was a gift to people who found themselves in desperate situations and knew that syntactic cocoons were of no use any more. Sorana Gurian was after all an agnostic, largely beyond the pale of religious tradition, and not a philosopher in the technical sense of the term. Whom could she read? Thomas Aquinas? Hegel? Treatises in mathematical logic? Or, better still, should she have tried solving crossword puzzles?

What does a creature that calls itself 'I' want for itself? It wants to be.

But Milosz keeps a cool eye on Shestov, well aware of the extent to which he has buried himself under the stone of his idea, and given even that stank idea its own metaphysical status. As Camus put it in *The Myth of Sisyphus:* 'For Shestov reason is useless, but there is something beyond reason. For the absurd mind reason is useless and there is nothing beyond reason.' But even that formula escapes total bereavement through its very neatness. Milosz's main emphasis, however, is on the need to ask 'why that?' about the position of any abstract thinker, to connect his attitude with his 'personal tragedy', never setting aside, as some have wished to do, 'Kierkegaard's sexual impotence, or Nietzsche's incurable disease'.

My guess is that Shestov, too, had his own drama, that of lacking the talent to become a poet, to approach the mystery of existence more directly than through mere concepts.

That would go some way to explaining his sardonic attitude to what the great creators, like Tolstoy and Dostoevsky, thought they were doing, and especially perhaps to Tolstoy's insistence that Ivan Illyich, who 'wants to *be*' but is pushed into death's black bag, none the less sees light at the bottom of that bag.

Milosz's point connects Shestov, like many another, with thwarted creators whose criticism insists on the authority that creation would have given it as of right. But unlike such a one as Leavis, Shestov was never a preacher. The stoicism which, as he pointed out, 'has survived under many disguises and is still with us' is also both a witty and – like so much Russian intellectualism – a basically irresponsible affair. Like Sidney Smith he might have urged us to take short views – no further than dinner or tea – for though cheerfulness should be the product of despair rather than of reason it is also a question of accepting the 'I'. Shestov destested Pascal's 'Le moi est haïssable.'

The Shestov essay goes with the one which gives the collection its title, an examination of the odd production by the Russian mystic Solovyov entitled *The Conversations on War, Progress and the End of World History, Including a Short Tale of the Antichrist and Supplements*. Solovyov's fantasy about the future (he was the generation before Shestov) imagines a figure whom both Shestov and Dostoevsky would instantly have recognized, the paramount symbolic figure, one might say in Russian mystics' 'science fiction' – the Grand Inquisitor, the benevolent and effective Antichrist who has both the will and the power to heal all human material ills. Milosz tells us that he became interested in Solovyov after seeing Signorelli's marvellous frescoes of the Antichrist legend in the cathedral in Orvieto:

Of the two Christian traditions concerning the Antichrist, one conceives of him as an incarnation of pure unconcealed evil, and the other as a liar feigning meekness, a wolf in sheep's clothing. Solovyov, as Luca Signorelli before him, adopted the second tradition, modifying it in his own way; his own idea was the Antichrist who strives and obtains much good, deceiving not only others but himself as well.

Milosz's sense of the application to eastern Europe is obvious enough, and we too, with our Wedgwood Benns and others, are habituated to leaders feigning meekness, who do good by deceiving us and themselves. But the historical interest of Solovyov, as of Shestov himself, is their opposition to all the numerous progeny of Fourier and of Tolstoyism. *Three Conversations* is essentially an anti-Tolstoyan tract – Tolstoy appears in it as the spokesman called the Prince. The superman of the twenty-first century combines enormous intellectual capacity with impeccable ethical standards, and not knowing he is Antichrist, considers his vocation to be the organizing of society so that the commands of the Gospel are implemented.

Solovyov wrote it – as Shestov contends and Milosz would agree – out of fright at the fact that he was himself beginning to come to some of the same conclusions as Tolstoy in a humanization of the Gospel, conclusions which from the best of motives, seek to 'sterilize' the essentially tragic nature of religion. Only a tragic religion can protect us from the final solution and the *apparatchiks'* paradise. The Shestovan centre of such a religion is to *be yourself*, like Dostoevsky's Underground Man – don't let reason or optimism make you into anything else. Neither he nor Solovyov are reactionaries in any obvious political sense, but both are sceptical of the happiness and well-being that comes from rendering both what is God's and Caesar's unto Caesar. The argument is familiar, but Milosz's eye on Poland gives it for him a special sardonic interest; Catholicism there does not want to be a Shestovan religion of despair, but is in a sense compelled to be by the logic of its resistance to the *apparatchiks'* regime.

A somewhat bizarre aspect of *Three Conversations*, incidently, which Milosz brings out in his essay 'Science Fiction and the Coming of Antichrist', is that the Antichrist will eventually be given his come-uppance by a Zionist state of thirty million Jews. A million-man-strong Jewish army will thwart his attempt to set up the government of the world in Jerusalem, and he and his troops will be swallowed up by a fiery crater near the Dead Sea. Orthodox Israelis might smile quietly at this and secular ones grimace; but Milosz points out that any such prediction and a *rapprochement* with non-humanist Christianity would have seemed grotesque at the time. Unfortunately Solovyov disregarded the Arabs.

The other essays in the collection are more marginal but no less interesting. 'On Pasternak Soberly' starts from a curiously Shestovan premise:

The paradox of Pasternak lies in his narcissistic art leading him beyond the confines of his ego. Also in his reedlike pliability, so that he often absorbed *les idées reçues* without examining them thoroughly as ideas, but without being crushed by them either.

Milosz goes on to develop a new theory about the structure of *Dr Zhivago*. According to the official doctrine in Soviet Russia vigorous fiction could only be produced by a vigorously ascending class, such as the English bourgeoisie in the eighteenth century. The victoriously burgeoning proletariat should produce an equally vigorous fiction, with socialist realism as its method. That this has not been a total success may be due to the fact that it is the bureaucracy rather than the proletariat which has burgeoned. But suppose Pasternak to have accepted the logic of the first part of the argument, and actually followed the party-line exhortation to learn from the early classics of the novel?

Nobody heeded the repeated advice to learn from the 'classics': an invitation to joyous movement addressed to people in straitjackets is no more than a crude joke . . . but what if somebody, in the spirit of spite, tried to learn? *Dr Zhivago*, a book of hide and seek with fate, reminds me irresistibly of one English novel: Fielding's *Tom Jones*.

The early days of the Revolution in fact saw something very like a picaresque society, a human anthill on fire which could produce any number of extraordinary meetings and unbelievable coincidences. And these are not symbolic. Distrusting modern Western fiction as supplied by tired magicians whose last trick is to tell how the trick is done, Pasternak went back to an early classic, suggests Milosz, and followed the party line in a literal but disconcerting sense.

There is a fascinating essay on Mayne Reid, the Ulsterman who emigrated to America, took enthusiastic part in all forms of American expansionism while denouncing the British Empire, and wrote tales of the Wild West which are still immensely popular in Poland and the Soviet Union. Milosz slyly suggests that the American expansionist concepts of 'manifest destiny' and the 'universal design of providence' may through the circulation of these stories have influenced the Russian intelligentsia at grassroots level and operated in much the same way as Hegelian and Marxist ideas of historical development. 'Holy Russia had the right to conquer and oppress other nations because the Spirit of History had assigned her a mission.' Polish intellectuals, who frequently ended up there, solaced themselves by seeing a Mayne Reid Wild West in Siberia. Not so, perhaps, Joseph Conrad's father, a remarkable man whose strong spiritual influence over his son's novels is traced by Milosz with sympathy and understanding. Both are Shestov men. Again and again in the son's novels we hear as it were the words of father Apollo Korzeniowski from his exile in Chernigov. 'Everything that surrounds me bids me doubt the existence of a divine omnipotence, in which I none the less place all my faith.'

Milosz recurs frequently to his Shestovan theme of the uncons-

cious duplicities in the greatest Russian fiction. Taking the term from
Anna Akhmatova, he describes both Tolstoy and Dostoevsky as
'heresiarchs' in their efforts, often 'fuzzy' and 'wild', to 'adapt
Christianity to what they believed to be the needs of modern
man'. Milosz conjectures that Dostoevsky is enough on the side of
his Grand Inquisitor to feel a secret despair at the certainty that he
will triumph, a despair only papered over by his attempt to find a
third way, 'clinging to Holy Russia with the peasant below and the
tsar above as the only possible mainstay of Christianity and
consequently of human freedom'. Dostoevsky's truer despair may
appear not in that genial solipsist the Underground Man, whom
Shestov considered his most significant character, but in the
appalling figure of Svidrigailov, the man who is 'nothing in
particular', and whom Milosz, himself born in Lithuania, notes to be
the only character in Dostoevsky with a Lithuanian name (Count
Svidrigaila was a well-known historical figure of the fifteenth
century) and thus with the provenance of his own family.

As can be seen, Milosz seldom loses the chance of a dig at the great
Russians, however much he admires them – they have an invigorat-
ing effect on his criticism as much as they had a curiously deadening
effect on Conrad's art – but it is fair to say that his preferred Polish
writers are those like Stanislaw Brzozowski – a 'one-man army' –
whose refusal to subscribe to the conventional Polish dismissal of all
things Russian makes him even now anathema to the *bien pensants*
of his country – 'even though there has hardly been one literary
discussion in Poland in which his name has not figured . . . there has
not even been such a memorial as a posthumous edition of his
collected works in his native country'.

Finally, one should not omit to mention the brief and moving
essay that begins the book, 'Brognart: A Story told over a drink'.
This is a story in the sense that Conrad would begin a story with a
victim of circumstance, like the foreigner who came out of the sea to
marry Amy Foster; but this story has neither art, meaning, nor
denouement, only the kind of bizarre and total pathos which a
Polish situation can produce and a Polish sensibility comprehend.
Brognart was a young French boy, high-minded, intelligent, and
enterprising, who had a pen-friend in Torun, Poland. He visited the
Polish family in summer 1939. When the Germans invaded he
managed to get out into neutral Russia, hoping to contact a French
consulate. He was arrested and sent to a camp in the east. He
survived until 1951, never accepting the fate that had befallen him,
and seeking successfully by many methods to let it be known back

home. His family petitioned Thorez, the Secretary of the French
Communist Party: in vain. It was an anomalous case, and nothing
was done. Nothing has ever been done, except that Milosz has now
put a name and a fate on record.

2. Return of the Native

'*Bin gar keine Russin, stamm' aus Litauen, echt deutsch.*' (I am not
Russian at all; I come from Lithuania, a true German.) The twelfth
line of *The Waste Land*, a fragment from the poet's reading in a
German memoir, raises more echoes than even T. S. Eliot was likely
to be aware of, and certainly more than are grasped by most of his
readers. The connection with the poem is minimal, but as in so many
of its other lines randomness has achieved an air of inevitability, in
its suggestion of unhappy and not-so-far-off things, unknown lives,
and fates, the product of complex histories, the inspissated rivalries
and relations of Lithuanians, Balts and Letts, Jews, Germans, and
Russians.

With them no one could have a more natural familiarity than the
poet and winner of the 1980 Nobel Prize for literature, Czeslaw
Milosz. He too stemmed from Lithuania. But not with any
conviction of purity; and during a century when the now small but
once enormous country has been successively Russian, German,
Polish, Lithuanian, Russian, German, and now Soviet Russian
again. Like most of the native sons of the town known in Polish as
Wilno (German and Russian *Wilna*, Lithuanian *Vilnius*), Milosz is a
Polish speaker, and it was in Polish that he began to write his poems.
With a hint of irony he remarks that natives of his province are more
inward, with the deeper intimacies of the Polish language, than are
their metropolitan cousins at the centre in Warsaw. The 'Polish
Pushkin', Adam Mickiewicz, foremost of native poets, began to
write under the inspiration of the land of Polish Lithuania.

But whereas a poet from Dublin or Edinburgh would advance in
all seriousness the proposition that the English language at its
liveliest and most sensitive was to be found in those towns (and a
bookish native of New York, Chicago, or Los Angeles might do the
same), Milosz is unquestionably amused by the complacency of his
own 'claim that languages are richest at their cultural edges.
Nationality is not a thing he can take seriously: it would be hard to
imagine a greater writer more emancipated from even its most subtle
pretensions.

Nevertheless his genius flourishes and finds its subject in the many degrees of consciousness nationality implies; and to feast on such things and yet remain free of them is in itself a gift of genius. Language and nationality are haunts of the irrational. They are also the root of the well-grown ego, the base of that *samodovolnost* – self-satisfaction – which Tolstoy (whose forebears, before rising in the Tsar's service, had themselves stemmed from Lithuania) perceived as the beginning of all lively and healthy human activity. Our natures grow and flourish by denaturing those who are not planted in the same bed. The snobberies of race and language are even more needful in us, more deeply intertwined in the unconscious, than the associated snobberies of class. And, so far from diminishing, this tribal metality is now everywhere more virulent, more local, than ever before.

Native Realm: A Search for Self-Definition – reissued – is thus an autobiography with a real title, and not just a fashionable quest for roots. The genius of Milosz is far too confident for him to wish to 'rediscover' himself: it is a question of seeking to embody in consciousness and in poetry the individual's complex and precious sense of itself. Looking back in 1968, when the book was first published in both Polish and English, he saw the forests and swamps of Lithuania as a rich manure heap out of which grows the butterfly of a detached and poetical awareness. With his secret fastidious humour, his natural delicacy, Milosz is fascinated by the vagaries of class in such a situation, no less than by those of race and language. Abruptly, when Milosz was a child, Lithuania became a sovereign state again, a minor result of the cataclysm of the First World War, which had severed one Tsarist province from another, as if New Jersey abruptly found itself an independent neighbour of New York, a contiguity that brought out every old sort of enmity and rivalry and fostered a whole lot of new ones.

Lithuanians now reserved their animus particularly for Poles, whom they assumed, not without justification, to be gentry, landlords, and oppressors, disaffected from the new state, as in the case of Ireland or Finland, but with a special degree of complication that could only be found in the marches of Eastern Europe. With the incomprehensible logic of time the Lithuanians, tardy converts to Catholicism, had slipped into the position of perpetual peasants, uncouth younger sons, their new religious devotion confirming their ineradicably junior status. In the days of their pagan ascendancy, worshippers of Peruna, the god of thunder, of the oak tree, and of Ragutis, the leering corpulent satyr hewn from it, had conquered all Eastern Europe to Kiev under their grand dukes Gudimin and Olgerd, and in the spirit of such a conquest had entered into partnership with the Poles. With the help of religion the Poles soon reduced them to the state of country cousins.

Northward, superiorities were of a Teutonic kind, bourgeois and Lutheran. It is significant that in Milosz's wonderful autobiographical novel, *The Issa Valley*, a Lithuanian peasant speaks admiringly of life in Sweden – the Swedes too, like everyone else in that quarter, have been through Lithuania in their time – and of the prosperous northern neighbour as a model state for rural egalitarianism. And though the gentry spoke Polish, Lithuania still had its language, one of the oddest and most ancient of Indo-Germanic survivals, akin to Sanskrit, the object of studious enquiry by philologists in Munich and Berlin. To have such a language was itself a form of superiority.

In *The Issa Valley*, which appeared in translation for the first time in 1981, Milosz portrays himself as Thomas, grandson of a minor landowner whose gentility is based on Poland and Polish, though his name and some of his forebears are Lithuanian. The novel is an idyll of immense charm and poetic depth, a story without much conventional plot about a boy growing up in the Lithuanian countryside and raised largely by grandparents proud of their Polish background. The sensitive translation by Louis Iribarne gives at least a good idea of what must be the quality of the original, first published by an émigré press in Paris in 1955. Its quality lies in its solidity – it is as solid as the oak-hewn figure of Ragutis himself.

The portraits in this novel will remind readers of those classic figures drawn from Tolstoy in *Childhood and Boyhood*, and by Aksakov in his family memoirs. But Milosz is more humane than Tolstoy and less 'creamy' (in literary historian Prince Mirsky's word) than Aksakov. The child of *The Issa Valley* accepts his elders with unconscious and uncomprehending love, but the pattern of their days and their being is created with a great poet's unobtrusively vivid power. As the book progresses we understand more and more of the nature and outlook of the hero's grandfather, who is at first a painting in words, like Ghirlandaio's *Old Man*. The hero's grandmothers are similarly memorable. One despises regular meals and nibbles titbits of sweet and sour, lifting her skirts to warm herself at the porcelain stove. The other, raised in cities, lives a more anxious life like a squirrel in its hole. Her death near the book's conclusion is a sign to the young hero – his first – of his true identification with the ground she goes to rest in.

Meantime he's growing up, hunting and dreaming, taking in portents both from nature and from the age-old accessibility of the human consciousness around him. He communes, too, with lives that form sub-plots to the novel: the mistress of the priest who killed herself with rat poison when he sent her away; the forester haunted by the Russian soldier he has stalked and killed in the forest; a Polish small land-owner who teaches the hero to shoot, and whose Lithuanian housekeeper – primitive, contemptuous, and bewitching – leads her own mysterious life in a corner of the narrative.

It is an ancient world over which Milosz has mastery here, but there is nothing self-conscious in its ancientness. I have stressed the Lithuanian provenance of Milosz because it seems to me the clue to something in his work that is unique today: the reality of the *thing*, the return of the *thing*. It is no accident that structuralism and deconstruction, as critical and reading techniques, have banished physical realities from literature, replacing them with the abstract play of language, 'the game of the signifiers'. They were on their way out anyway; they were leaving literature; and the critical process, as usual, found ways of explaining and rationalizing their departure, even of suggesting they had never been there.

Why 'things', in this profound sense, should have faded out of literature, leaving not even the grin of a Cheshire cat, is a question of great complexity, but one reason is certainly what has to be termed the Americanization of the field of literature itself. Things, in the sense in which the nineteenth-century novel – Dickens and Hardy and Tolstoy – both assumed and created them have not been central to the American literary consciousness. In their place have been legends and ideas and consciousness itself. The Deep South and Wild West with its Indians and cowboys which captivated the European imagination (Milosz often refers to them as part of his own boyhood awareness) did so because they had never existed. Like so many other American stories these were an effort of consciousness to create experience, to give itself something to live by.

In Europe things preceded consciousness; in America they had to be created and commemorated by it. Most literary creation in

America is factitious, in the sense that it has to be an advertisement for itself; and this leads naturally to the world of actual advertising – of news, of lifestyles, of literary fields – which dominates the modern consciousness. New styles of reading and of analysing texts represent a recognition and an intellectualization of this process, which has come to be the norm in every contemporary culture.

It takes a masterpiece to reveal the sheer unreality of our modern creative modes and poses, and Milosz's novel is such a masterpiece. Its account of childhood in a valley inhabited by an 'unusually large number of devils' has no obvious originality, nor is it in any sense a strikingly distinctive work; but, strangely enough, even the fact that it is a translation only appears to accentuate its closeness to real things, for it seems to be about those things and not about the author's invention of them, odd or novel. It makes us realize the extent to which an American masterpiece tends to be about itself only, and has to be. *Winesburg, Ohio; Appointment in Samarra; The Great Gatsby; The Heart Is a Lonely Hunter* – they all have to clutch their discoveries to themselves, creating a new consciousness that does duty as a new world. Such comparisons are not wholly invidious; it is a fact that a writer like Milosz is effortlessly master of a primeval world, of which the art of the West no longer has any conception, and can only reconstitute in solipsistic magic, the supermarkets gothicism of Edna O'Brien or Joyce Carol Oates. Even Faulkner's world is as willed as theirs, crafted straight from vacancy into myth and symbol.

The significance of this was touched on accidentally by Milosz himself in his essay 'On Pasternak Soberly', printed in the collection entitled *Emperor of the Earth*, published in 1977. *Dr Zhivago*, he writes, has been misunderstood in the West because we have forgotten how to read and to recognize a primitive work. All those events and objects and people, the products of that hymn 'Eternal Memory' which is being chanted in the first sentence – these are real, with the reality conferred by primary art; they are not the 'web of symbols' ingeniously discovered by Edmund Wilson, just as they are not the soap opera, with the 'Lara theme' and the sword-waving Cossacks dashing over the snow, into which the publicity agents of the West converted them. But *Dr Zhivago* is a primitive tale about a society in an ageless state of barbarism now grown dynamic, full of the chances, the coincidences, the collisions that actually occur in such a society and thus in a story about it. Milosz points out, for example, that Yuri Zhivago's half-Asiatic natural brother Yevgraf, who appears mysteriously from time to time to sort out his problems, and who has been taken as some kind of symbolic figure, is in fact just the kind of person you find both in Soviet and in primitive heroic societies – the archetypal Great One who offers some protection against perpetual threats and hazards.

Of course there is a strong element of pastiche in *Dr Zhivago*, an element of *fin-de-siècle* fantasy, and *The Issa Valley* is not free from pastiche either. It could hardly be otherwise with a book written today about a boy growing up in the small valley, the countryside of the author's childhood. But both Pasternak and Milosz are poets, poets of the first class though of very different kinds, and this difference is shown in the texture of their prose. In the case of Milosz experience emerges as a quality that overrides the impossibilities of translation. A poet so good that he can be translated is a supreme paradox, one which many poets today, and readers of poetry, would refuse to recognize, so strong is the tendency now for poetry only to congeal and inhere in the carefully exploited accuracies and idiosyncrasies of a language.

But if nobody thought Dante and Shakespeare untranslatable it was because of what they said; how they said it was of course another matter. The fact that what Milosz says comes across with such primary force and impact is itself an indication that, as a poet in the largest sense, he is an ideal kind of recipient of the Nobel Prize. It is possible that there are real differences here, though of a wholly indefinable kind, in the nature of languages themselves: some are more amenable than others to moving sideways, to acquiring a kind of international potential. Not for nothing, perhaps, was Esperanto invented in Poland.

In *Native Realm* Milosz writes with admirable humour and dispassion about the lightness of his native tongue, its adaptability, its centuries-old cultivated Westernness, as contrasted with the poise and weight, the inevitability, as it were of Russian syllables and syntax. Observing that his countrymen are fascinated by Russian because it 'liberates their Slavic half', because in its menace and seduction it 'is all there is to know about Russia', Milosz tells how he and his friends used to perform a certain exercise which gave them 'a good deal to think about'. First they uttered in a bass voice the Russian words for 'A deep hole dug with a spade', and then chattered quickly in a tenor the verbally very similar Polish equivalent.

The arrangement of accents and vowels in the first phrase connotes gloom, darkness, and power; in the second, lightness, clarity, and weakness. In other words, it was both an exercise in self-ridicule and a warning.

Be that as it may, it is certainly true that such Russian syllables, if they become poetry, are untranslatable in consequence. Milosz discovered Pushkin on his own, which is the right way to do it, and was captivated. 'My native tongue was incapable of such power of expression, of such masterful iambs, and I had to admit it.' But as an embryonic poet he soon began to distrust the lyricism 'which seemed to unfold from itself as if born of the very sounds themselves'. Pushkin doesn't happen to talk about a deep hole dug with a spade, though if he did it would become poetry, as it does when he writes of 'the sea where ships were running', or 'a forest on the banks of the Dnieper'. Such poetry is untranslatable because it says nothing, but exists merely and absolutely in its own tongue, and so in another language is flat and banal.

The poetry of Milosz, as of Mickiewicz, is not like that; it has a timbre, a clarity of desire, an urgency of sense which forces itself out of its own language into others. The Spanish of Neruda, the Italian of Montale, can today still do the same, availing themselves of the Latin camaraderie which is so immanent also in Polish religion and culture, if not in the language itself. In the lines of Mickiewicz's 'Forefather's Eve', which Milosz quotes, there is an acoustic forcefulness which proclaims itself as poetry in whatever language. The poet's hatred for Russian tyranny contrasts with his sympathy for its victims, whom he sees not from the inside, as Pushkin and Gogol did, but with the brutally lucid incredulity of an outsider. He contrasts the faces of Europeans, an articulate record of intelligible emotion and feeling, with the Russian face.

> Here, people's eyes, like the cities of this country
> Are large and clear; never does the soul's tumult
> Move the pupil with an extraordinary glance;
> Never does desolation cloud them over long.
> Seen from a distance they are splendid, marvellous;
> Once inside, they are empty and deserted.
> The body of this people is like a fat cocoon,
> Inside which sleeps a caterpillar-soul . . .
> But when the sun of freedom shall rise,
> What kind of insect will fly out from that shroud?

A poem written by the young Milosz, before the war, will serve as an example of his special quality, as well as of his extraordinary translatability. Written in 1936 and collected in *Bells in Winter* (1978), it is called 'Encounter'.

We were riding through frozen fields in a wagon at dawn
A red wing rose in the darkness.
And suddenly a hare ran across the road.
One of us pointed to it with his hand.
That was long ago. Today neither of them is alive,
Not the hare, nor the man who made the gesture.
O my love, where are they, where are they going
The flash of a hand, streak of movement, rustle of pebbles.
I ask not out of sorrow, but in wonder.

Even more striking than the fact that this poetry remains poetry in another language – with the advantage, it is true, of having been translated in collaboration with the poet himself – is the sense of a shared experience that Milosz manages to give, a limpid repose upon the way things are that is no less than our sense of wonder at them. What prompted the writing of *The Issa Valley* in 1955 was the same kind of emotion that found expression in this poem, and Milosz was then an exile in America, collecting and perpetuating the wonderings of his adolescence.

There is in a way nothing personal about them. Milosz's world is collective – a place for everything and everything in its place. He is one of the few poets who do not give the impression of seeing something in his own special way. The self in his poetry is not impersonal but effortlessly manifold, like the emotions and sensations in its records. As he puts it in his poem 'Ars Poetica?' which appears in *Bells in Winter*:

The purpose of poetry is to remind us
how difficult it is to remain just one person,
for our house is open, there are no keys in the doors,
and invisible guests come in and out at will.

We become our relations, our moments, each other, even our graves; at least we do so if we live in the kind of dense and populous relation with the world which Milosz records and celebrates. The relation to the past moment in his poem is the same as that to his grandmother's grave in *The Issa Valley*. In *The Issa Valley* too we see the beginnings of the poem 'Diary of a Naturalist', however much later on that poem was written, in an experience of the young boy.

One winter Thomas spotted an ermine on the bank of the river Issa. Frost and sunlight made the twigs of the bushes on the steep shore of the opposite bank stand out like bouquets of gold, lightly tinged with gray and bluish purple. It was then that a ballet dancer of remarkable grace and ability would appear on the ice, a white sickle that would arch and straighten again. With a gaping mouth Thomas stared at it in bewilderment and ached with desire. To have. If he had had a rifle with him he would have shot it, because one could not simply stand still when one's wonder demanded that the thing arousing it be preserved for ever.

The overwhelming impulse that wished to have the creature – shoot it if need be – later became the impulse of the poet. Milosz does not sentimentalize the adolescent's worship of nature, as predatory as the beasts it moves among. *The Issa Valley* is full of hunting and hunting expeditions, as memorable as those in *Pan Tadeusz*, or Aksakov and Turgenev. Of particular note is the stalking of the capercailzie (the translation, in most respects excellent, calls it a grouse – quite a different bird) when that fabulous fowl of the spruce woods, as wary as a cat throughout most of the year, is temporarily deafened by the noise of its own ritual mating call.

The characters in *The Issa Valley* – grandfather, grandmothers, neighbours, the local forester, are all members of a household, even though the Lithuanian peasant shows at moments an atavistic hostility to the Polish *pan*, or local gentry. As in Tolstoy, the more closely integrated the members of a family, the more peculiarly individual they appear. In this pre-American melting pot the racial and social mix produces not uniformity but a matured exactness of distinction, of the kind found in nature itself and worshipped by Milosz when he writes as a botanist and ornithologist.

That habit of exactness explains the twin paradox of Milosz's distinction as a poet: his sense of things as they are, and yet his power – almost a conscious power it sometimes seems – of projecting what he writes out of the absolute linguistic form which poetry usually demands. His own poetic temperament and upbringing again offer a clue. He has a sense of a poet as 'not just one person', an instinct akin to Keats's perception of the poet as a man in whom personality has been exorcised in the intensities of negative capability. But Keats's poetry, in all its richness, its vulnerability as language, is held down to the very words in which it was first uttered. Milosz's seems to aspire to some ideal language, almost to Wordsworth's 'ghostly language of the ancient earth', and not the earth only – the sky too, the steady rationale of a sentient universe.

It is the same with the novel. Despite its immensely local subject and setting there is nothing in the least provincial about it. A friend of Milosz, the poet Tomás Venclova, a native of Vilnius Wilno, notes the same characteristic about it from the viewpoint of a native professional, a connoisseur, as it were, of the interplay of linguistic factors, and of their transcendence.

It always seems to me that this novel belongs to a certain conceivable, ideal Lithuanian literature. In that literature [as in the work of Donelaitis] we have these types and motifs, there are these landscapes and seasons, but, alas, we have no novel in which everything could be united into such an integral and beautiful entity. The novel belongs to Polish literature. However, from a certain point of view, this is ultimately unimportant. (Tomás Venclova, 'Despair and Grace', from the *Literary Quarterly* of the University of Oklahoma, Summer 1978.)

Unimportant because a true transcendence of nationalism is produced not by simplification and standardization but precisely by the linguistic interplay, rivalry and synthesis of which the background of Milosz's writing affords such a remarkable example.

There is another factor involved. The whole movement of American and English poetic writing, of such writing in the West in general, has tended towards the linguistic justification of the individual, of the poet as self-explorer and self-proclaimer. In proclaiming himself, Walt Whitman gave a voice to America, but the modern poet has for the most part settled to invent only his own language and his own self. By belonging to themselves – and to the poet – so completely, his poems elude any authenticity other than their own personal one; they not only avoid any other and wider version of themselves but disown it. Their art is devoted to remaining just one person, one poem, one life study. This is as true of Lowell and Berryman as it is of Philip Larkin and Seamus Heaney. The Irish poet writes fondly and with devout precision of the nature of bogs, of their soft dark provenance in his soul; but this is bog as he owns it, and he has found it – as Yeats found and made his own Ireland. That bog so dependent on its personal verbal artifact ('The squelch and slap / Of soggy peat, the curt cuts of an edge') is a far cry from the forest swamps of Lithuania, which, through Milosz's mediation and advocacy, are an open place alive with invisible guests and no longer centered in his own self.

This is not to attempt a qualitative judgement. Milosz is not better than the best poets of the West, but he is certainly different, and the difference declares itself as a question of open poetry and an open mind, an openness manifesting itself out of a society now closed by the Iron Curtain. The formidable talent of an American artist in our time seeks in one sense relief from freedom: it needs the prison of its own self-creation, one suggested in that grimly revealing little exchange between the painter Edward Hopper and an admirer – 'What are you after?' 'I'm after me.' Perhaps one can pay too high a price for one democratic tongue and one democratic kind of solitude.

Milosz is not after himself but after the old European goal of cultivation and understanding, enlightenment and *humanitas*. Often, no doubt, his open poetic pronouncements upon that goal may look like cliché, to poets and their readers conditioned to come at it – if at all – through the honing and perfecting of the ego. And there is a certain irony in the fact that while a poet and critic like Donald Davie may have learned from Milosz and deeply understood his old-fashioned creative intellectualism, Milosz is also admired in America by an open tradition of poetry which is the reverse of intellectual. As Milosz himself has recognized by quoting it in his own poetry, Ginsberg's *Howl* is paradoxically closer to his own poetic outlook than is that of the sophisticated and egocentric poetic styles of today.

Openness in Milosz as an artist is also rare in terms of his openness of genre. By writing in every form, he writes virtually in one: and he instructs in all. *Native Realm* and his earlier essay *The Captive Mind*, which first appeared in English in 1953, are among the most illuminating books to come out of recent history and its debate on ideology. It is so much an index of how good Milosz is as a critic, historian, and philosophical commentator that if one knew his work only in those reflective forms one would not guess that he is also a novelist and poet. Only very good poets and novelists have these comprehensive and Goethean abilities, though Milosz's creative outlook has none of Goethe's deliberative importance. He excels at the rapid focus, the quick glimpse that finds the inner dimension of a subject.

In one of his essays, 'Brognart: A Story Told Over a Drink', collected in *Emperor of the Earth*, he relates almost as Conrad might have done the story of a young Frenchman of peasant origins, who visited a friend in Poland in 1939 and was caught by the war. Because he remained bent, in his logical French fashion, on finding a consul and repatriating himself, because, in effect, he persisted in behaving as if he were not in a world where civilization had ceased to have meaning, he was eventually picked up by the Russians and shipped off to a camp near Archangelsk, where he lasted until 1951, still making efforts to get in touch with a French consul.

As a Pole, eternally caught between two incompatible power centres, Milosz profoundly understands the total incomprehension that exists between states and individuals of quite different provenance. No other phenomenon is historically more important, and its importance today continues to increase. It made any mutual understanding impossible between Neville Chamberlain and Hitler in 1939, and equally impossible between poor Brognart and his persecutors. Incidentally, this terrible little true story has something in common with Conrad's meticulous tale, 'Amy Foster', in which a shipwrecked immigrant pathetically attempts to adapt himself to life in an English village.

Milosz's essay on Apollo Korzeniowski, in *Emperor of the Earth*, the doomed, tormented, and idealistic father of Conrad the English novelist, is more illuminating in a few pages than most of the critical books on Conrad's novels. So, in a different way, is his passing reference to the fact that the Poles who would not let Jews join their first partisan detachments during the war would have been genuinely amazed if their behaviour had been criticized as racial discrimination – not that this was any comfort to the Jews. Such things to them were facts of nature; and as such were intimately connected with the fact that prewar Poland had nothing resembling the fanatical and hysterical anti-Jewish policy carried out in Germany. The 'gentrification' of that great Polish-Lithuanian *respublica* which stretched from the Baltic to the Black Sea may have been politically disastrous, as was shown in its easy liquidation by the servile empires of the Teutons and Slavs, but it also means that an idea of civilized behaviour, of moral *comme il faut*, penetrated from above into the humblest reaches of Polish society.

And yet Milosz's uncle, Oscar Milosz, himself half Jewish and a distinguished French poet, used to admonish his young nephew on his rare visits to the East to remember that 'in Europe there is nothing more stupid or more brutal in its petty hatreds than the Polish gentry'. And that was true too. The remarkable father of this cosmopolitan poet, who became the first Lithuanian delegate to the League of Nations, had been a Polish land-owner who saw a portrait of his future bride – she happened to be a beautiful Jewess – in a Warsaw shop. The fact that he determined on the spot to marry her was itself a manifestation of the proud independence befitting a Polish gentleman, but it also meant that his caste ostracized him and his family. For all his French domicile and reputation the son expressed as plangently as Chateaubriand a home-sickness for what he regarded as his native Lithuania – 'une vaste étendue de lacs obscurs, verdâtres et pourissants, envahis par une folie des tristes nymphéas jaunes, . . . O Maison, Maison! pourquoi m'avez-vous laissé partir?'

Milosz regained that home through writing about it in *The Issa Valley*. He was conscious always of the precarious and provisional nature of the country in which he grew up, and how complete would be its extinction when the moment came. France, he points out, survived a German invasion and conquest without undue discomfort, and would have done so even if the Germans had remained the winning side. For Poland – the new nation – defeat would mean calamity and extinction. The young Milosz got the nickname of 'catastrophist' from the tone of the poems he wrote in the years before the war, but, though history was to prove him altogether too accurate a prophet, his own survival during the time of apocalypse chastened him. He was too honest not to see that survival is its own form of humiliation, one that subdues not only the pride of the ideological visionary – and Milosz then was a believing Marxist and revolutionary – but the impulse to denunciation of such ideology, a counter-attitude.

Life itself, and the reverence for it, becomes then the precious thing to be explored and celebrated. It is this lucid humility which sets Milosz apart from Solzhenitsyn, a self-martyred soul who inhabits a country where conviction is more important than reflection, where the vowels are deeper, the shapes of speech more minatory. Solzhenitsyn's power as a writer demands that life should be intensified, directed and organized in the Russian style; Milosz's provenance makes him conservative and freedom-loving in a wholly different sense. In his novels and poetry, life and time are caught in an unending study of awareness: the gesture of a man pointing to a hare that runs across the road.

Life studies: Vasko Popa, *Collected Poems, 1943–1976*

Translating a good poet into poetry is a thankless task. When you have finished he will not look so good and, worse, he may seem to approximate to the manner of a number of other poets, whether foreign or writing in English. This loss of absolute individuality is bound to flatten in its turn the reader's powers of response, and give him nagging doubts about whether the poetry possessed it in the first place. Philip Larkin's straightforwardly insular objection to what is claimed to be distinguished foreign poetry is that it sounds so like the mediocre stuff that is always being produced at home. The 'once only' quality has vanished.

All the more remarkable that it has survived in this version (translated by Anne Pennington) of the complete poems of Vasko Popa, one of the best European poets writing today. The translation is in its way as good as Charles Johnston's recent version of *Evgeny Onegin*: that is to say it does not try any tricks but succeeds by sheer skill in keeping to the spirit, verve, and economy of the original. Its success does not look hard to achieve, but is; and that is the test. In this translation the precision and economy of Popa's poetry come alive, as in this example:

A CONCEITED MISTAKE
Once upon a time there was a mistake
So silly so small
That no one would even have noticed it

It couldn't bear
To see itself to hear of itself

It invented all manner of things
Just to prove
That it didn't really exist

It invented space
To put its proofs in
And time to keep its proofs
And the world to see its proofs

All it invented
Was not so silly
Nor so small
But was of course mistaken

Could it have been otherwise

As this shows, Popa's poetry is highly formalized. But it is not formalization in the senses of imagism or surrealism, though Popa (who is fifty-seven) was finding his style at a time when more or less precise and intelligent versions of surrealism were a common fashion in European poetry.

Cycles of poems link up in Popa's work to form both a human and a legendary landscape, the one included in the other. One of the most potent of Serbian legends is that of St Sava and the wolves, the wolves whom he tamed to become his flock and pastoral following. He is celebrated in a sequence beginning with the poem 'St Sava's Spring'.

. . . At the bottom of this water
Shines the crystal wolf-head
With a rainbow in its jaws

To wash in this water
Heals all pain of death
To drink of this water
All pain of life

Clear eye in the stone
Open for all
Who leave their black teardrop here

This sequence forms part of 'Earth Erect', a meditation on Serb history and the legendary figures of St Sava, Stephen the Tall, poet and warrior of the short-lived Serbian empire, and Prince Lazar, defeated and killed by the Turks at the decisive battle of Kossovo Polye – the Blackbirds' Field. Lazar before the battle is said to have had a vision in which he was offered victory and an earthly crown or defeat and a heavenly crown, and chose the latter: one might compare this part with Aleksandr Blok's poetic meditation on the field of Kulikovo, where Prince Dimitri of Moscow encountered the Tartars. In both cases history and myth seep naturally into the poet's apprehension of the present, without any feeling that he is making use of nationalism and folklore.

The poet–pilgrim of Popa's sequence returns to Belgrade, the white city, and to those questions of the present and future which in the medium of this poetic culture are at one with the past. In the same way the Marxist and materialist aspirations of a modern state and society mingle naturally with popular religious traditions and practices in the culture, the wolves of St Sava – his Serbian flock – and the fortified monastery with its miracle-working icon of the Mother of God with her three hands, two painted and the third, a votive offering, worked in silver. In the life of the poems these merge too into the life of the provincial town of Vershats, where the poet was born and brought up. The more personal poems are as effective in their domesticity, their saturation in friends and family affairs, as any of the other 'life studies' we are now accustomed to in contemporary poetry.

THE LAST DANCE
I am burying my mother
In the old overcrowded
New cemetery of Belgrade

The coffin is laboriously lowered
Into the shallow slit of grave
And rests on my father's

It soon disappears under the first clods

Two hatless young grave-diggers
Leap round on the invisible coffin
And pack down the earth

On their upraised spades
Shine two afternoon suns

My laughing mother
Would have been thrilled to watch
This dance in her honor

Serbo-Croat was only organized as a literary language at the beginning of the nineteenth century. In this it resembles another

Balkan language – otherwise wholly different – Rumanian. A sense of the young instrument and the old tradition makes affinities between Popa and such Rumanian poets as Blaga or Sorescu. In both cases the country's myths and its modernity blend together in a language which for poetry is both old and new. Serbo-Croat, a Slav language and close to Russian, shares the same history of Church Slavonic, and the same familiarity between the legendary uses of a language and its modern organized state. Although, and even because, it is in a sense 'new', such a language can be more at home over the whole stretch of a culture than would be possible in the more highly compartmented and stylized idioms of poetry written in English.

There is another important difference for the amateur of poetry to take into account. In whatever ways it may seem to resemble ours, this sort of European poetry is in fact far more *public* than anything now being written in English. One reason is simple: poetry – even good poetry – has in Eastern Europe the blessing of the state, however reluctantly given. Its relation with its audience is as close as that of propaganda, however little like propaganda it is. Its audience will not necessarily be either 'for' or 'against' the regime, and yet poems will excite an essentially public response to questions about life under state control, questions irrelevant in the private response of his readership to a poet writing today in English. And that public readership will be a much larger one. A printing of fifteen or twenty thousand would disappear from the bookshops of Belgrade or Bucharest in a couple of days. It would be the same in the case of Polish or Czech poets – Holub or Herbert – or the Hungarian Istvan Vas – all near contemporaries of Popa, and still more so in the case of new and younger poets coming on.

It is admirable that people should still want poetry and need it, whatever the reason. One reason, in fact, must be the enforced absence of variety, that great mass of surrogate and often degraded culture with which we are surrounded in the West. Few know the highest when they see it, and fewer of those invariably prefer it to the many alternatives available. In Eastern Europe it is sometimes only the best that is available. But the best is read by many without any real capacity to appreciate it, and this can be bad for a poet and his poetry. Through no fault of its own poetry may become too much a part of local and national culture. How is this not a good thing? Perhaps it is, or can be, but the fact remains that the best contemporary poetry in English – say Larkin's or Lowell's – has its life very much out of the way of official culture, very much out of the way of the *idea* of poetry in society. Its indeterminate privacy resists mass readership and popular integration – resists it involuntarily, since it is itself so much the product of a disintegrated culture.

Ted Hughes, who contributes a thoughtful introduction to these collected poems, is a great admirer of Popa and indeed may well have been influenced by him. Hughes has always had a nostalgia for vatic poetry, poetry that while appearing to be recondite can tap some deep vein of folk response. He attempted something of the sort in *Crow*, and even more so in *Gaudete*, a kind of melodrama of the national unconscious, a blood ritual which the reader was invited to join in. Popa is not like this: he has far more restraint, fastidiousness, and humour. It is only the culture he writes in that gives him something of the appearance of a successful popular poet. His leading characteristics are an extreme precision and tautness, yet he does not seem to be trying to be taut and precise; on the contrary, he seems friendly, relaxed, and forthcoming. Justly, if somewhat overdramatically, Ted Hughes refers to his 'intensely bracing moral vigilance'. And more generally of the poets of that generation who were involved in the destruction of Europe and its ambiguous rebirth, Hughes remarks that 'like men come back from the dead they have an improved perception, an unerring sense of what really counts in being alive'. What they have gone through has 'purged them of rhetoric'.

Their poetry is a strategy of making audible meanings without disturbing the silence, an art of homing in tentatively on vital scarcely perceptible signals, making no mistakes, but with no hope of finality, continuing to explore. Finally, with delicate maneuvering, they precipitate out of a world of malicious negatives a happy positive.

Though it is a fancy way of putting it, that may accurately describe how a poet like Hughes apprehends the creative process. Yet it does not ring quite true. Hughes has a nostalgia for the poetry of extreme situations that leads him, I think, to falsify the ways in which such experience was actually used by good poets who were in the midst of it. He seems sure that such poetry is quite different from any other, and by implication superior to any other – 'brought down to such precisions, discriminations and humilities that it is a new thing'.

I think it was Milosz, the Polish poet, who when he lay in a doorway and watched the bullets lifting the cobbles out of the street beside him realized that most poetry is not equipped for life in a world where people actually do die. But some is. And the poets of whom Popa is one seem to have put their poetry to a similar test.

Isn't 'In Memoriam', or 'A Nocturnall upon St Lucy's Day', or 'The Eve of St Agnes', or almost any good poem one can think of, 'equipped for life in a world where people actually do die'? I suspect that both Milosz and Popa would be deeply embarrassed by the curious claim Hughes is making on their behalf: so perhaps even would the Jewish Hungarian poet Miklos Radnoti, who died on a forced march to a German camp, and whose last remarkable poems were found on his body in a mass grave after the war.

But apart from this muddle – the product of stylized, tough, neo-realistic longings – there is a more empirical fallacy in Hughes's argument. For there is no especially strenuous kind of poetry that 'equips' us for a strenuous and dangerous kind of life – quite the contrary. In war situations, as I remember, the few people who depended upon poetry found *The Faerie Queene* or *The Prelude* or some poems of Hardy particularly relevant to their situation, and equipped to help them.

Popa's poetry is emphatically not 'equipped' in the sense Hughes means, and I think Hughes, naturally enough, is reading his own fantasies and preoccupations into it. The strength, humour, and flexibility in its closely constructed cycles seem to have matured and grown together over a number of years, always suggesting a lack of finality and a further modulation into cycles of poems yet to come. Particularly moving is the relation between the visionary, almost psalm-like sequence on the 'lame wolf' as symbol of Serbia, and the homely sequences in which national and cultural symbolism have merged into the simple routines and relations of Vershats, past and present. It says much for Anne Pennington's translation that she is able to convey the nature and tempo of these transitions in a version as sensitive as it is unpretentious, as successful as the translations which she and Andrew Harvey have already made of Macedonian poetry.

This leads back to the vexed question of translation in general. With no wish to be a poet at all, the translator is often compelled to look like an unsuccessful one. When a poet 'translates' – FitzGerald his *Rubaiyat*, Robert Lowell his 'Imitations' of European poets, Robert Graves his superb versions from the Hungarian of Gabor Devecseri – the original is turned into a counterpoint variation of the translator's own idiom; and this can give new insight into an original that in being taken from one poet is added to by another. One can feel this even when there is a gap of more than a thousand years, as in Yeats's rendering of choruses from Sophocles.

But for the amateur of poetry who wants to penetrate a little – whatever his linguistic inadequacies – into the physical being of a foreign poet's work, there is no substitute for a dual version, the text on one side and a translation on the other, even though the translation need not be into the literal prose preferred by the Penguin European series. There are some excellent and important poets in the Persea Series of Poetry in Translation, including Mandelstam and the remarkable Turkish poet Nazim Hikmet. This collected version of Popa makes the worthiest possible addition. But I wish the general editor would consider a policy of printing the real text as well. To the poetry lover even the original's incomprehensibility has a sort of eloquence; and its verbal appearances, shape, guessed-at rhythms, do something to bring us more closely into contact with the poet himself.